Google Nexus 7 & 9

CHRIS KENNEDY

Questing Vole Press

Google Nexus 7 & 9
by Chris Kennedy

Copyright © 2015 by Questing Vole Press. All rights reserved.

Editor: Kevin Debenjak
Proofreader: Diane Yee
Compositor: Birgitte Lund
Cover: Questing Vole Press

Contents

1 Getting Started with Your Nexus 1
    Hardware & Specifications 2
    Using and Updating Android 8
    Powering On and Off 11
    Using Multitouch Gestures 13
    Using the Navigation Buttons 14
    Setting Up Your Nexus 16
    Adding Other Users 18
    Adding Restricted Profiles 21
    Viewing and Changing Settings 22

2 Touring Your Nexus 25
    Navigating and Organizing the Home Screen 26
    Creating Home-Screen Folders 30
    Viewing the Status Bar 31
    Setting the Date and Time 32
    Adjusting Screen Brightness 33
    Changing the Wallpaper 34
    Changing Screen Orientation 35
    Adjusting the Volume 36
    Using Earphones and Speakers 37
    Charging the Battery 38
    Conserving Power 40
    Screen Mirroring and External Displays 41

3 Securing Your Nexus 43
    Setting the Screen Lock 44
    Locating a Lost or Stolen Nexus 46
    Encrypting Your Nexus 48
    Verifying Apps 48

4 Typing & Editing 49
Using the Onscreen Keyboard 50
Typing with Gestures 52
Using a Physical Keyboard 53
Setting Typing Options 54
Checking Spelling 55
Using International Keyboards 56
Selecting and Editing Text.. 58
Dictating Text 59
Printing from Your Nexus 60

5 Wireless & Network Connections 61
Wi-Fi Connections 62
Cellular Connections.. 66
Virtual Private Networks 67
Bluetooth Devices 68
Android Beam & NFC 71
Airplane Mode... 72

6 Managing Your Accounts & Data 73
Adding and Removing Accounts 74
Configuring Sync Options.. 76
Backing Up or Erasing Your Data 78

7 Connecting to Computers 79
Connecting to a Windows PC via USB... 80
Connecting to a Mac via USB 81

8 Getting Notifications 83
Viewing Notifications 84
Managing Notifications.. 85

9 Google Now... 87
Using Google Now.. 88
Controlling Location Privacy 89
Displaying and Managing Cards... 90
Settings Reminders in Google Now.. 92

10 Google Search.. 93
Using Google Search 94
Running Sample Search Queries.. 96
Using Voice Actions 98
Setting Search Options 100

11 Browsing the Web with Chrome 103
Using Chrome 104
Signing In to Chrome 105
Searching the Web 106
Navigating Webpages 108
Working with Tabs..110

    Browsing Privately 111
    Bookmarking Webpages 112
    Downloading Files 114
    Changing Chrome Settings 116

12 Watching YouTube Videos 117
    Using the YouTube App 118
    Finding and Watching Videos 119

13 Email, Messaging & Keeping in Touch 121
    About Gmail 122
    Touring Your Inbox 123
    Reading Mail 126
    Working with Attachments 128
    Managing Conversations in Bulk 128
    Writing and Sending Mail 130
    Changing Gmail Settings 132
    Hangouts 134

14 Organizing Your Life 135
    Maintaining Contacts 136
    Setting Up Calendars & Events 144
    Taking Notes 149
    Using the Clock 152

15 Shopping for Apps, Games & Media 155
    Accessing the Google Play Store 156
    Getting Apps and Games 158
    Playing Music 161
    Playing Movies and TV Shows 162
    Reading Books 163
    Reading Magazines and News 164

16 Maps & Navigation 165
    Using Google Maps 166
    Navigating the Map 168
    Viewing Location Details 169
    Finding Your Location 170
    Using Compass Mode 171
    Exploring Street View 172
    Searching for a Location 174
    Exploring Map Views 176
    Saving Offline Maps 177
    Getting Directions 178
    Using Other Mapping Apps and Services 179
    Using Location Services 180

17 Shooting, Viewing & Managing Photos 181
    Getting Photos onto Your Nexus 182

18	Nexus Care & Troubleshooting	185
	Getting Information About Your Nexus	186
	Restarting Your Nexus	187
	Managing Apps and Services	188
	Monitoring Internal Storage and RAM	190
	Optimizing Data Usage	191
	Resetting Your Nexus to Factory Settings	192

Index **193**

CHAPTER 1

Getting Started with Your Nexus

To use a Nexus tablet, you need to know a few basics. This chapter brings you up to speed with a few terms and concepts, and shows you how to set up a new, out-of-the-box Nexus.

Hardware & Specifications

The following figures label the Nexus's physical controls and ports, which are covered in detail later in this chapter and beyond. You can refer to these figures to jog your memory.

The Nexus comes with several accessories:

- A **USB charging unit**, used to provide power and charge the battery. This unit varies by country or region.

- A **Micro-USB cable**, used to connect your Nexus to the USB charging unit or to your computer.

Tip: To see the guts of a dismantled Nexus, go to *ifixit.com* and search for *nexus*.

Nexus 9 (2014)

Table 1.1 lists some key specifications for the Nexus 9 (2014) and Figure 1.1 labels its front and back controls.

Table 1.1 Nexus 9 (2014) Specifications

Specification	Nexus 9 (2014)
Dimensions	8.98 × 6.05 × 0.31 inches (228.25 × 153.68 × 7.95 mm)
Weight	0.94 pounds (425 grams)
Display size	8.9 inches (226.1mm) diagonal
Display resolution	2048 × 1536 pixels (287 pixels per inch)
Processors	64-bit NVIDIA Tegra K1 Dual Denver @ 2.3GHz; 192-core Kepler GPU
Memory (RAM)	2 GB
Storage	16 or 32 GB flash memory
Wireless	Dual-band wi-fi (2.4GHz/5GHz) 802.11 a/b/g/n/ac, Bluetooth 4.1, NFC, and LTE/HSPA+ cellular networks (on some models)
Battery life	Up to 9.5 hours
Cameras	1.6 megapixels front facing, fixed focus; 8 MP rear facing, autofocus, LED flash

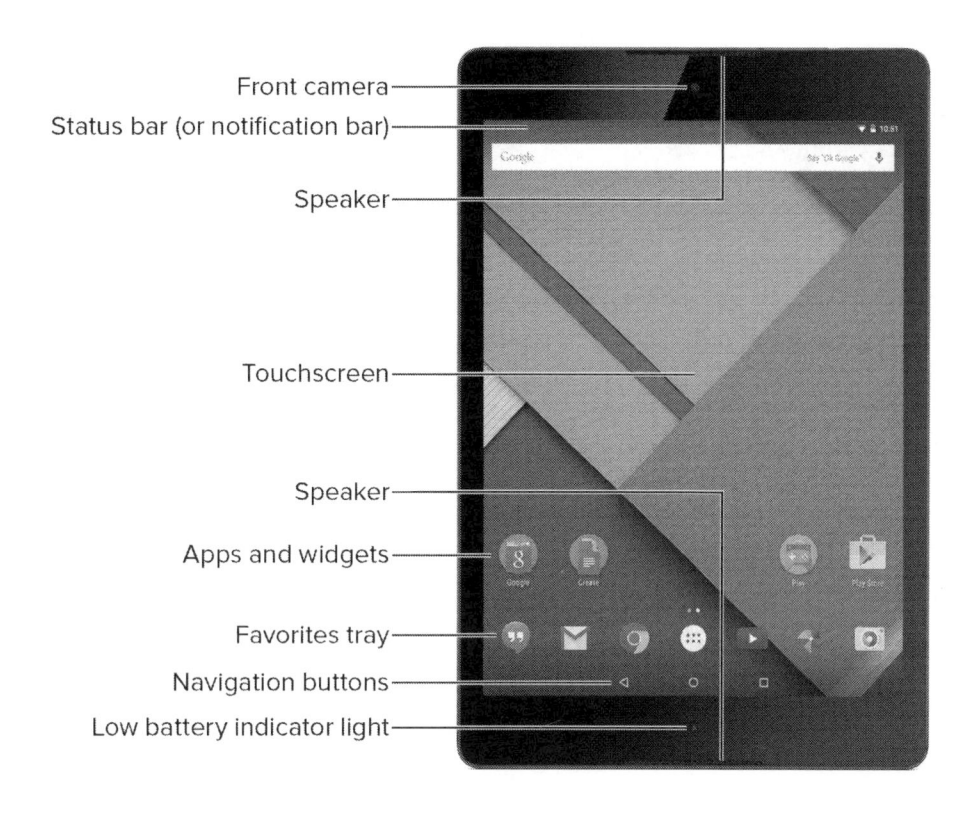

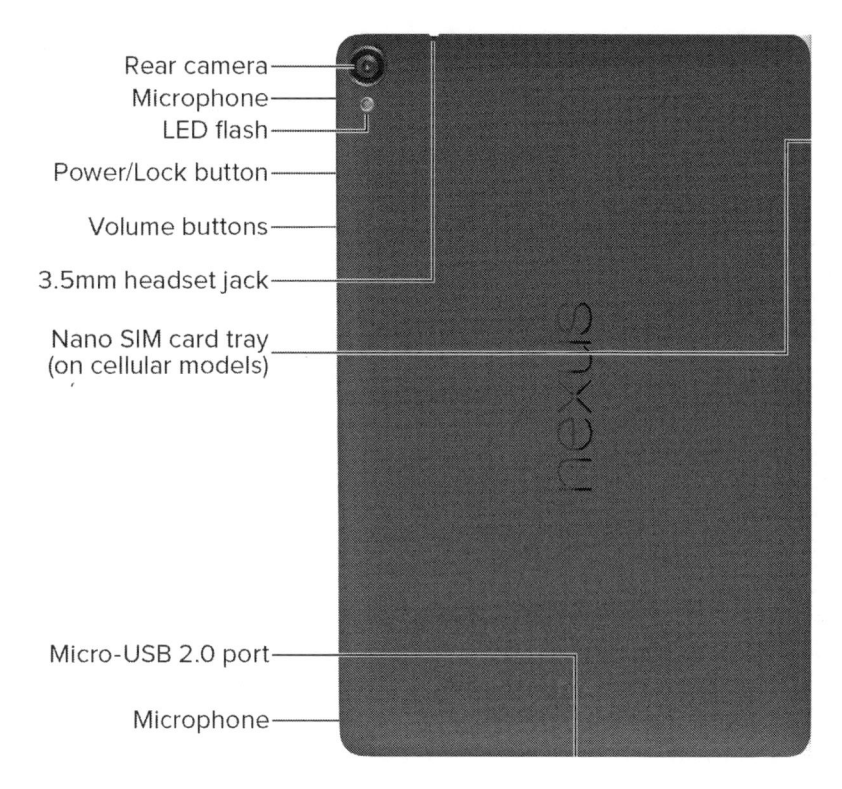

Figure 1.1 Front and back controls for the Nexus 9 (2014).

Nexus 7 (2013)

Table 1.2 lists some key specifications for the Nexus 7 (2013) and Figure 1.2 labels its front and back controls.

Table 1.2 Nexus 7 (2013) Specifications

Specification	Nexus 7 (2013)
Dimensions	7.87 × 4.49 × 0.34 inches (200 × 114 × 8.65 mm)
Weight	0.64 pounds (290 grams)
Display size	7.02 inches (178.3mm) diagonal
Display resolution	1920 × 1200 pixels (323 pixels per inch)
Processors	Qualcomm Snapdragon S4 Pro, 1.5GHz
Memory (RAM)	2 GB
Storage	16 or 32 GB flash memory
Wireless	Dual-band wi-fi (2.4GHz/5GHz) 802.11 a/b/g/n, Bluetooth 4.0, NFC, and LTE/HSPA+ cellular networks (on some models)
Battery life	Up to 9 hours
Cameras	1.2 megapixels front facing, fixed focus; 5 MP rear facing, autofocus

Figure 1.2 Front and back controls for the Nexus 7 (2013).

Nexus 7 (2012)

Table 1.3 lists some key specifications for the Nexus 7 (2012) and Figure 1.3 labels its front and back controls.

Tip: The 4-pin connector on the Nexus 7 (2012) is used with Nexus 7 dock accessories, which cradle the Nexus for charging, hands-free viewing, and line-out audio.

Table 1.3 Nexus 7 (2012) Specifications

Specification	Nexus 7 (2012)
Dimensions	7.81 × 4.72 × 0.41 inches (198.5 × 120 × 10.45 mm)
Weight	0.75 pounds (340 grams)
Display size	7 inches (177.8mm) diagonal
Display resolution	1280 × 800 pixels (216 pixels per inch)
Processors	Nvidia Tegra 3 quad-core, 1.2 GHz
Memory (RAM)	1 GB
Storage	8, 16, or 32 GB flash memory
Wireless	Single-band wi-fi (2.4GHz) 802.11 b/g/n, Bluetooth 3.0, NFC, and HSPA+ cellular networks (on some models)
Battery life	9–10 hours
Cameras	1.2 MP front facing, fixed focus; no rear facing

Figure 1.3 Front and back controls for the Nexus 7 (2012).

Using and Updating Android

The Nexus's operating system, called **Android**, is the same OS that runs on many other (non-Apple, non-Microsoft) tablets and smartphones.

Android adapts to the hardware and screen on which it's running but retains its basic personality across all devices, so if you've used an Android smartphone (such as those from Samsung, LG, HTC, or Motorola), you have a head start with the Nexus.

Android was developed by the Open Handset Alliance (OHA), a group of firms that develops and advances open standards and is led by Google. By *led*, I mean that it's really the iron fist of Google that steers and develops Android; all the rest are hangers-on.

Android is based on Linux (a flavor of the industrial-strength Unix operating system) and is **open source**, meaning that it's developed in a public manner, and others can study, change, improve, and at times distribute it.

Google regularly releases free updates and bug fixes for Android. Some changes refine or add features to Android and the built-in apps and services, whereas others plug security holes or fix stability problems. Your Nexus will notify you automatically when an update is available, but you can check manually at any time. You can update to the latest version of Android over wi-fi. Before you update your Nexus, plug it in or make sure that it has a significant battery charge.

Tip: To change the size of the text used throughout Android, tap Settings > Display > Font Size. If you have vision, hearing, or mobility problems, tap Settings > Accessibility to make Android easier to use.

Pure Android

Because the Nexus is a Google-branded product, its Android software is "pure", meaning that it's exactly how Google designed it, with no extra changes or add-ons.

Google gives away Android, however, and any company can use the OS on its smartphones, tablets, and other hardware. To differentiate their products, manufacturers modify standard Android by adding custom Home screens, controls, apps, widgets, and other doodads. These "enhancements" are often user-hostile, self-promoting, or poorly designed. My Samsung Galaxy Tab tablet, for example, is stuffed with Samsung-only apps that let me chat with *only* Galaxy Tab users, share photos with *only* other Samsung owners, and so on. What's more, this crapware occupies about 25 percent of already-tight storage and can't be deleted without **rooting** the machine (a tricky technical procedure on Samsung hardware).

Pure Android, also called stock Android, offers advantages besides peace of mind. You can always update your Nexus to the latest version of Android, whereas updating non-Google devices is often an adventure. And virtually every app that you buy from the Google Play store will work on pure Android, which isn't true of the many fragmented, nonpure versions.

Rooting a pure Android device is easy, should you want to experiment, install custom or rogue apps, or customize the interface. Pure Android is one of the Nexus's best features, but Google doesn't trumpet it so as not to step on the toes of the other hardware vendors.

Tip: Some tablets and phones from manufacturers other than Google are designated **Google Play Edition** devices, meaning that they run pure Android.

To get system information:

- Tap Settings > About Tablet (Figure 1.4).

    The About Tablet screen gives hardware, software, and status information about your Nexus and Android.

Figure 1.4 The About Tablet screen.

Shorthand Instructions

Throughout this book, you'll find shorthand instructions like "Tap Settings > Display > Adaptive Brightness", which means this: on the Home screen or All Apps screen, tap the Settings app; then, on the Settings screen that opens, tap Display; and then tap Adaptive Brightness on the Display screen. (To see the Settings icon, you may have to tap the All Apps icon ⊞ in the Favorites tray.) Each name between the > symbols refers to an app, widget, icon, button, link, or control; just look on the screen for a matching label.

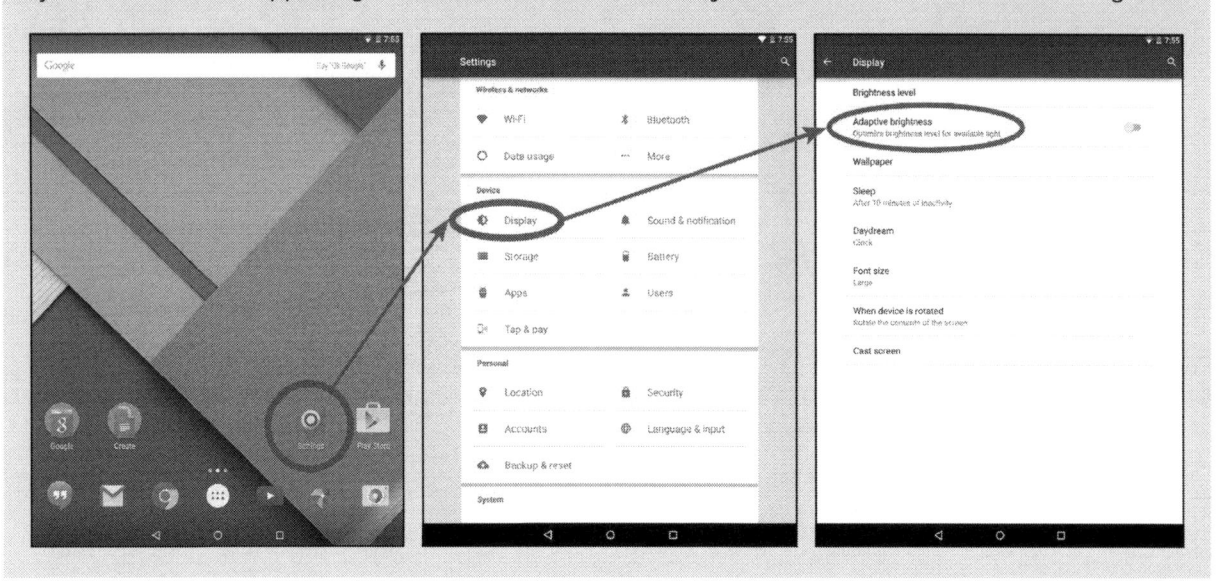

Chapter 1   Getting Started with Your Nexus   9

To update Android:

1. Tap Settings > About Tablet > System Updates (Figure 1.5).

2. If an update is available, tap Download or Restart & Install.

   The System Updates screen tells you whether an updated version of Android is available and, if so, describes its changes.

Tip: Android versions (and significant incremental updates) are named after desserts or sweets. This books covers Android 5.0, better known as **Lollipop**.

Figure 1.5 The System Updates screen.

Figure 1.6 The Power/Lock button on the Nexus 9 (left) and Nexus 7 (right).

Powering On and Off

Putting a Nexus to **sleep** locks it in standby mode: the screen turns off and doesn't respond to single taps, but audio keeps playing, and the volume buttons still work. The battery drains slowly but noticeably. A sleeping Nexus wakes instantly to where you last left off. You may also need to wake your Nexus if you leave it untended for a few minutes, because it goes to sleep by itself to save power.

Tip: The Nexus locks itself because, as with any touchscreen device, an unintended tap on the screen while it's in your bag or backpack can launch a program and drain the battery.

Powering off a Nexus shuts it down: no power is used, though the battery still drains imperceptibly over days or weeks. A powered-off Nexus takes a minute to **power on** and show the Lock screen (page 44). In day-to-day use, you don't need to power off; sleep suffices in most cases.

To put your Nexus to sleep:
- Press the Power/Lock button (Figure 1.6).

To wake your Nexus:

- Press the Power/Lock button or double-tap the screen, and then unlock the screen (Figure 1.7).

  The first time that you use a new Nexus, you unlock it by dragging the lock icon 🔒 up. For details, see "Setting the Screen Lock" on page 44.

Tip: To adjust how long your Nexus screen stays on before it sleeps (and displays the Lock screen when you wake it), tap Settings > Display > Sleep.

To power off your Nexus:

1. Press and hold the Power/Lock button for a moment until a window opens.
2. Tap Power Off.

To power on your Nexus:

- Press the Power/Lock button.

Tip: To set a secure screen lock that you must enter each time that you wake or power on your Nexus, see "Setting the Screen Lock" on page 44.

Drag lock up to unlock

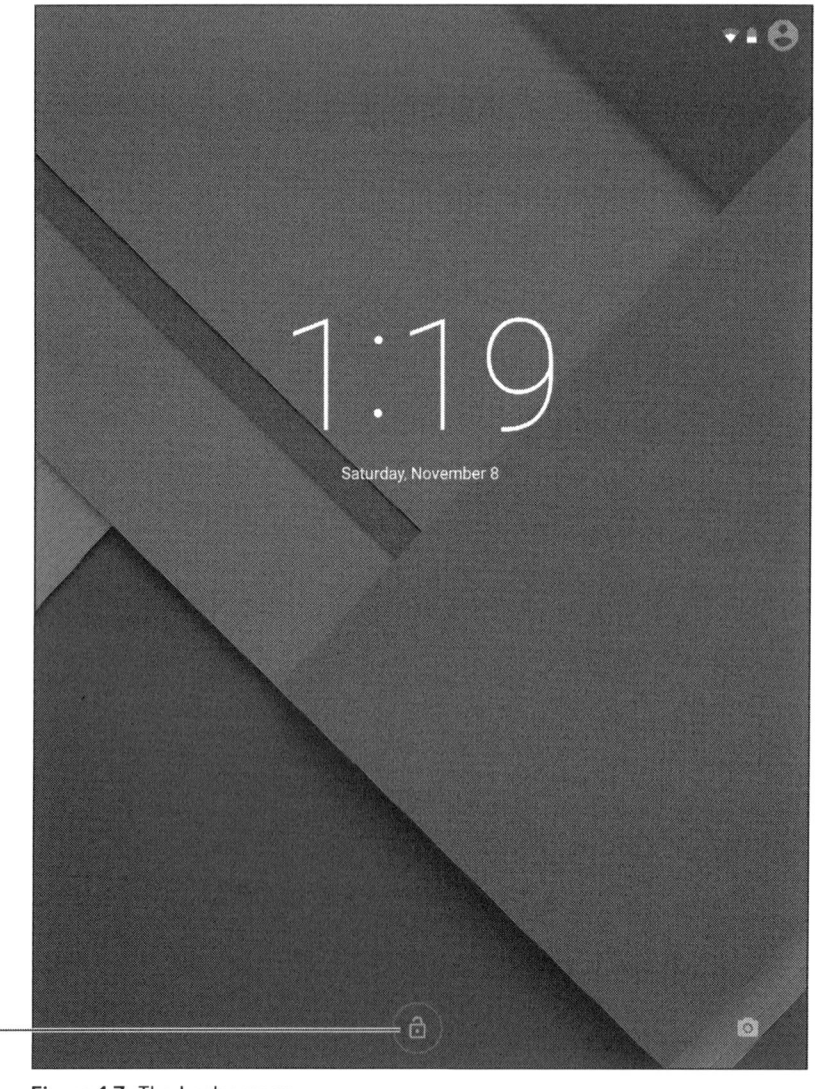

Figure 1.7 The Lock screen.

Using Multitouch Gestures

The Nexus is designed for your fingertips. You interact with the software on the screen by performing the **multitouch gestures**, or simply **gestures**, described in Table 1.4. If you've used a computer mouse, learning these gestures will be easy because tapping and dragging correspond to similar mouse actions. Unfamiliar motions like swiping and pinching quickly become natural.

Tip: To hear a sound or vibrate the tablet when you tap the screen, tap Settings > Sound & Notification > Other Sounds.

The Nexus's **capacitive** screen contains a dense grid of touch sensors that responds to the electrical field of your fingers. The screen won't respond to a traditional stylus or gloves. Increasing finger pressure on a capacitive screen, as opposed to a resistive screen, won't increase responsiveness.

> **Tips for Multitouch Gestures**
>
> The frame surrounding the screen, called the **bezel**, doesn't respond to gestures; it's just a place to rest your thumbs.
>
> Feel free to use two hands. You can use both hands to type on the Nexus's onscreen keyboard (page 50), for example. In some apps, you can touch and hold an item with a finger of one hand and then use your other hand to tap other items to select them all as a group.
>
> If you're having trouble with a gesture, make sure that you're not touching the screen's edge with a stray thumb or finger (of either hand).

Table 1.4 Multitouch Gestures

To	Do This
Tap (or touch)	Gently tap the screen with one finger. A tap triggers the default action for a given item.
Double-tap	Tap twice quickly. (If you tap too slowly, your Nexus interprets it as two single taps.) A double tap is a quick way to zoom in on a photo or webpage. **Tip:** If Settings > Accessibility > Magnification Gestures is turned on, you can triple-tap (or triple-tap and hold) to enter full-screen magnification.
Touch and hold (or long press)	Touch the screen with your finger, and maintain contact with the glass (typically, until some onscreen action happens). To change the duration for which touch-and-hold gestures are recognized, tap Settings > Accessibility > Touch & Hold Delay.
Drag	Touch and hold a point on the screen and then slide your finger across the glass to a different part of the screen.
Swipe (or flick or slide)	Fluidly and decisively whip your finger across the screen. If you're on a webpage or a list, a faster swipe scrolls the screen faster.
Pinch	Touch your thumb and index finger to the screen; then pinch those digits together (to zoom out) or spread them apart (to zoom in).
Rotate	Spread your thumb and index finger and touch them to the screen; then rotate those digits clockwise or counterclockwise. (Or keep your fingers steady and rotate the Nexus itself.)

Using the Navigation Buttons

On the Home screen and All Apps screen and in most apps, you'll find three **navigation buttons** at the bottom of the screen (Figure 1.8). In some apps, these buttons shrink to dots, disappear with disuse, or vanish when the app is in full-screen mode. To bring them back, tap their location or swipe down from the top edge of the screen (start the gesture from the bezel, just beyond the screen edge). If that doesn't work, exit the current app to the Home screen.

- ◁ **Back button**. Opens the preceding screen that you were working in, even if it was in a different app. If you back up to the Home screen, you can't go back any further.

Tip: The Back button doesn't behave consistently and takes some getting used to. Depending on the app and context, the Back button can jump to the Home screen, the previously used app, or the preceding screen within the same app. Some apps (Settings and Play Store, for example) also have an icon in the top-left corner that backs up a screen within the app.

Using a Mouse

You can connect a mouse (or trackpad) to your Nexus via USB or Bluetooth and then use it just as you would with a computer. For USB connections, you'll need an adapter to connect the mouse to the Nexus's Micro-USB port. To connect a Bluetooth mouse, see "Bluetooth Devices" on page 68. Bluetooth and unpowered USB connections drain the battery quickly. To connect multiple USB devices, use a powered USB hub.

When you connect a mouse to your Nexus, a pointer appears, just like on a computer. Use it as follows:

- Moving the mouse moves the pointer. To adjust the pointer speed, tap Settings > Language & Input > Pointer Speed.

- Clicking, holding down, or dragging with the mouse button is equivalent to tapping, touching and holding, or dragging with your finger. (Only one mouse button is supported.)

- The mouse trackball or scroll wheel (if present) scrolls vertically or horizontally.

Tip: See also "Using a Physical Keyboard" on page 53.

Back button   Overview button
       Home button

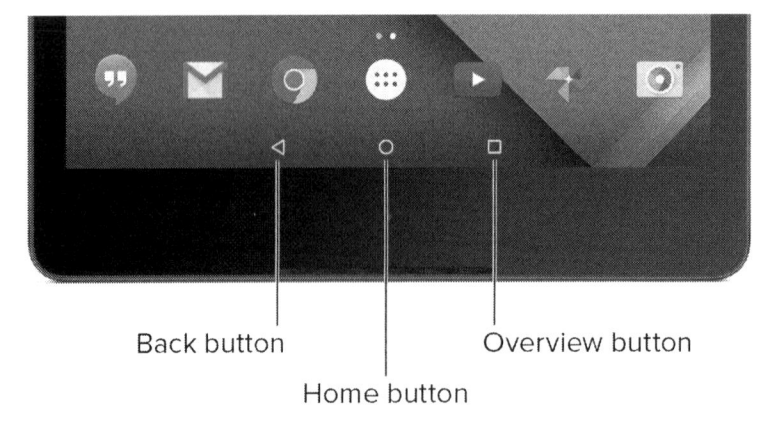

Figure 1.8 The navigation buttons.

Figure 1.9 The Home screen.

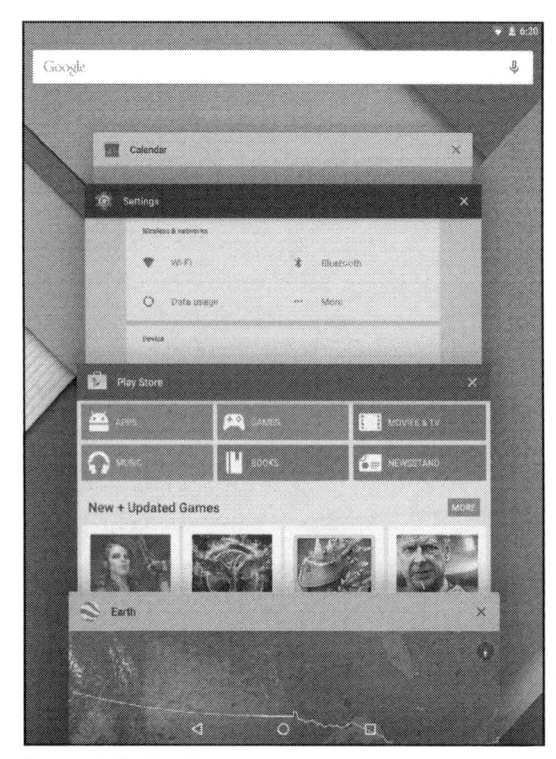

Figure 1.10 The Overview screen.

- ◯ **Home button**. Opens the Home screen. If you're viewing Google Now or a secondary Home screen, it jumps to the main Home screen (Figure 1.9).

- ☐ **Overview button**. Opens a list of apps, settings, documents, and other items that you've viewed recently (Figure 1.10). Apps can add more than one item to the Overview list. You might see multiple items for Settings or Gmail, for example. To scroll the list, swipe it. To open an item, tap its thumbnail image (each thumbnail shows the item in the state in which you last left it). To remove an item, swipe its thumbnail off the screen or tap × in the corner of the thumbnail. To return to the item that you were using, tap the Overview button again.

Tip: When you're typing on the onscreen keyboard, the Back button changes to the Hide button ▽, which you can tap to hide the keyboard.

Because the Nexus displays only one app at a time, you can use the navigation buttons to switch among apps. If you're browsing the web in Chrome, for example, when your Nexus chimes an incoming email alert, tap a navigation button to close Chrome and then open Gmail, where you can read your mail. If the desired app isn't visible, tap ◯ and then tap ⊞ in the Favorites tray (above the navigation buttons) to view all your apps.

Tapping a navigation button always saves your current position or work in progress automatically. (Unlike Windows and OS X programs, Android apps have no manual Save command.) If you're watching a video in Play Movies & TV or typing a message in Gmail and then tap Home, you can return to Play Movies & TV or Gmail at any time, exactly as you left off.

Chapter 1 Getting Started with Your Nexus 15

Setting Up Your Nexus

The first thing to do with a new, out-of-the-box Nexus is set it up. To do so, you need a nearby wireless internet connection. (Don't wander away from the wi-fi signal with your Nexus during setup.) Your Nexus will also need a significant battery charge if the battery drained while sitting in the cargo container or on the store shelf.

The Nexus is self-contained. You don't need a computer to set it up or use it. Everything that you need is downloaded over the internet. Your account data and settings are backed up wirelessly to the **cloud** (free online storage).

To set up your new Nexus, turn it on and then follow the onscreen instructions, which step you through the setup process. If you need to backtrack a step during setup, tap < at the bottom of the screen. If you need help typing on the onscreen keyboard, see "Using the Onscreen Keyboard" on page 50.

The exact steps vary depending on whether you're a new Google user or restoring a previous backup, Setup asks you to:

- Choose your preferred language (possibly including country or region) for the Nexus's screens, keyboard, and interface.

- Connect to a wi-fi network. Setup lists in-range wi-fi networks. A secured home network is safer than a public network at a café or library, where intruders can sniff out your passwords and personal information as you type. A lock icon 🔒 indicates a secure network (which requires a password), and a wi-fi icon 📶 indicates the signal strength (more bars = stronger signal). For details, see "Wi-Fi Connections" on page 62.

Tip: To join a closed network—one whose name is hidden so that it isn't shown in the list of scanned networks—tap Add Another Network.

- Download and install any pending system updates. If any updates are available, the Nexus restarts automatically to apply them.

- Sign in with or create a Google Account. Your Google Account is a unique user ID (email address) and password that lets you use the Google Play store, back up and sync your data, and use other Google apps and services. For details, see the "Google Accounts" sidebar.

  To sign in to your Google Account, enter the email address that you use for Gmail, YouTube, Google Apps, AdWords, or any other Google product. If you have multiple Google Accounts, you can add the others later by tapping Settings > Accounts > Add Account (for details, see Chapter 6).

- Restore a backup. If you previously backed up your Google Account, you can restore it by choosing a backup from the Restore From this Backup menu. If you don't want to restore a previous backup, choose Set Up as a New Device.

- Choose which Google services to use, such as backup and location services.

Tip: Location services let built-in apps such as Maps and Google Search, as well as third-party apps such as weather apps, use your physical whereabouts via the Nexus's built-in positioning service. These services are a convenience for some people and a privacy invasion for others. For details, see "Using Location Services" on page 180.

- Choose whether Google Now (Chapter 9) can access your personal and location data.

- Enter payment info to shop in the Google Play store for apps, books, music, movies, and other media. If you like, you can skip this step and set up your store account later in the Play Store app.

When you're done, Setup takes you to the Home screen. Your Nexus is set up and ready to use. The Home screen's exact appearance depends on whether you set up your Nexus as a new device or restored it from a Google Account backup.

Tip: Google+ (Google Plus) is Google's social network—basically, Google's version of Facebook. If you're not interested, you can safely skip any requests to join Google+.

Google Accounts

A Google Account lets you organize and access your personal information from your Nexus or any computer or mobile device, as follows:

- **Google Play store**. You can shop for and download movies, TV shows, books, music, magazines, apps, and more. Your Google Account lets you reach any of your content from any of your devices.

- **Google Wallet**. You can connect your Google Account with Google Wallet to pay for purchases in Google Play and other online stores. Google Wallet is a secure mobile payment system (similar to PayPal) that lets you store debit cards, credit cards, loyalty cards, gift cards, and more. For details, see *google.com/wallet*.

- **Back up and sync**. Google securely and continually backs up your email, text messages, calendar events, contacts, and more, and it syncs your data across computers and devices on which you use the same Google Account. You can access your stuff no matter what computer or device you're using.

- **Google apps and services**. Your Google Account gives you personalized access to Google apps and services, including Gmail, Google Maps, Navigation, Google Play, YouTube, and Hangouts.

Tap & Go

After Android updates itself during setup, you may be able to use Tap & Go to quickly finish setting up your Nexus. Tap & Go copies backed-up apps, data, account details, and settings from your old Android device (if you have one) to your new one. It uses NFC (page 71) to pair a Bluetooth connection between the devices. To start the process, tap the two devices back-to-back until you hear a tone, and then follow the onscreen instructions. The new device requires Android 5.0 or later, but the old device needs only the latest version of Google Play Services, which can run on Android 2.3 and later. Turn on NFC on the old device (Settings > More > NFC).

Changing Settings After Setup

If you change your mind or skip a step during setup, you can change the setup options later by using the Settings app. To change the system language, tap Settings > Language & Input > Language. To sign in to, change, or create a Google Account, tap Settings > Accounts. To toggle Location services, tap Settings > Location. To change backup settings, tap Settings > Backup & Reset.

Selling Your Old Nexus

Before you sell or give away a Nexus, reset it to erase all your personal data, accounts, and settings so that the new owner can't access your stuff. Resetting a Nexus returns it to its factory settings without reinstalling Android. Tap Settings > Backup & Reset > Factory Data Reset > Reset Tablet. Charge the battery before a reset.

Adding Other Users

Several people can use the same Nexus without being able to see or change each other's files or settings. You can add other **users** if you want to share your Nexus with your family, friends, coworkers, or guests. The person who first sets up the Nexus is designated as the tablet **owner** and can add, edit, or delete other users at will (nonowner users can only modify or delete their own accounts). Network settings and app permissions are universal and shared among all users on the tablet, but all other settings—including wallpaper, Home screen and Lock screen layouts, passwords, screen brightness, documents and photos, and individual app settings, among others—are unique to each user.

Here are a few tips for sharing a tablet with other users:

- Tap ⊖ at the top of the Lock screen to list each user's image and nickname (Figure 1.11). To use the tablet, tap your image and then unlock your Lock screen.

- Each user's apps are segregated from every other user's apps, though apps that have been downloaded by one user don't occupy extra storage space when downloaded by a second user. If one user updates an app, it's updated for all users who share the app.

- Users can't share data with one another directly. If you want to transfer a picture to other users, for example, you must email it to them or share it through a third-party service.

- The new-user setup process is similar to the first-time setup routine that you go through when you unbox your Nexus: you associate your Google Account with the user profile, decide which services to turn on, and so on.

- New users and guests can be added from the Lock screen: choose Settings > Users > ⋮ > select Add Users When Device is Locked. This setting is handy for letting other people create personal spaces without bothering you or accessing your account.

Figure 1.11 Users are listed on the Lock screen.

Figure 1.12 The Users screen.

Guests

You can let another person use your Nexus as a **guest**. A guest can't access the information of any other user on the device. Guests profiles are meant to be temporary spaces that the guest can delete when finished. After switching to the built-in Guest profile, the guest can work with the tablet in most of the usual ways:

- Sign in to a Google Account and other types of accounts.
- Customize the Lock screen, Home screen, and other settings.
- Add, update, and delete apps.

A guest's information remains on the tablet until it's deleted. When switching to the Guest profile, the guest is asked whether to continue from the previous guest session or start over (the latter choice deletes guest info from the previous session). To delete guest information explicitly, tap 😊 on the Lock screen and then tap Remove Guest. Alternatively, switch to the Guest profile, swipe down with two fingers from the top of the screen, tap 😊 in the Quick Settings menu, and then tap Remove Guest. The tablet owner can add a new guest in Settings > Users or in Quick Settings.

- You can create up to eight users on your Nexus. Only three users can remain active at a time, however. The system inactivates the least recently active user when necessary to maintain this limit. An inactive user's account won't sync in the background. To make an inactive user active again, switch to that user.

- A brand-new user account with no email, apps, or other configured settings initially occupies only a few megabytes of storage. Other users' background services take up a small amount of memory (RAM).

- If you connect your Nexus to a computer, you can view the files of only the current user. Switching users while the Nexus is connected to the computer unmounts the Nexus and then remounts it to give you access to the other user's files. For details, see Chapter 7.

To add a user:

1. Tap Settings > Users (Figure 1.12).

    Only the tablet owner can add new users.

2. Tap Add User or Profile.

3. In the Add screen, tap User.

4. In the Add New User screen, tap OK.

5. If the new user is available, tap Set Up Now and then ask that person to set up the Google Account and other details.

    or

    If the new user isn't available, tap Not Now.

    A generic new user appears in the Users list. When the new user becomes available, tap the user image on the Lock screen and then give your Nexus to that person to set up.

Tip: Another way to add a user: swipe down with two fingers from the top of the screen, tap 😊 in the Quick Settings menu, and then tap Add User.

To change your user information:

1 Tap Settings > Users.

2 Tap your user name (Figure 1.13).

3 Do any of the following:

   ▸ To change your nickname, edit the text in the Nickname field.

   ▸ To change your user image (picture), tap the icon next to your nickname.

To change the information that appears on the Lock screen:

1 Tap Settings > Security > Owner Info (or User Info).

   The Owner Info (or User Info) screen opens (Figure 1.14).

2 Select Show Owner Info on Lock Screen, and then type any text that you want to appear on the Lock screen.

Tip: If you enter your phone number or email address and then lose your tablet, the finder can contact you without needing to unlock it.

---

3 When you're done, tap the icon in the top-left corner.

To delete a user:

1 Tap Settings > Users.

2 To delete a different user, tap 🗑 next to that user's name. (Only the tablet owner can delete other users.)

   or

   To delete your own (nonowner) user space, tap ⋮ > Delete *username* From This Device.

To switch users:

- On the Lock screen, tap 😊 at the top of the screen, tap a user image in the list, and then unlock the screen (refer to Figure 1.11).

Tip: If you're already signed in as a user, you can switch quickly to the Lock screen for a different user: swipe down with two fingers from the top of the screen and then tap 😊 in the Quick Settings menu.

Figure 1.13 The Profile Info screen.

Figure 1.14 The Owner (or User) Info screen.

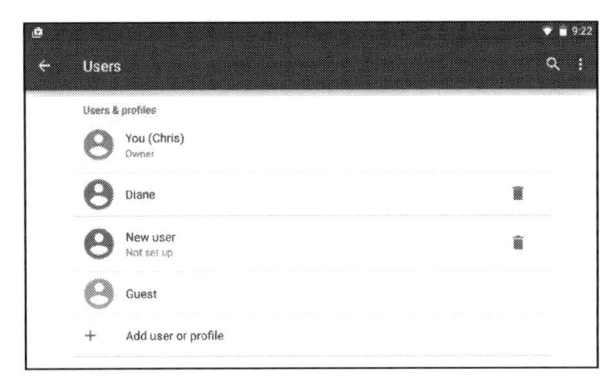

Figure 1.15 The Users screen.

Figure 1.16 The App & Content Access screen.

Adding Restricted Profiles

Restricted profiles let you (the tablet owner) limit the apps, content, and settings that are available to certain other users. This feature is ideal for children, guests, retail kiosks, and point-of-sale devices.

To add a restricted profile:

1. Tap Settings > Users (Figure 1.15).

   Only the tablet owner can add restricted profiles.

2. Tap Add User or Profile.

3. In the Add screen, tap Restricted Profile.

   The App & Content Access screen opens, showing a list of settings for the new profile (Figure 1.16).

4. Use the on/off toggles and other controls to select the features and settings that you want to grant access to.

5. To set up the new profile, press the Power/Lock button twice to return to the Lock screen, tap 😊 at the top of the screen, and then tap the new profile icon.

   When the restricted user finishes setting up, the Home screen is almost empty, and the granted apps appear in the All Apps screen.

Tip: To edit or delete a restricted user, you must be the tablet owner.

Chapter 1 Getting Started with Your Nexus 21

Viewing and Changing Settings

Settings is the central screen for changing systemwide settings and getting information about your Nexus, similar to System Preferences in OS X or Control Panel in Windows. If you've used your Nexus for even a little while, you've probably visited Settings.

If you want to tweak the way your Nexus works, poke around in Settings to see what's available.

To view or change settings:

1. Tap the Settings icon on the Home screen.

   If the Settings app isn't visible, tap ◯ and then tap ⊞ in the Favorites tray (above the navigation buttons) to view all your apps.

   or

   Swipe down with two fingers from the top of the screen and then tap the Settings icon ✱ in Quick Settings.

   The Settings screen opens (Figure 1.17).

Tip: To change the text size in Settings (and elsewhere throughout Android), tap Settings > Display > Font Size.

---

2. Tap an item to view or change a setting. Or tap ◯ to search for a setting.

   If necessary, swipe up or down to scroll to the desired setting. Tapping an item may take you to yet another Settings screen or launch a window where you can view or change the current settings.

3. To backtrack to the previous screen, tap the icon in the top-left corner of the screen.

Tip: To change the settings for a specific app, open the app and then tap the menu icon ⋮ or ≡ (if it appears) at the top or bottom of the screen.

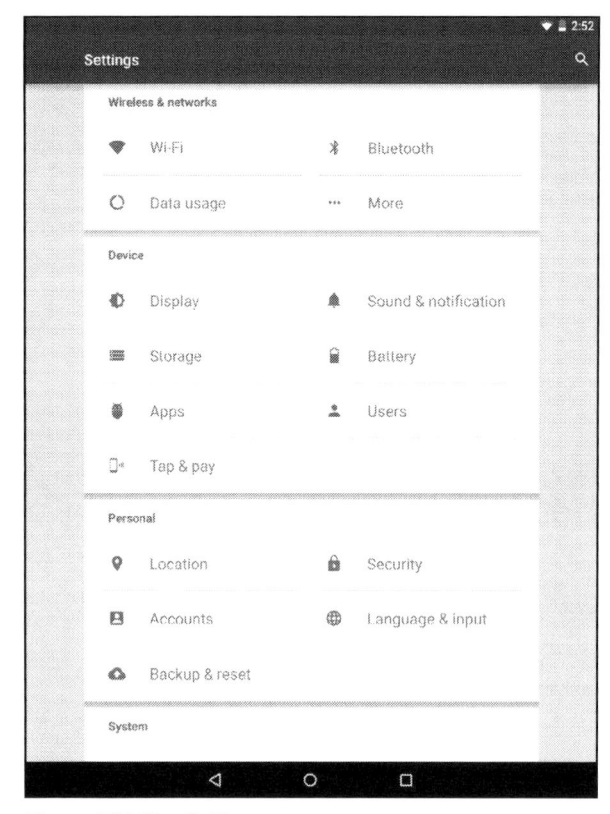

Figure 1.17 The Settings screen.

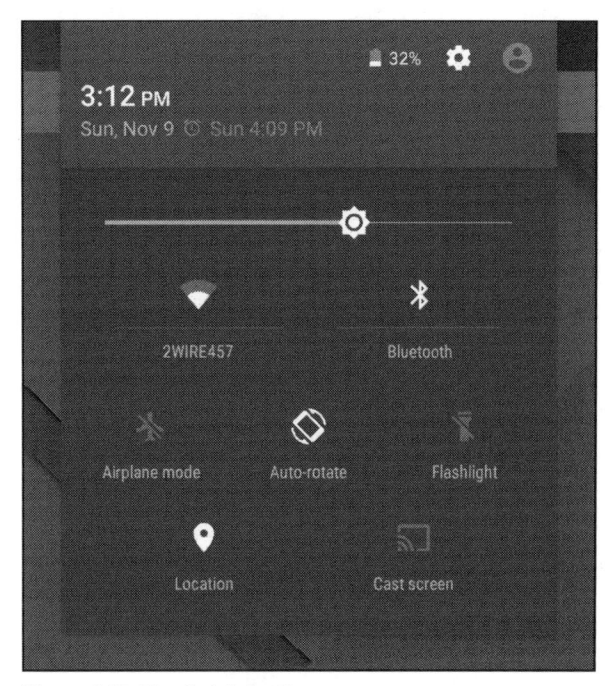

Figure 1.18 The Quick Settings menu.

Tip: You can access Quick Settings on the Lock screen.

Quick Settings

The Quick Settings menu grants you instant access to frequent tasks, saving you the taps needed to get to common settings buried in other screens.

To open Quick Settings:

- Swipe down with two fingers from the top of the screen (Figure 1.18).

  or

  Swipe down with one finger twice in succession from the top of the screen. Swiping down the first time opens the notification shade (Chapter 8).

To dismiss Quick Settings without using it, swipe up or tap off the Quick Settings menu.

Quick Settings lets you:

- Display battery life (tap to open the Battery screen)
- Open the Settings app
- Switch or add users
- See the current local day, date, and time
- See any upcoming alarms (tap to open Clock)
- Adjust screen brightness
- Tap the icon to turn wi-fi on or off, or tap the text label (network name) to open the Wi-Fi screen (a ! indicates a connectivity problem)
- Tap the icon to turn Bluetooth on or off, or tap the word *Bluetooth* to open the Bluetooth screen (a ! indicates a connectivity problem)
- Turn airplane mode on or off
- Lock or unlock screen rotation
- Turn the flashlight on or off (for tablets with an LED flash)
- Turn Location services on or off
- Toggle tablet-to-TV screen mirroring via Chromecast (page 41) or Google Nexus Player

Google Settings

On the All Apps screen, tap Google Settings to open the central settings screen for Play Games, Location services, Google Now, Google Search, and other Google-specific apps and services (Figure 1.19). You can also reach many of these settings from within the relevant apps themselves.

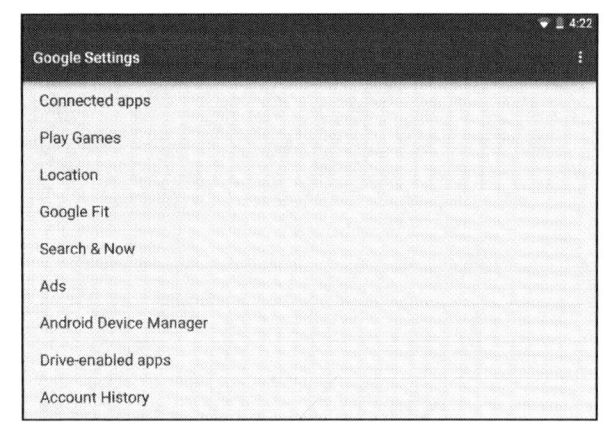

Figure 1.19 The Google Settings screen.

CHAPTER 2

Touring Your Nexus

The Nexus offers the features of modern tablets: you can surf the web; play games; find your way with maps; download and play media; keep in touch via email, messaging, or video chat; and much more (including a few Google-specific touches). Yet the Nexus is a true computer running complex programs on a modern operating system. Fortunately, Google has given the Nexus a consistent, simple design that lets you wield a lot of power with only a little learning. Even complete beginners can't easily stumble into any ravines. This chapter gets you up and running.

Navigating and Organizing the Home Screen

After you unlock your Nexus, the **Home screen** appears, displaying icons for your apps and widgets (Figure 2.1). The Nexus comes with built-in apps and widgets (Gmail, Settings, and My Library, for example), and you can download more from the Google Play store, Google's online store for media and Android apps and games. You can customize the layout of apps icons and widgets on the Home screen and in the Favorites tray.

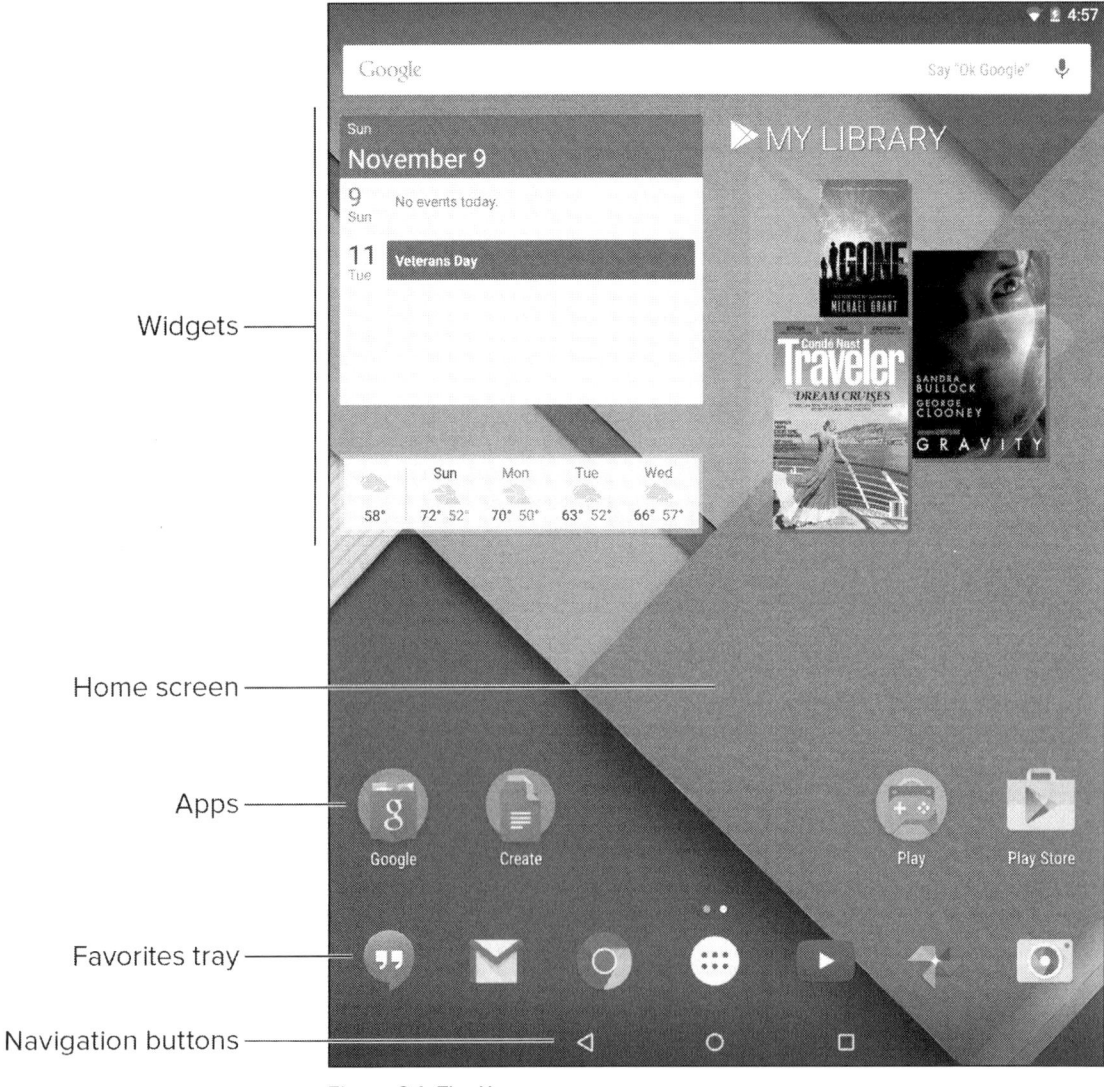

Figure 2.1 The Home screen.

Tap to open the Google Play store to learn more

Tap to suppress future suggestions like this one

RECOMMENDED FOR YOU
Agora Go
Weiqi, Igo, Baduk
Popular with Tsumego Pro (Go Problems) users

Tap to see a new suggestion

Figure 2.2 The Recommended Apps widget suggests featured apps, popular apps, and apps based on the ones that you already have installed.

View all your apps

Figure 2.3 The Favorites tray.

Apps. **Apps** (short for **applications**) are conventional programs that occupy the entire screen when opened. Applications added to the Home screen appear as icons. To open an app, tap its icon.

Widgets. **Widgets** are single-purpose miniprograms. Widgets added to the Home screen appear as icons that you can tap to open or activate or as tiles that you can resize to occupy part or all of the Home screen. Every widget is different, so you may have to experiment with its links and controls to figure out how it works (Figure 2.2).

Tip: For PC or Mac users: Android widgets are similar to Windows gadgets or OS X widgets and extensions.

Home screen. If you install lots of apps and widgets, you can spread them over the multiple Home screens that reside to right of the main Home screen. The main Home screen appears by default.

Favorites tray. You can put your most frequently used apps in the **Favorites tray**, which is visible at the bottom of every Home screen (Figure 2.3). Anchored to the center of the tray is the All Apps icon ⊕, which shows all your installed apps.

Navigation buttons. The three navigation buttons at the bottom of the screen take you to the previous screen ◁, the Home screen ◯, or the Overview screen ☐. For details, see "Using the Navigation Buttons" on page 14.

To show the Home screen:

- Tap the Home button ◯.

Tip: If the navigation buttons shrink to dots or fade away, tap their location to bring them back. If that doesn't work, exit the current app to return to the Home screen.

To switch Home screens:

- Swipe left or right on the Home screen. On a Nexus 9, the leftmost screen is Google Now (Chapter 9), if Google Now is turned on.

  As you switch screens, indicators above the Favorites tray glow to show which Home screen you're on.

Tip: If you're on any Home screen, tapping ◯ switches to the main Home screen.

To rearrange apps and widgets on the Home screen:

- Touch and hold an app or widget icon for a moment and then drag it slowly to a new location within a screen or off the edge of one screen and onto the next.

  As you drag, other icons move aside (if there's room).

Tip: If you drop an app icon on top of another app icon, you create a folder (page 30).

To resize a widget on the Home screen:

1. On the Home screen, touch and hold the widget for a moment until it rises slightly out of the screen; and then lift your finger.

   A border appears on the widget.

2. Drag any of the dots on the widget's border (Figure 2.4).

   As you drag, other apps and widgets move aside (if there's room).

3. When you're done resizing, tap an empty area on the Home screen.

Figure 2.4 Drag the dots to resize the widget.

Switching Apps

The Nexus displays only one app at a time, full-screen. You can't have, say, Chrome on one side of the screen and Gmail on the other, as you can in Windows or OS X. Fortunately, Android supports **multitasking**, which lets multiple apps run in the background at the same time, and you can quickly open, switch among, and close apps.

Most apps are effectively frozen when you switch away from them, but certain apps (such as Play Music and Gmail) continue working in the background. Switching back to an app lets you resume where you left off. To switch apps, use the navigation buttons at the bottom of the screen.

See also "Managing Apps and Services" on page 188.

Figure 2.5 All Apps screen.

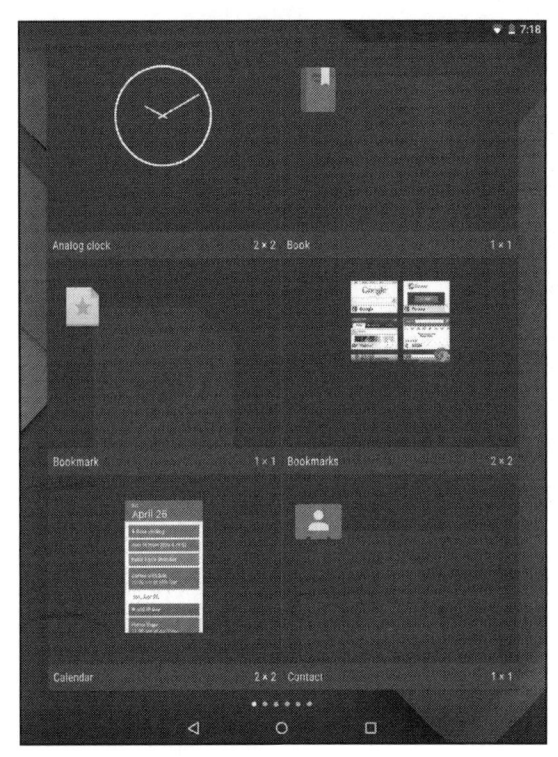

Figure 2.6 Widgets screen.

To add an app or widget to the Home screen:

1. If necessary, tap ○ to go to the Home screen.
2. To add an app, tap ⊞ in the Favorites tray.

    The All Apps screen opens, showing your installed apps (Figure 2.5).

    or

    To add a widget, touch and hold an empty area on the Home screen for a moment until icons appear near the bottom of the screen, and then tap Widgets.

    The Widgets screen opens, showing your installed widgets (Figure 2.6).

Tip: On a Nexus 7, widgets are added from All Apps: tap Widgets at the top of the All Apps screen or swipe to the widgets.

---

3. Swipe left or right to find the desired app or widget.
4. Touch and hold the app or widget icon.

    The display jumps to the Home screen.

5. Drag the icon to the desired Home screen location and then lift your finger.

    You can drag off the edge of one screen and onto the next. You can't drag an icon to a screen that lacks the room to hold it.

To remove an app or widget from the Home screen:

1. Touch and hold the app or widget icon for a moment until the word *Remove* appears at the top of the screen.
2. Drag the icon to *Remove* and then lift your finger.

    The app or widget is removed from the screen (but isn't uninstalled from your Nexus).

Creating Home-Screen Folders

If too many icons are crowding your Home screens, you can group them into **folders** rather than drag them around to different screens. It's a common practice to create multiple folders, each holding similar types of apps (games, media, travel, and so on). Folders save a lot of screen space and reduce excessive screen-switching. Folders can hold apps but not widgets or other (nested) folders.

To create a folder:

1. Touch and hold an app icon for a moment and then drag it on top of an app icon that you want to store in the same folder.

   A new folder containing the two icons is created (Figure 2.7).

2. If you like, drag other icons to the folder.

3. Do any of the following:

   ▶ To open the folder, tap it (Figure 2.8).

   ▶ Tap an app icon in the folder to open that app.

   ▶ Drag icons within the folder to rearrange them.

   ▶ Drag icons out of the folder. Removing the last icon from a folder deletes the folder.

   ▶ To rename the folder, open it, tap the default name (*Unnamed Folder*), and then type a new name. The onscreen keyboard appears when you tap the name.

   ▶ To close the folder, tap off the folder.

Tip: By default, the Home screen comes with a folder containing popular Google apps. As with any folder, you can customize its contents.

Figure 2.7 A folder appears on the Home screen as a circle containing small icons.

Figure 2.8 An open folder.

30   Google Nexus 7 & 9

Viewing the Status Bar

The **status bar** (also called the **notification bar**) is the narrow strip that runs along the top of the Home screen, the Lock screen, and many application screens (Figure 2.9). The status bar shows the current time and displays icons that indicate the current state of your Nexus, including pending notifications (Chapter 8), Bluetooth status, Clock alarms, location requests, wi-fi network connectivity and signal strength, and battery level and charging status.

Tip: If you can't see the status bar (or navigation buttons) in an app, then the app might be in full-screen mode. To reveal the controls, swipe down from top edge of the screen (start the gesture from the bezel, just beyond the screen edge).

Pending notifications

Location, Bluetooth, alarm, wi-fi, battery status, and clock

Figure 2.9 The status bar.

Setting the Date and Time

The time of day appears in the status bar at the top of the screen. By default, the time and time zone are set automatically, based on your internet connection. By tapping Settings > Date & Time to display the Date & Time screen (Figure 2.10), you can switch between the 12-hour (AM/PM) clock and 24-hour clock, and also choose a date format (the order of the year, month, and day). If you're traveling, you can choose a time zone and set your Nexus's date and time manually. Keep your Nexus's time accurate; apps use it to time-stamp files and messages, schedule tasks, record events, and sound alerts.

Tip: To display the time, day, and date in large format on the Home screen, open the Clock app (page 152). An Analog Clock widget is also available. Both app and widget also let you set alarms.

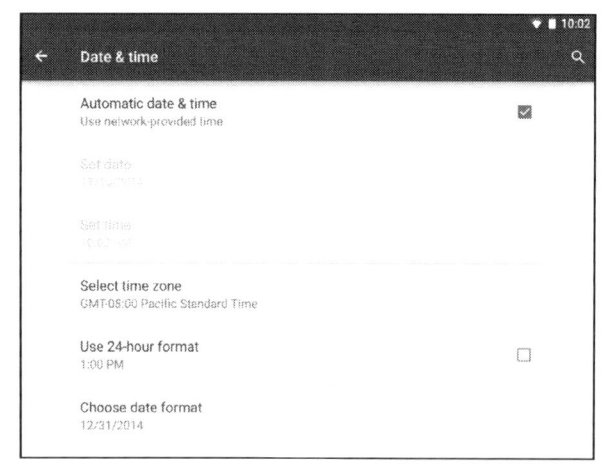

Figure 2.10 The Date & Time screen.

Figure 2.11 The brightness slider.

How Adaptive Brightness Works

When adaptive brightness is turned on, the Nexus autoadjusts brightness by using its built-in **ambient light sensor**. This sensor, located near the front camera, is barely visible behind the screen's bezel. If the screen doesn't dim automatically, check whether something (your hand, a protective film, or a case) is blocking or obscuring the sensor. Adaptive brightness doesn't disable the brightness slider—you can still make manual adjustments as your eyes adapt.

Adjusting Screen Brightness

You can make the Nexus's screen brighter or dimmer, or have it adjust the brightness automatically for ambient light.

To adjust screen brightness:

- To adjust brightness manually, swipe down with two fingers from the top of the screen and then drag ✲ in Quick Settings (Figure 2.11). Alternatively, tap Settings > Display > Brightness Level.

    or

    To make the Nexus autoadjust brightness for current light conditions (subject to manual adjustments), tap Settings > Display and then turn on Adaptive Brightness.

Changing the Wallpaper

You can choose the picture or animation that you want to use as a background image, or **wallpaper**, that sits behind the icons and widgets on your Home screen and Lock screen (Figure 2.12). The Nexus comes with some stock images for use as wallpaper, but you can use your own pictures. You can also download additional wallpapers from the Google Play store: open the store and then search for *wallpaper* or browse the Live Wallpaper category in the Apps store.

Tip: When you're not using a docked or charging Nexus, you can have it display a digital or analog clock, a slideshow of photos, a pattern of shifting colors, or other screensaver: tap Settings > Display > Daydream.

To change the wallpaper:

1 Touch and hold an empty area on the Home screen for a moment until icons appear near the bottom of the screen, and then tap Wallpapers.

Tip: On a Nexus 7, tap a wallpaper location in the pop-up list, tap a picture, and then tap Set Wallpaper.

2 To use a stock (built-in) wallpaper, tap one of the images in the scrolling gallery, and then tap Set Wallpaper.

   or

   To use your own picture, tap Pick Image and then choose a wallpaper in the image browser (Figure 2.13). You can pinch-zoom or drag the image to set the crop area. When you're done, tap Set Wallpaper.

Tip: You can also change the wallpaper by tapping Settings > Display > Wallpaper.

Figure 2.12 Wallpaper sits behind the icons and widgets.

Figure 2.13 Browse for a wallpaper image.

Figure 2.14 Portrait and landscape views.

Changing Screen Orientation

The Nexus's built-in accelerometer senses how you're holding the Nexus in physical space and then orients the screen to either portrait (tall) or landscape (wide) view (Figure 2.14).

Tip: In Chrome (Chapter 11), webpages scale automatically to the wider screen, making the text and images larger.

To change the view, rotate the Nexus. Most apps self-adjust to fit the new orientation. Some apps support only one view. Many games and video players, for example, work only in landscape view.

If you don't want the screen to change its orientation, such as when you're reading while lying on your side, you can lock the current view to stop it from rotating. To do so, swipe down from the top-right corner of the screen and then tap ◊ in Quick Settings. Tap it again to unlock rotation.

To disable screen rotation, tap Settings > Accessibility > clear Auto-Rotate Screen.

Adjusting the Volume

The buttons on the right edge of the Nexus control the volume (Figure 2.15). The volume control is a rocker switch with two buttons that adjust the audio level of anything that makes noise, such as songs, videos, audiobooks, apps, notifications, and alarms.

Volume adjustments affect the Nexus's built-in speaker, earphones or headsets plugged into the headphone jack, and external speakers connected wirelessly or through the Micro-USB port (or the 4-pin connector on a Nexus 7 (2012)).

To change the volume, press the Volume Up or Volume Down button. To raise or lower the volume quickly, press and hold the button. A volume overlay appears briefly onscreen as you adjust the volume (Figure 2.16).

To set the volume levels of media, alarms, and notifications independently, tap Settings > Sound & Notification. To stop some or all notifications (Chapter 8) indefinitely or for a fixed duration, tap None or Priority on the volume overlay or choose Settings > Sound & Notification > Interruptions. When sound is muted, a mute icon appears in the status bar at the top of the screen.

Figure 2.15 The volume buttons on the Nexus 9 (left) and Nexus 7 (right).

Figure 2.16 Volume slider.

Figure 2.17 Headset jack.

Using Earphones and Speakers

The Nexus doesn't come with earphones, but it does have a headset jack on its top-right edge (Figure 2.17), or bottom-right edge on the Nexus 7 (2012). More precisely, it has a standard 3.5mm stereo headphone minijack. You can plug in any earphones or headsets that come with the 3.5mm miniplug (including iPod and iPhone earphones). Push the plug firmly into the jack so that it fully connects.

Certain audio accessories, such as stereo-audio docks and external speakers, plug into the Nexus's Micro-USB port, or connect wirelessly via Bluetooth (page 68). To pair wireless speakers with your Nexus, tap Settings > Bluetooth > On. After the Nexus finds and lists your accessory, tap its name; then, if required, type a passkey (which you'll find in the gadget's manual).

The Nexus's built-in speakers are silenced when you use earphones or external speakers.

Charging the Battery

Charge your Nexus by using the USB charging unit and Micro-USB cable that came with it (or that you bought separately from Google). The charging unit varies by country or region, so don't risk using foreign charging units even if they look compatible.

The battery icon in the status bar at the top of the screen shows the battery strength and charging status (Figure 2.18). A lightning bolt indicates that the battery is charging. A red battery icon means the battery is running low.

You can also charge your Nexus via a USB port on your computer, which takes longer than charging with the USB charging unit. The Nexus charges fastest when it's sleeping or powered off.

The Nexus 7 (2013) supports **Qi wireless charging**, if you have a Qi-compliant inductive charger.

Figure 2.18 Battery icon.

Tip: A drained Nexus lacks sufficient power to show the Home screen. You may have to charge it for a few minutes to see the Home screen.

To check the battery level and usage details, tap Settings > Battery, or swipe down with two fingers from the top of the screen and then tap in Quick Settings (Figure 2.19).

Near the top of the Battery screen are the battery level (as a percentage of full charge), charging status, and power source if charging (USB or AC). The discharge graph shows battery level over time and how long you've been running on battery power. Below the graph is a list that breaks down battery usage by apps and services. The biggest power hog is usually a bright screen (page 33).

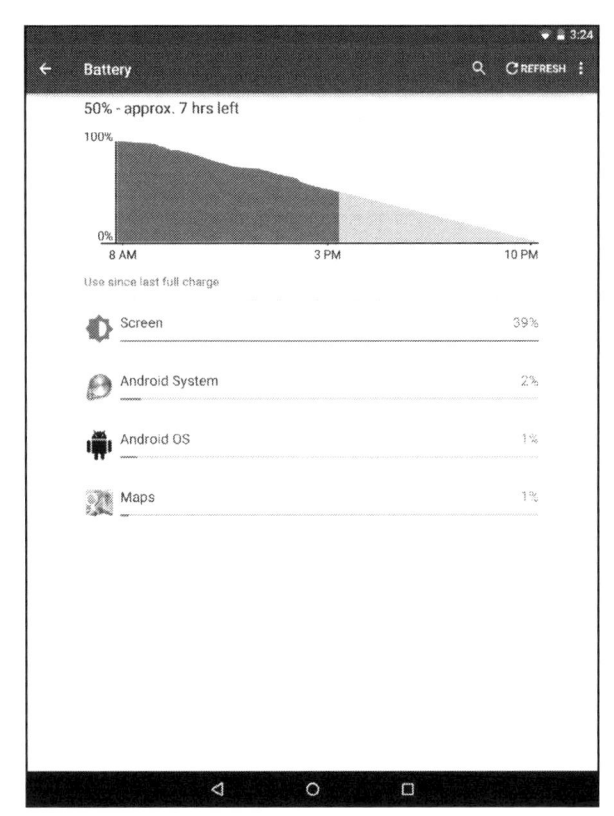

Figure 2.19 The Battery screen.

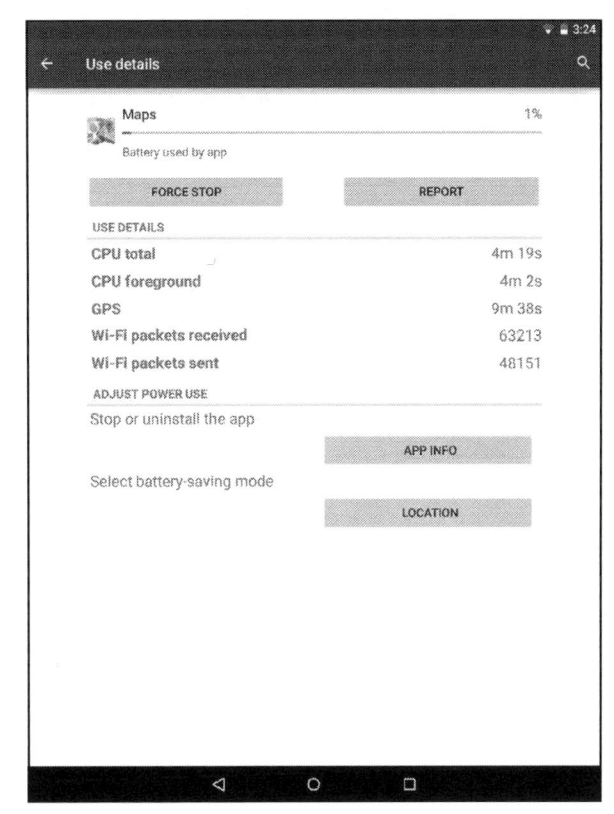

Figure 2.20 The Use Details screen.

On the Battery screen, tap an item in the list for more details (Figure 2.20). The Use Details screen varies by app or service. Some apps include buttons to let you change settings that affect power usage, or stop the app completely.

Tip: When you're not using a docked or charging Nexus, you can have it display a digital or analog clock, a slideshow of photos, a pattern of shifting colors, or other screensaver: tap Settings > Display > Daydream.

Conserving Power

When you're not using your Nexus, put it to sleep (by pressing the Power/Lock button) to conserve power. When you're using it, the battery drains more slowly if you:

- Turn on Battery Saver: tap Settings > Battery > ⋮ > Battery Saver.

- Dim the screen brightness. Swipe down with two fingers from the top of the screen and then drag ⚙ in Quick Settings. Alternatively, tap Settings > Display > Brightness Level.

- Turn off wi-fi, VPN, and Bluetooth connections when you're not using them (Chapter 5).

Tip: You can switch to airplane mode to turn off all wireless connections in one shot. Swipe down with two fingers from the top of the screen and then tap ✈ in Quick Settings.

- Turn off or minimize the use of Location services (page 180). Tap Settings > Location.

- Don't leave mapping or navigation apps open onscreen when you're not using them. They use GPS (and, thus, more power) only when they're running.

- Shorten sleep timeout. Tap Settings > Display > Sleep.

- Sync manually. Turn off automatic syncing for all apps by tapping Settings > Accounts > Google > *account_name*. When automatic syncing is turned off, you won't receive notifications of new messages, new email, and recently updated information.

> **Battery Saver**
>
> Battery Saver mode, which is intended for low-power situations, slows your tablet's processor, limits background activity (like email downloading), and dims the screen. You might be able to eke out an extra hour per charge this way. You can turn on this mode manually or automatically when the battery reaches either 5 or 15 percent charge. When Battery Saver is turned on, orange bars flank the screen. Battery Saver turns itself off when you charge your Nexus.

Screen Mirroring and External Displays

You have a few ways to use your Nexus with an external display such as an HDTV or digital projector.

- To **mirror** (duplicate) whatever is on your Nexus's screen to a high-definition television (HDTV), you can use a Nexus 7 (2013) and a **SlimPort** Micro-USB–to–HDMI cable (Figure 2.21). After you connect your Nexus to your HDTV, the Nexus screen is mirrored to your HDTV, with the audio playing on your HDTV. Don't forget to change the TV's input source to the correct HDMI connection.

- Google **Chromecast** (*google.com/chromecast*) can stream content wirelessly to your HDTV from Chromecast-aware apps (*chromecast.com/apps*), including Netflix, HBO GO, WatchESPN, WATCH Disney, Hulu Plus, Pandora, Plex, Avia, YouTube, Google Play (TV, movies, and music), and Chrome. Chromecast is a separately available two-inch dongle that plugs into the HDMI port of your HDTV (Figure 2.22). It plays media from apps by connecting to the same wi-fi network as your Nexus. Third-party developers can use the Google Cast toolkit to make their apps Chromecast-aware. Chromecast streams media directly from the internet, a server, or local storage while your Nexus acts as a remote control. On your Nexus, tap Settings > Display > Cast Screen. You can also cast from your tablet to your TV by using a Google **Nexus Player** (*google.com/nexus/player*).

Tip: To cast (mirror) your Nexus's screen to your TV, swipe down with two fingers from the top of the screen and then tap in Quick Settings.

- The Nexus 7 (2013) is compatible with devices that support **Wi-Fi Certified Miracast** (*wi-fi.org/wi-fi-certified-miracast™*) for wireless display. You can mirror your Nexus's screen and wirelessly stream video and audio to displays and other devices that support Miracast, even when a standard wi-fi network isn't available. You can show your Nexus's screen on an HDTV equipped with a Miracast adapter, for example. For more information, see the documentation that came with your Miracast-compatible display. To start mirroring, on your Nexus, tap Settings > Display > Cast Screen > > Enable Wireless Display.

Tip: Even though Miracast is a standard, individual vendors are free to call it whatever they want. Miracast isn't uniformly labeled on devices that support it. Google calls it "Wireless Display", Sony calls it "Screen Mirroring", Panasonic calls it "Display Mirroring", Samsung calls it "AllShare Cast", and LG calls it "SmartShare".

Figure 2.21 SlimPort adapter.

Figure 2.22 Google Chromecast.

CHAPTER 3

Securing Your Nexus

You can use the Nexus's security features to protect your data from co-workers, thieves, cops, spouses, lawyers, busybodies, governments, and other snoops.

Setting the Screen Lock

You can set an automatic screen lock to prevent other people from accessing your Nexus. You must unlock your tablet each time you power on or wake it (page 11). If you've created multiple users, each user has a separate Lock screen.

Tip: To change when your tablet goes to sleep, tap Settings > Display > Sleep.

To set the screen lock:

1. Tap Settings > Security > Screen Lock (Figure 3.1).

2. Tap the type of lock you want, and then follow the onscreen instructions.

    If you've previously set a lock, you must enter the pattern, personal identification number (PIN), or password to unlock it. The following screen locks are available, listed in approximate order of strength, from least secure (None) to most secure (Password):

    ▶ **None** provides no protection, not even a Lock screen. None isn't available if the tablet has multiple users (page 18).

    ▶ **Swipe** provides no protection, but you must swipe a lock icon to dismiss the Lock screen.

    ▶ **Pattern** lets you draw a simple connect-the-dots pattern to unlock.

    ▶ **PIN** requires you to type four or more digits to unlock. Longer PINs tend to be more secure.

    ▶ **Password** requires you to type four or more characters to unlock.

Tip: If your Nexus is playing music when the screen locks, you can continue listening or pause the audio without unlocking.

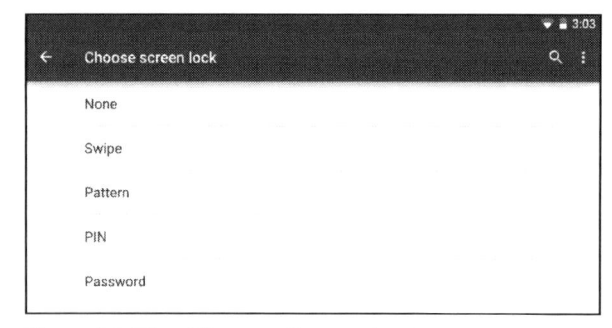

Figure 3.1 The Choose Screen Lock screen.

> ### Screen Pinning
>
> Screen pinning lets you set your Nexus to display only a specific app, which stays in view until you unpin it. Pinning is useful for playing games that you don't want to dismiss with accidental taps on the Home button. It's also handy for handing your tablet to a child to play a game, and *only* that game.
>
> **To turn screen pinning on or off:**
>
> - Tap Settings > Security > Screen Pinning > On/Off switch.
>
> **To pin a screen:**
>
> 1. Turn on screen pinning.
> 2. Open the screen that you want to pin.
> 3. Tap ☐.
> 4. On the Overview list, swipe up to reveal the pin icon on the bottom-right corner of your selected screen.
> 5. Tap the pin icon and then tap Start.
>
> **To unpin a screen:**
>
> 1. On the pinned screen, touch and hold ◁ and ☐ at the same time for a moment.
> 2. Release both buttons to unpin the screen and return to the Overview list.

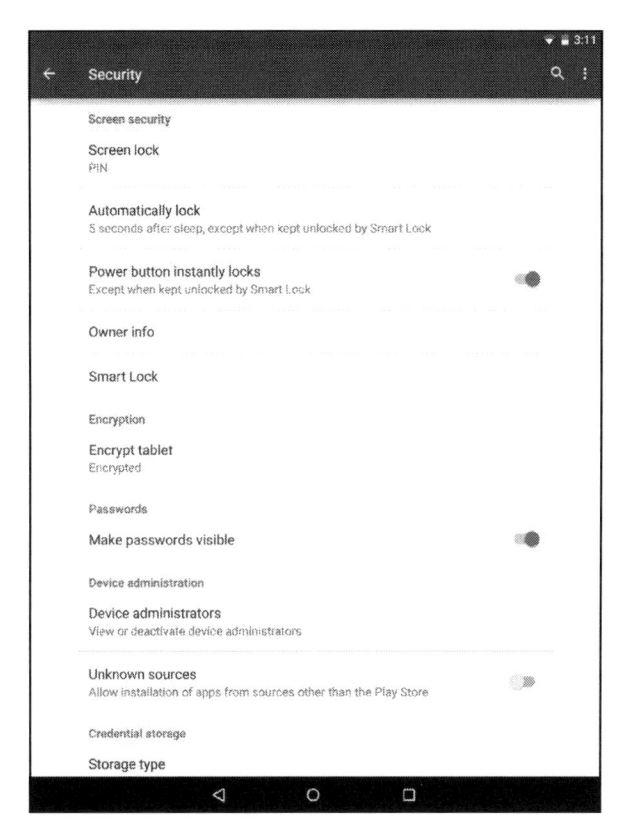

Figure 3.2 The Security screen.

You can fine-tune the screen lock by setting the following options in the Security screen (tap Settings > Security) (Figure 3.2).

- **Automatically lock**. Locks your tablet a specified amount of time after it goes to sleep. Shorter durations are more secure but less convenient.

- **Power button instantly locks**. Determines whether pressing the Power/Lock button instantly locks the tablet. If this setting is turned off, the tablet locks after the time interval specified by Automatically Lock.

- **Owner info**. Lets you show owner information or a custom message on the Lock screen.

Tip: If you enter your phone number or email address and then lose your tablet, the finder can contact you without needing to unlock it.

- **Smart Lock**. Bypasses the Lock screen when a trusted Bluetooth or NFC device is nearby. You can also bypass the Lock screen by using facial recognition with the tablet's front camera.

- **Make passwords visible**. Displays each PIN or password character briefly as you type it.

- **Make pattern visible**. Displays a pattern as you draw it.

Tip: To hear a sound when the screen locks or unlocks, tap Settings > Sound & Notification > Other Sounds > Screen Locking Sounds.

Smart Lock

Smart Lock unlocks the Nexus automatically when in the vicinity of a trusted device, such as when your Nexus is connected to a known Bluetooth device (page 68) or near an authorized NFC sticker (page 71). For example, you can tell your Nexus to remain unlocked as long as a certain Bluetooth gadget—your headphones, watch, or wearable—is within Bluetooth range. If that gadget ventures far enough away, then your Nexus realizes that you've left the room and locks itself automatically. You can even use Smart Lock with a Bluetooth-equipped car.

Locating a Lost or Stolen Nexus

You can use **Android Device Manager** to track down a lost or stolen Nexus by showing its approximate location on a map, provided that the missing Nexus is turned on and connected to a wi-fi or cellular network. You must turn on Android Device Manager *before* you lose your Nexus.

Figure 3.3 Android Device Manager settings.

To turn on Android Device Manager:

1. Tap the Google Settings app on the Home screen or All Apps screen. (The Google Settings app is different from the main Settings app.)

2. Tap Android Device Manager (Figure 3.3).

Tip: If your Nexus has multiple users, only the tablet owner can set up Android Device Manager.

---

3. Turn on the following options:

   ▶ **Remotely locate this device** lets you find your Nexus on Google Maps.

Tip: You must also turn on Location access in Settings > Location.

   ▶ **Allow remote lock and erase** lets you lock your Nexus or erase everything on it remotely (a factory reset). You can also change the Lock screen password.

To find your missing Nexus, open a browser, go to *www.android.com/devicemanager*, and then sign in to your Google Account. If you have more than one device linked to your account, click the arrow next to the device name to change the one that's displayed. To rename a device, click ✏️.

When your Nexus is found, its approximate location appears on a map, with the time it was last used (Figure 3.4).

You can select the following actions:

- **Ring**. Ring your Nexus at full volume for 5 minutes—even if it's set to silent.
- **Lock**. Lock your Nexus with a new password.
- **Erase**. Delete all your data permanently.

If your Nexus is offline (or turned off), the selected action will be performed after it's back online.

If you own another Android device, you can use the Android Device Manager app to find your missing Nexus. Download it for free from the Google Play store.

Tip: If you hide a device on Google Play, then it won't appear in Android Device Manager. You can hide or show devices on Google Play by going to *play.google.com/settings* and then selecting a device in the Visibility column.

Figure 3.4 Android Device Manager map.

Locating a Friend's Device

If a friend loses his device, he can sign in to Android Device Manager on Chrome on your Nexus, without adding his account to your tablet.

To locate a friend's device:

1. Open Chrome, open an incognito tab (page 111), and then go to *www.android.com/devicemanager*.
2. Have your friend sign in to the Google Account that he uses on his device.
3. Ring, lock, or erase the device remotely.
4. Close the Chrome tab.

Encrypting Your Nexus

Setting a PIN or password screen lock is moderately secure, but to stop a determined enemy, you must also encrypt your Nexus. **Encryption** makes data unreadable to anyone without the key and scrambles everything on your tablet: Google Accounts, app data, music and other media, downloaded information, and so on.

The Nexus 9 is encrypted automatically on first use and encryption can't be turned off. If you're using a Nexus 7, your tablet will keep its encryption settings when you update to the latest version of Android.

Encryption is irreversible. The only way to revert to an unencrypted Nexus 7 is to do a factory data reset (tap Settings > Backup & Reset > Factory Data Reset), which erases all your data and settings stored on the tablet.

Tip: If your screen-locked but unencrypted Nexus 7 is stolen, the thief can still read your data by accessing the tablet's internal storage directly, a technically sophisticated but not uncommon procedure.

Before you encrypt a Nexus 7, charge the battery and keep the tablet plugged into a power source. Schedule some free time—encryption can take an hour or more. To encrypt your Nexus 7, tap Settings > Security > Encrypt Tablet. (The Encrypt Tablet button is dimmed if your battery isn't charged or your tablet isn't plugged in.) Don't touch the tablet or interrupt the encryption process, during which your tablet may restart several times.

Verifying Apps

You can protect yourself against harmful apps by preventing the installation of apps that aren't from the Google Play store, or by scanning apps for malware (viruses) and blocking installation if a threat exists.

When you verify apps, Google receives log information, URLs related to the app, and general information about your tablet, including your device ID, version of the operating system, and IP address. App verification is turned on by default, but no data is sent to Google unless you agree to allow this when asked in the window that opens prior to installing the first app from an unknown source.

To allow or prohibit non-Play Store apps, tap Settings > Security > Unknown Sources. To scan apps for malware, tap Google Settings > Verify Apps. Verify Apps is available only when Unknown Sources is turned on. (Note that the Google Settings app is different from the main Settings app.)

Using Digital Certificates

You can use **digital certificate** files to identify your Nexus for security purposes. Some organizations use certificates to let mobile devices access private wi-fi or VPN networks, or to authenticate certain apps (such as Email or Chrome) to servers. To use a certificate to identify your Nexus, get the certificate file from your system administrator and then install it on your Nexus by following the administrator's instructions. You can manage certificates in the Credential Storage section of the Security screen (tap Settings > Security).

CHAPTER 4

Typing & Editing

The Nexus isn't all scrolling, dragging, and zooming; it also offers an onscreen keyboard and other tools for working with text.

Using the Onscreen Keyboard

An onscreen keyboard (Figure 4.1) pops up automatically when you tap any area that accepts text. The Nexus offers alphabetic, numbers-and-punctuation, and symbols keyboards, which you can switch among as you type.

Use the keyboard to type notes, email, messages, web addresses, passwords, search terms, contact information, or any other text. Typing is straightforward: tap a character to make it appear in the editing area. The target key changes color when you tap it.

The onscreen keyboard has much in common with its physical counterpart, plus a few tricks:

- **Keyboard orientation**. The keyboard reorients for portrait (tall) and landscape (wide) views. The latter view is roomier for typing. For details, see "Changing Screen Orientation" on page 35.

- **Uppercase letters**. To type an uppercase letter, tap the Shift key ⬆. This key changes color when it's active and then returns to normal after you type a letter. To turn on Caps Lock, double-tap or touch and hold ⬆. Tap again to return to lowercase.

- **Character deletion**. To delete the last character that you typed, tap the Backspace key ⌫. To delete multiple characters quickly, touch and hold the Backspace key.

- **Keyboard hiding**. To hide the keyboard, tap the Hide button ▽ below the keyboard, or tap off an editable area.

- **Double-space period shortcut**. Double-tap the spacebar at the end of a sentence to end it with a period, move one space to the right, and start the next sentence with an uppercase letter.

- **Accents and diacritical marks**. You can touch and hold certain keys to see variants of their characters in a pop-up box (Figure 4.2). Slide your finger to the target character in the box and then lift your finger to type it. The E key, for example, lets you type not only the standard e, but also ê, è, é, and other diacriticals.

Figure 4.1 The alphabetic keyboard.

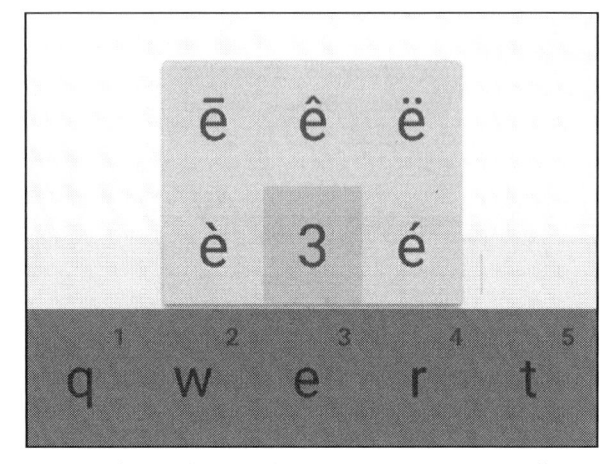

Figure 4.2 Touch and hold a key to see whether it offers additional letters or symbols.

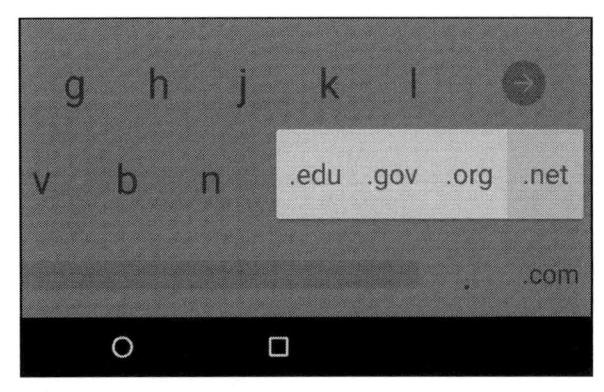

Figure 4.3 Top-level domains.

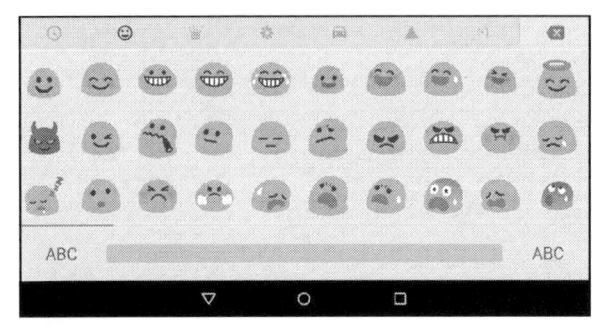

Figure 4.4 Emoticons and graphics.

- **Alternative key characters.** Some keys have tiny characters in their corners. Touch and hold one of these keys to type its alternative character.

- **Keyboard switching.** On the alphabetic keyboard, tap the ?123 key to see numbers and most punctuation. Within that layout, tap the ~[< key to see less-common symbols, tap ?123 to return to the numbers-and-punctuation layout, or tap the ABC key to return to the alphabetic keys.

- **Momentary keyboard switching.** You can quickly type a character in a different keyboard without switching away from the current one. On the alphabetic keyboard, for example, touch and hold the ?123 key; still touching the screen, slide your finger up to the numeric character that you want; and then lift your finger. Characters are typed only when you lift your finger.

- **Context-sensitive Return key.** The Return key changes to Go, Done, Next, ⬅, or 🔍, depending on whether you're typing ordinary text, a web or email address, a password, a search term, and so on. If a tiny ellipsis (...) appears on the Return key, you can tap (or touch and hold) the key to jump to the previous or next text field.

- **Web and email addresses.** When you type a web address (URL) or email address in Chrome, Gmail, or a similar app, the keyboard includes a .com key. Touch and hold the .com key to get your choice of .net, .org, .edu, and other top-level domains (Figure 4.3), depending on what country or region you've set your Nexus for.

- **Smileys and symbols.** In email, messaging, Chrome, and some other apps, you can tap the 🙂 key to type a smiley (emoticon) or graphic symbol (Figure 4.4).

Tip: Classic **emoticons**—such as the **:-)** symbol—represent facial expressions by using punctuation marks and letters, usually written to express a person's mood. Emoticons are read sideways, most commonly with the eyes on the left, followed by an (optional) nose and then a mouth.

Typing with Gestures

Drag your finger around the onscreen keyboard, and the Nexus will guess what word you're trying to spell and display it in a floating preview or in the middle of the suggestion strip (Figure 4.5). Lift your finger and that word will be typed, or tap one of the other words in the suggestion strip. You don't have to use the spacebar—just continue to glide your finger over the letters of the words you want.

Gesture typing works in the standard alphabetical keyboards, not for numbers or symbols, and it tends to work better for common dictionary words. This feature doesn't interfere with standard touch typing: if the word you want isn't shown while using Gesture Typing, you can type it manually.

To change Gesture Typing settings, tap Settings > Language & Input > Google Keyboard > Gesture Typing.

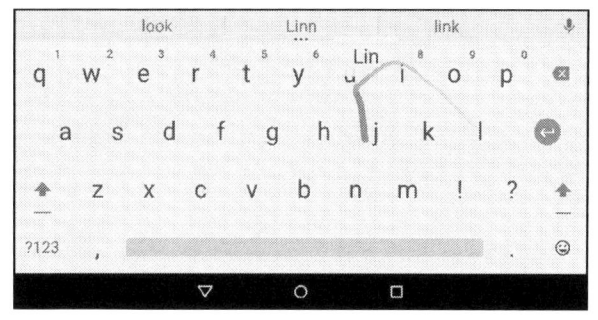

Figure 4.5 Drag your finger on the keyboard to gesture type.

> **Using Gamepads and Other Input Devices**
>
> You can connect gamepads, joysticks, and other input devices to your Nexus. If they work without special drivers or adapters on your computer, they will likely work with your tablet. To take advantage of any special controls (such as dedicated buttons) on an input device, games and apps must be designed explicitly to support them.

Using a Physical Keyboard

If you type a lot of text, work with large documents, or just don't like typing on glass, you can use a physical keyboard. You can connect the keyboard to your Nexus via USB or Bluetooth and then use it just as you would with a computer. For USB connections, you'll need an adapter to connect the keyboard to the Nexus's Micro-USB port. To connect a Bluetooth keyboard, see "Bluetooth Devices" on page 68. Bluetooth and unpowered USB connections drain the battery quickly. To connect multiple USB devices, use a powered USB hub.

When you connect a keyboard to your Nexus, you can use it to navigate as well as type text:

- Use the arrow keys to select items.
- Pressing Return when an item is selected is equivalent to tapping that item.
- Pressing Escape is equivalent to tapping Back.
- Pressing Tab or Shift+Tab jumps to the next or previous text field.

Tip: See also "Using a Mouse" on page 14.

Setting Typing Options

The onscreen keyboard has several built-in shortcuts and tricks that you can turn on or off. Tap Settings > Language & Input > Google Keyboard > Preferences (Figure 4.6). After you get the hang of typing on the onscreen keyboard, you'll know whether a particular typing option is helpful or irritating.

You can set the following options:

- **Auto-capitalization.** Capitalize the first letter after a period automatically.

- **Double-space period shortcut.** Double-tap the spacebar at the end of a sentence to type a period and start a new sentence.

- **Vibrate on keypress.** Vibrate the tablet each time you press a key. To adjust the vibration duration, tap Settings > Language & Input > Google Keyboard > Advanced.

- **Sound on keypress.** Play a sound each time you press a key. To adjust the keypress volume, tap Settings > Language & Input > Google Keyboard > Advanced. See also "Adjusting the Volume" on page 36.

Figure 4.6 The Google Keyboard Preferences screen.

Auto-correction

As you type, auto-correction automatically suggests words and corrections, which appear at the top of the keyboard. Touch and hold the center suggestion to see additional suggestions (Figure 4.7). To adjust auto-correction settings, tap Settings > Language & Input > Google Keyboard > Text Correction. You can set the following options:

- **Personal dictionary.** Manage a list of personal or specialized words and auto-expanding text snippets that you want auto-correction to know about.

- **Add-on dictionaries.** Install, disable, or delete auto-correction dictionaries for various languages.

Tip: Emoji dictionaries add suggestions for smiley faces and other picture characters.

- **Block offensive words.** Don't suggest naughty words.

- **Auto-correction.** Turn off auto-correction or adjust its aggressiveness. In modest mode, tap a suggestion to accept it; to reject it, finish typing the word. In aggressive mode, auto-correction replaces typos with suggestions automatically when you tap a space or punctuation character at the end of a word.

- **Show correction suggestions.** Determines whether auto-correction suggestions appear.

- **Personalized suggestions.** Suggest words based on your email, location, and other personal data.

- **Suggest Contact names.** Suggest names from the Contacts app.

- **Next-word suggestions.** Suggest the next word based on the word that you just typed.

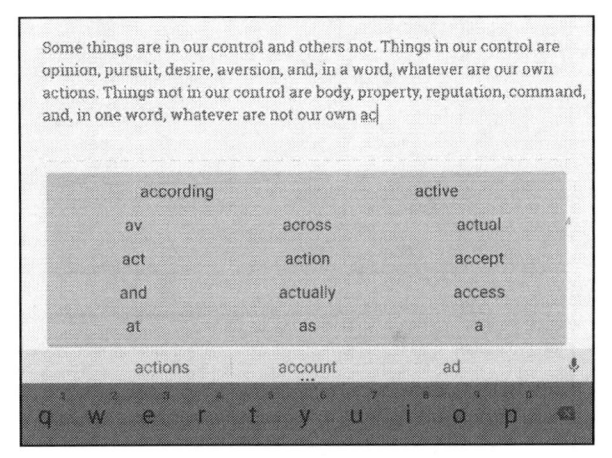

Figure 4.7 Touch and hold the center suggestion to see additional auto-correction suggestions.

Figure 4.8 Spelling replacement options.

Checking Spelling

A misspelled word is flagged with an underline. To see replacement options, touch and hold the word and then tap Replace in the pop-up menu (Figure 4.8).

Tap one of the alternative spellings to replace the misspelled word. If the word you want doesn't appear, just retype it. To configure the spell checker, tap Settings > Language & Input > Spell Checker.

Your **personal dictionary** contains a list of words that you don't want to be autocorrected or flagged as misspellings. This dictionary starts out empty. Words are added to it when you tap Add to Dictionary in the spell checker, but you can also edit the dictionary manually: tap Settings > Language & Input > Google Keyboard > Text Correction > Personal Dictionary.

Using International Keyboards

If you communicate in more than one language, you can add keyboards to type in Spanish, Italian, French, German, Chinese, Japanese, Russian, and many more. You can switch keyboards at any time.

The **system language**, which you chose when you set up your Nexus, is used for the screens, keyboard, and interface. Switching keyboards doesn't affect the system language.

To view or change the system language:

- Tap Settings > Language & Input > Language.

To add an international keyboard:

1   Tap Settings > Language & Input (Figure 4.9).

2   To add a Hindi, Japanese, Korean, or Chinese keyboard, tap Current Keyboard, and then tap Choose Keyboards.

    or

    To add keyboards for other languages, tap Google Keyboard, tap Languages, turn off Use System Language, and then select the desired keyboard language(s) (Figure 4.10).

Figure 4.9 The Language & Input screen.

Figure 4.10 The Languages screen.

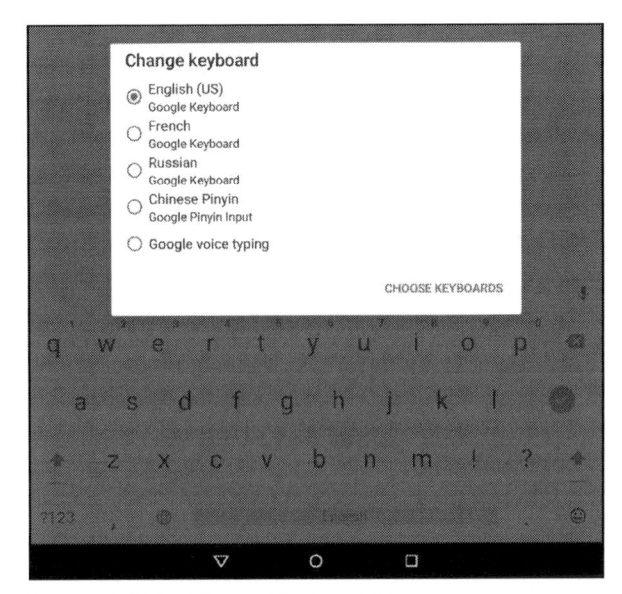

Figure 4.11 The Change Keyboard list.

To switch keyboards:

- Tap the Location key 🌐 repeatedly to cycle through your keyboards. Stop when you see the name of the desired keyboard on the spacebar.

    or

    Touch and hold the Location key 🌐 and then tap the desired keyboard in the pop-up list (Figure 4.11).

Tip: The Location key (next to the spacebar) appears only if you've added multiple keyboards.

Printing from Your Nexus

You have a few ways to print from your Nexus.

- **Google Cloud Print**. Google Cloud Print is a Google service that connects your printers to the web. You can make your printers available to you and anyone you choose, from a variety of apps. To get started, download the free Cloud Print app from the Google Play store. For details, go to *google.com/cloudprint/learn/*. To configure printing, tap Settings > Printing.

- **Wi-fi or cloud-hosted services**. An app can print any type of content over wi-fi or cloud-hosted services (like Google Cloud Print), provided the developer has added printing support to the app. In a print-enabled app, you can discover available printers, change paper sizes, choose specific pages to print, and print almost any kind of document, image, or file. Android provides a print manager that mediates between apps requesting printing and installed print services that handle print requests. Printer manufacturers can develop their own print services that communicate with specific types of printers. These print services plugins are available in the Google Play store, where you can find and install them on your tablet. Print services are listed in Settings > Printing.

- **Bluetooth printer**. After pairing your Nexus with a Bluetooth printer (page 68), you can print from a variety of apps. View the document, webpage, or image that you want to print. Choose Share (look for a Share icon or a > Share command). Tap Bluetooth and then select your Bluetooth printer on the Bluetooth Device Chooser screen. If a prompt appears on the printer, confirm that the Nexus is printing a document. The document is uploaded (sent from the tablet to the printer), and then it prints. Check notifications for the upload status.

Tip: Not everything on your Nexus can be printed on a Bluetooth printer. If you can't find the Share command or Bluetooth isn't available on the Share menu, then you can't print via Bluetooth.

CHAPTER 5

Wireless & Network Connections

The Nexus can access the internet over a wi-fi connection. You can jump online from a wireless network at home, work, or school, or from a public wi-fi hotspot at a library, café, or airport.

This chapter also covers the Nexus's other wireless features: cellular connections, Bluetooth, VPNs (virtual private networks), and more.

Wi-Fi Connections

Wi-fi—also known by its technical name, **IEEE 802.11**—is the same technology that laptop computers and handheld gadgets use to get online at high speed. After your Nexus is connected to a wi-fi network, you can browse the web, send and receive email, view maps, and do other tasks that require an internet connection. Wi-fi also lets you interact with other devices and computers on the same network.

When wi-fi is turned on, your Nexus scans continually for nearby networks. You can connect to a wi-fi network (and view or change network settings) by tapping Settings > Wi-Fi; alternatively, swipe down with two fingers from the top of the screen and then tap the text label (network name) below the icon in Quick Settings. When your Nexus is joined to a wi-fi network, the Wi-Fi icon in the status bar at the top of the screen shows the signal strength. The more bars, the stronger the signal (Figure 5.1).

You can also connect to a **closed** network—one whose security-minded owner has hidden the network name so that it isn't shown in the list of scanned networks.

Some wireless networks use **MAC address** filtering to restrict access to preapproved computers, devices, and other hardware. To find your Nexus's MAC address, tap Settings > Wi-Fi > ⋮ > Advanced. (MAC stands for Media Access Control and isn't related to Apple Mac computers specifically.)

After you join a wi-fi network, your Nexus automatically reconnects to it whenever the network is in range. If more than one previously used network is in range, your Nexus rejoins the one last used. You can make your Nexus "forget" specific networks (and their passwords) so that it doesn't join them automatically.

If you join a public, unsecured wi-fi network, it's easy for the network owner or nearby intruders to collect the unencrypted data (passwords, credit-card numbers, web addresses, and so on) flowing between your Nexus and the wireless router. Don't shop, bank, or pay bills on such networks. If you have no choice, use a VPN service like WiTopia.

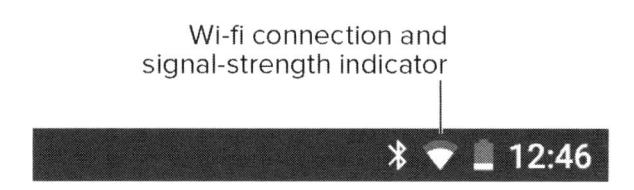

Figure 5.1 The status bar shows your wi-fi status.

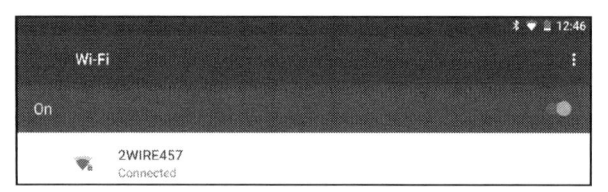

Figure 5.2 The Wi-Fi toggle on the Wi-Fi screen.

Mobile Hotspots

If you don't have a cellular Nexus, then your tablet can't connect directly to cellular networks—the networks used to make mobile phone calls—but you can still connect to a cellular network over wi-fi by using a **mobile hotspot** (a practice also known as **tethering**). A mobile hotspot is a pocket-size gadget or smartphone that offers wireless internet connections to multiple devices at the same time (like your Nexus, mobile phone, and laptop). If you have a cellular Nexus, then your tablet can serve as a mobile hotspot for other devices.

To share your mobile data connection (cellular models):

- Tap Settings > More > Tethering & Portable Hotspot.

Signal-strength indicator

Lock indicates that network requires a password

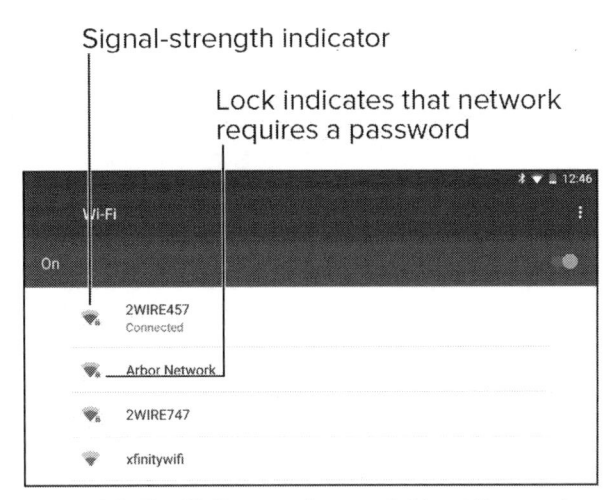

Figure 5.3 The Wi-Fi screen lists available wi-fi networks.

Figure 5.4 A secured network requires a password.

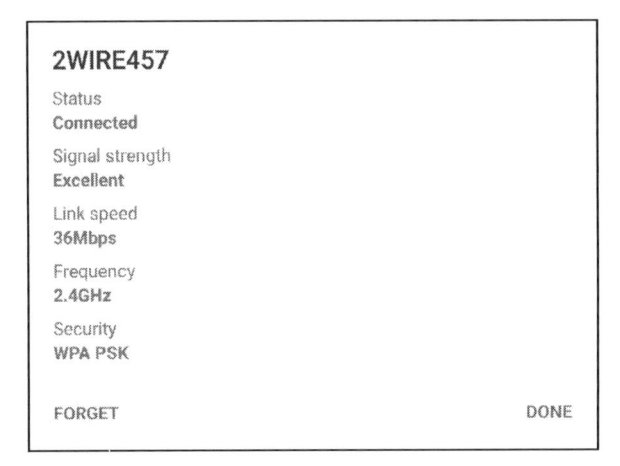

Figure 5.5 Tap a network name to view or clear its settings.

To turn wi-fi on or off:

- Tap Settings > Wi-Fi and then tap the On/Off switch (Figure 5.2).

    or

    Swipe down with two fingers from the top of the screen and then tap ▼ in Quick Settings.

Tip: If you're not using the internet, you can turn off wi-fi to conserve battery power.

To connect to a wi-fi network:

1 Tap Settings > Wi-Fi (Figure 5.3).

   The Nexus scans for active wi-fi networks within range and lists them.

Tip: To scan for networks manually at any time, tap Settings > Wi-Fi > ⋮ > Refresh.

2 Tap the name of a network that you want to connect to.

3 If the network is secured, as indicated by a lock icon 🔒, type its password and then tap Connect (Figure 5.4).

Tip: If your wi-fi router supports Wi-Fi Protected Setup (WPS), tap Settings > Wi-Fi > ⋮ > Advanced and then tap WPS Push Button or WPS Pin Entry.

To forget a network so that your Nexus doesn't join it automatically:

1 Tap Settings > Wi-Fi.

2 Tap the name of the target network. To see out-of-range networks to which you've previously connected, tap ⋮ > Saved Networks.

3 Tap Forget (Figure 5.5).

Tip: You can also touch and hold the network name in Settings > Wi-Fi and then tap Forget Network.

To join a closed (hidden) wi-fi network:

1. Get the network's name and security settings from the network's owner or administrator.
2. Tap Settings > Wi-Fi > ⋮ > Add Network (Figure 5.6).
3. Enter the network name (SSID), security (encryption) type, and (if required) password.
4. Tap Save.

   The network appears in the Settings > Wi-Fi screen.

To view or change a network's settings:

1. Tap Settings > Wi-Fi.
2. Touch and hold the network name, and then tap Modify Network to view or change its settings (Figure 5.7).

Tip: To connect to a network via a proxy server, turn on Advanced Options when you connect to, add, or modify a network.

To configure general wi-fi network settings:

1. Tap Settings > Wi-Fi > ⋮ > Advanced (Figure 5.8).
2. The following settings and information are available:

   Network notification. Determines whether you receive notifications in the status bar at the top of the screen when your Nexus detects an open (unsecured) wi-fi network.

   Scanning always available. Determines whether apps and services can use Location services (page 180) to scan for wi-fi networks to determine your location, even when wi-fi is turned off.

   Keep Wi-Fi on during sleep. Determines whether your Nexus stays connected to wi-fi when it sleeps. If you're using a mobile hotspot, you can use this option to reduce mobile data usage.

   Wi-Fi frequency band. Choose a specific wi-fi band or let your Nexus determine automatically which band has the best signal.

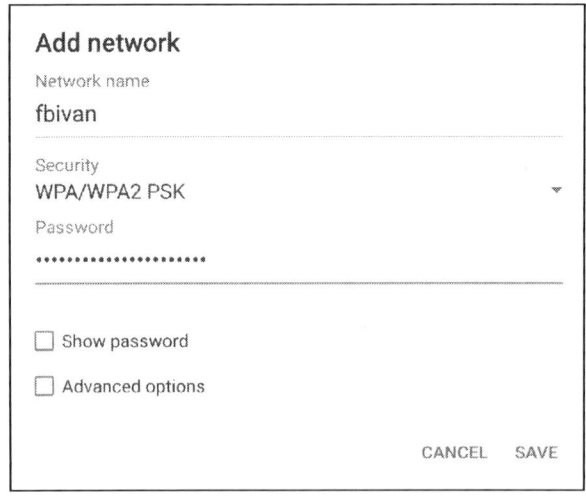

Figure 5.6 Before you can join a closed network, the network's owner or administrator must tell you its settings.

Figure 5.7 Touch and hold a network name to view or change its settings.

Figure 5.8 The Advanced Wi-Fi screen.

Figure 5.9 A wi-fi network login notification.

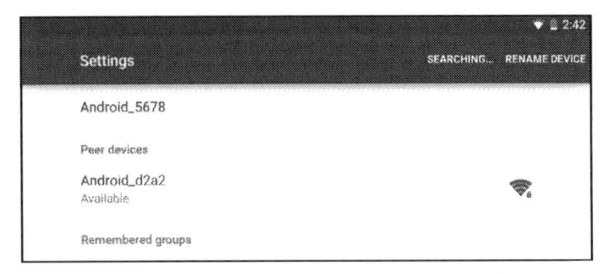

Figure 5.10 The Wi-Fi Direct screen lists nearby devices.

Install certificates. Installs any certificate files (page 48) found in USB storage.

Wi-Fi Direct and WPS settings. Use specialized wi-fi and router features.

MAC address. Shows the Media Access Control (MAC) address of your Nexus.

IP address. Shows the Internet Protocol (IP) address assigned to your Nexus by the wi-fi network you're connected to (or your static IP address, if you've set one by tapping Advanced Options).

Tip: Some of the preceding settings aren't available on the Nexus 7 (2012).

Login screens

Many public-access wi-fi hotspots don't require a password but do need you to log in or accept terms of use by completing a web form after you connect. After you join the network, open Chrome, and enter any valid web address. After a few seconds, a login page should appear if you need to sign in (or pay) for access. You can also drag down the notification shade from the top of the screen and then tap the notification to log in (Figure 5.9). Many commercial networks in large public places, such as airports and hotels, charge an hourly or daily fee to your credit card.

Wi-Fi Direct connections

You can use **Wi-Fi Direct** to connect directly to other nearby devices that support Wi-Fi Direct. These simple peer-to-peer (P2P) connections, also called ad-hoc networks, need no internet access points or passwords, and are handy for sharing files or playing head-to-head games. To use Wi-Fi Direct, tap Settings > Wi-Fi > ⋮ > Advanced > Wi-Fi Direct. The Wi-Fi Direct screen lists nearby devices that are available to connect to (Figure 5.10). Both parties must authorize the connection. (Wi-Fi Direct works much like Bluetooth.)

Cellular Connections

If you have a cellular (LTE/HSPA+) Nexus, you don't need a wi-fi hotspot to connect to the internet. You can connect wherever your chosen carrier provides cellular network coverage. Before you can start using a cellular network, you must sign up for a pre-paid data plan. Plans vary by carrier and country; in the United States, for example, plans are available from AT&T, T-Mobile, and Verizon. The Nexus isn't "locked" to any particular carrier.

A **SIM card** (Subscriber Identity Module) is used for cellular data and stores information about your cellular account. You can install the card yourself or replace it if you change carriers. The Nexus 7 uses a micro-SIM card and the Nexus 9 uses a nano SIM card.

Look for the small, looped piece of wire—called a SIM card ejection tool—that came with the Nexus. Insert the pin into a tiny hole on the edge of the Nexus to pop open the SIM tray. Pull out the SIM tray to install or replace the SIM card. You may have to power off and restart your Nexus.

Tip: To check whether a SIM card is installed, tap Settings > SIM Cards.

To activate the SIM card, turn off wi-fi (Settings > Wi-Fi > Off) and then wait for a notification to appear at the top of the screen. Drag down the notification shade from the top of the screen and then tap the notification. Follow the activation instructions provided by your carrier. Carriers can take a minute or more to activate your SIM card. If activation is taking too long, try restarting your tablet or entering and then exiting airplane mode (page 72).

To manage mobile network connections, tap Settings > More.

Figure 5.11 The VPN screen.

Figure 5.12 The Edit VPN Profile screen.

Figure 5.13 The Connect To screen.

Always-on VPNs

An **always-on VPN** prohibits network traffic from getting through unless a secure VPN connection has been established. If your tablet loses its connection to the VPN server (or if the VPN server ends the session), traffic doesn't begin flowing over an unprotected network connection. To designate a VPN to always remain connected to, tap Settings > More > VPN > ⋮ > Always-On VPN.

Virtual Private Networks

A **virtual private network** (VPN) lets you connect from your Nexus to an organization's network securely and privately by using the internet as a conduit. VPN works over wi-fi network connections. You can add multiple VPN profiles and switch among them on the VPN screen (tap Settings > More > VPN) (Figure 5.11).

Tip: To use a VPN, you must first set a PIN or Password screen lock. For details, see "Setting the Screen Lock" on page 44.

To add a new VPN profile:

1. Tap Settings > More > VPN > ＋.
2. Configure the VPN connection based on information you get from your network administrator or your IT department (Figure 5.12).

Tip: If you've set up a VPN on your computer, you may be able to use the same VPN settings for your Nexus.

3. Tap Save.

    The VPN profile is added to the list on the VPN screen.

To connect to a VPN:

1. Tap Settings > More > VPN.
2. Tap the name of the VPN profile.
3. In the Connect To screen, enter your credentials.

    If you don't want to type your credentials every time you connect, turn on Save Account Information (Figure 5.13).

4. Tap Connect.

    While you're connected to a VPN, a status-bar icon and notification are displayed. To disconnect, tap the notification for the VPN connection.

To edit or delete a VPN profile:

1. Tap Settings > More > VPN.
2. Touch and hold the name of the VPN profile, and then tap Edit Profile or Delete Profile.

Chapter 5 Wireless & Network Connections

Bluetooth Devices

Bluetooth is a wireless technology that provides short-range (up to 32 feet/10 meters) radio links between a Nexus and external keyboards, mice, headphones, speakers, wearables, or other Bluetooth-equipped devices. It eliminates cable clutter while simplifying communications, sharing, and data synchronization between devices. Bluetooth doesn't need a line-of-sight connection, so you can, say, use a handsfree headset to listen to music playing on the Nexus in your backpack or pocket.

A **passcode** (or personal identification number [PIN]) is a number that associates your Nexus with a Bluetooth device. For security, many Bluetooth devices make you use a passcode to ensure that your Nexus is connecting to your device and not someone else's nearby. Check the device's manual for a passcode. (The most common passcodes are 0000 and 1234.)

Before you can use a Bluetooth device, you must make it **discoverable** and then pair it with your Nexus; the device will come with instructions. **Pairing** (or **passcode exchange**) gets the Nexus to positively identify the device that you want to connect to. After it's paired, the device autoconnects whenever it's within range of your Nexus. You can pair your Nexus with multiple devices at the same time (say, a headset and a keyboard).

Your Nexus comes with a generic Bluetooth name, visible to other Bluetooth devices when you connect them. You can change the name to something more meaningful.

To turn Bluetooth on or off:

- Tap Settings > Bluetooth and then tap the On/Off switch (Figure 5.14).

    or

    Swipe down with two fingers from the top of the screen and then tap ✱ in Quick Settings.

    When Bluetooth is on, a Bluetooth icon ✱ appears in the status bar at the top of the screen.

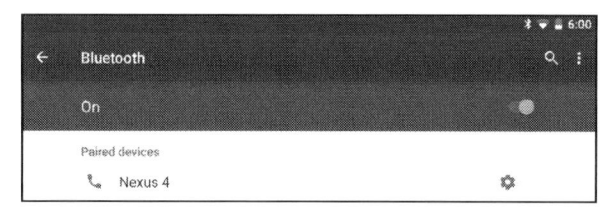

Figure 5.14 The Bluetooth toggle on the Bluetooth screen.

Tip: If you're not connected to a Bluetooth device, you can turn off Bluetooth to conserve battery power.

Figure 5.15 The Bluetooth screen.

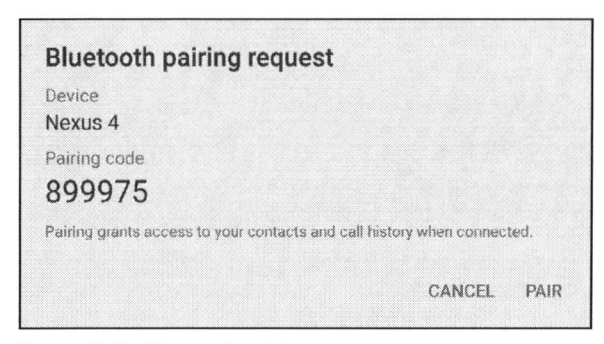

Figure 5.16 Bluetooth pairing request.

To change your Nexus's Bluetooth name:

1. Tap Settings > Bluetooth

2. Make sure Bluetooth is turned on.

3. Tap ⋮ > Rename This Device.

To pair a Bluetooth device with your Nexus:

1. On your Nexus, make sure Bluetooth is turned on.

2. Turn on your Bluetooth device and then follow the instructions that came with it to make it discoverable.

3. On your Nexus, tap Settings > Bluetooth.

   or

   Swipe down with two fingers from the top of the screen and then tap the word *Bluetooth* in Quick Settings.

   The Bluetooth screen lists nearby discoverable devices (Figure 5.15). If you don't see your device, tap ⋮ > Refresh.

4. Tap the device in the Available Devices list and then follow the onscreen instructions (Figure 5.16).

   If requested, type the passcode (PIN) to complete the pairing. (Check the pairing request or the device's manual for the passcode.)

   After you've paired with a Bluetooth device, you can connect to it manually (to switch devices, for example, or to reconnect after it's back in range).

Tip: Some Bluetooth audio devices come with a small separate transceiver that plugs into the Nexus's headset jack. If you have one of these transceivers, you don't need to turn on Bluetooth; the plug-in takes care of the connection.

To connect to a Bluetooth device:

1 Tap Settings > Bluetooth.

2 Make sure Bluetooth is turned on.

3 In the list of devices, tap a paired but unconnected device.

   When the Nexus and the device are connected, the device is shown as connected in the list.

Tip: If you transfer files to your Nexus via Bluetooth, you can see them by tapping ⋮ > Show Received Files.

To unpair (forget), rename, or configure a paired Bluetooth device:

1 Tap Settings > Bluetooth.

2 Make sure Bluetooth is turned on.

3 Tap ✲ next to the device name.

Tip: You can use Smart Lock (page 45) to unlock your Nexus automatically when it's near a trusted Bluetooth device.

Figure 5.17 NFC and Android Beam must be enabled on both devices.

Tip: You can also instantly pair your Nexus to Bluetooth devices (like headsets or speakers) that support the Simple Secure Pairing standard just by tapping the devices together.

Android Beam & NFC

Android Beam lets you easily share your photos, videos, contacts, webpages, YouTube videos, directions, apps, and other content with a simple tap. Touch your Nexus to another Android device (smartphone or tablet) and then tap to beam whatever's on your screen to your friend's device (or vice versa).

Both devices must be NFC-enabled to use Android Beam. **NFC** (Near Field Communication) lets devices establish radio communication with each other when they're touching or in close proximity. The Nexus supports NFC. If the other device doesn't support NFC, you can't use Android Beam.

To beam screen content:

1. Make sure NFC is enabled on both devices.

   To enable NFC on your Nexus, tap Settings > More > NFC > On.

2. Make sure Android Beam is enabled on both devices (Figure 5.17).

   To enable Android Beam on your Nexus, tap Settings > More > Android Beam > On.

3. Open a screen containing what you want to share (photo, video, map, whatever). You may have to use the app's Share menu to initiate Android Beam.

4. Move the back of your Nexus toward the back of the other device.

   When the devices connect, you hear a sound, and your screen image shrinks and shows an instructive message.

Tip: To make a connection, you may have to experiment with positioning the devices relative to each other.

---

5. Tap your screen anywhere.

   The open app determines what's beamed. Your friend's device displays the transferred content.

   If the necessary app isn't installed, Google Play opens to a screen where your friend can download the app.

Chapter 5 Wireless & Network Connections 71

Airplane Mode

If an airplane's cabin crew asks you to turn off electronic devices to avoid interfering with the flight instruments, you can turn on **airplane mode** to suppress your Nexus's wi-fi, cellular, Bluetooth, NFC, GPS, and other wireless signals.

You can still play downloaded music and videos, read books, play games and do other things that don't involve wireless data transmission.

To turn airplane mode on or off:

- Tap Settings > More > Airplane Mode (Figure 5.18).

    or

    Swipe down with two fingers from the top of the screen and then tap ✈ in Quick Settings.

When airplane mode is on, ✈ appears in the status bar at the top of the screen.

If the plane offers in-flight wi-fi, tap Settings > Wi-Fi > On. If you're using a Bluetooth accessory, tap Settings > Bluetooth > On.

Tip: When you're not using the internet, airplane mode is also a quick way to turn off all your Nexus's battery-draining wireless services in one shot.

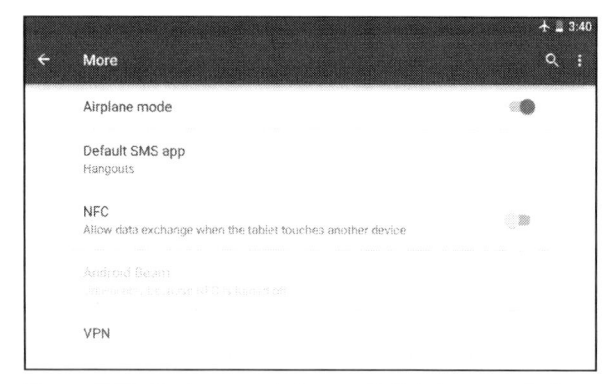

Figure 5.18 Airplane mode turns off all data transmission from your Nexus.

CHAPTER 6

Managing Your Accounts & Data

When you first set up your Nexus, you created a Google Account or signed in to an existing one. (If you skipped that step, this chapter shows you how.) If you have multiple Google Accounts, you can add them all. The Nexus also supports third-party accounts for internet-based mail and other online services, such as Facebook, Yahoo, Microsoft Exchange, and Skype. Moreover, you can **sync** (synchronize) some or all data associated with accounts, ensuring that information is kept up to date in multiple locations (such as on the web and locally on your Nexus). For Google Accounts, online backups let you restore your data and settings to any Android tablet or smartphone.

Adding and Removing Accounts

You can add, edit, and remove accounts by using the Settings > Accounts screen, which shows accounts that you're signed in to (Figure 6.1). By default, Accounts lets you add Google, Microsoft Exchange, and web-based email accounts. You can add other types of accounts, depending on which apps you've installed. Accounts for some apps—such as Skype, Facebook, Twitter, and Dropbox—appear in Settings only after you sign in to the app directly. In other apps, such as Amazon Kindle, you manage your account entirely within the app, without tapping Settings > Accounts.

Adding accounts is usually painless, but for some accounts, you may need to get details from the system administrator or service provider. Most accounts request a username and password, but depending on the service you're connecting to, you may also have to provide a domain or server address.

To add an account:

1   Tap Settings > Accounts > Add Account.

2   On the Add an Account screen, tap the type of account to add (Figure 6.2).

    To add a Google Account, tap Google. To add a Microsoft Exchange account, tap Exchange. To add a web-based mail account, tap Personal IMAP or POP3 (typically, IMAP; see page 122). Other types of accounts may also be available, depending on which apps you've installed.

3   Follow the onscreen instructions, which vary by account type.

    Depending on the kind of account, you may be asked to name the account, specify which data to sync, and supply other details.

    When you're done, the account is added to the Accounts screen.

Tip: You can also add a Google or email account from directly within the Gmail app, either in the initial screen or the ≡ > Settings screen.

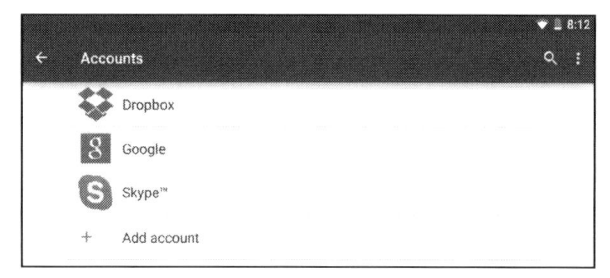

Figure 6.1 The Accounts screen shows accounts that you're signed into.

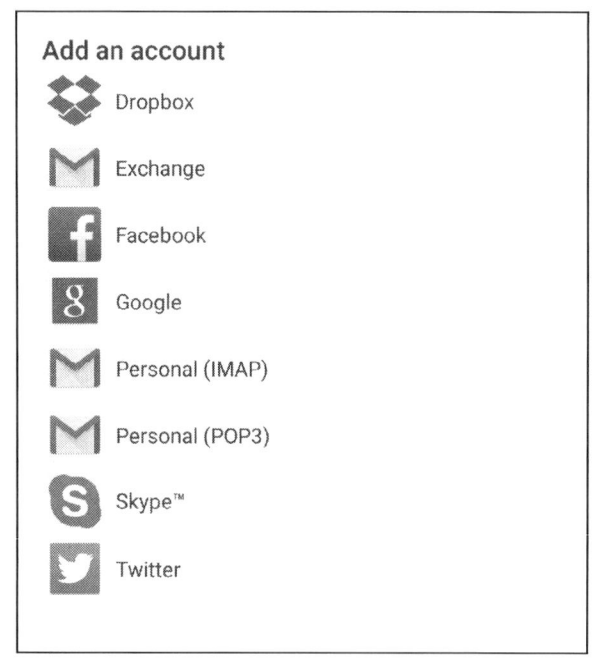

Figure 6.2 The list of available account types depends on which apps you've installed.

To edit an account:

1 Tap Settings > Accounts.

2 Tap the account type, and then, if necessary, tap the account name.

You can view or change the account's current settings, which vary by account.

To remove an account:

1 Tap Settings > Accounts.

2 Tap the account type, and then, if necessary, tap the account name.

3 Tap ⋮ > Remove Account.

All information associated with the account (email, contacts, settings, and so on) is removed as well.

Tip: For some types of accounts, the ⋮ > Remove Account command isn't available. In that case, look for a Remove option in the account's settings screen or within the app itself.

Configuring Sync Options

You can configure sync options for any of your apps and decide what kinds of data to sync for each account.

If an account does **two-way sync**, changes that you make to the information on your Nexus are also applied to the copy of that information on the web, and vice versa. Most accounts, including Google Accounts, work this way. Changes that you make in the Contacts app on your Nexus, for example, are made automatically to your Google contacts on the web. If an account does only **one-way sync**, the information on your Nexus is read-only.

Tip: Some apps let you fine-tune sync settings within the app. In Gmail, for example, tap ≡ > Settings > *account_name* > Manage Labels, tap a label, and then tap Sync Messages.

You can sync manually or automatically by using the autosync feature. To toggle autosync, tap Settings > Accounts > ⋮ > Auto-Sync Data. If autosync is turned off, you won't receive notifications when updates occur; you must sync manually (by using the Sync screen or the app's own tools) to collect recent email, messages, and so on. Sync options vary by account type; this section shows you how to configure Google Account sync settings. For other accounts, tap the account name in the Settings > Accounts screen to see what's available.

Tip: If you don't need to sync automatically, you can turn off autosync to conserve battery power.

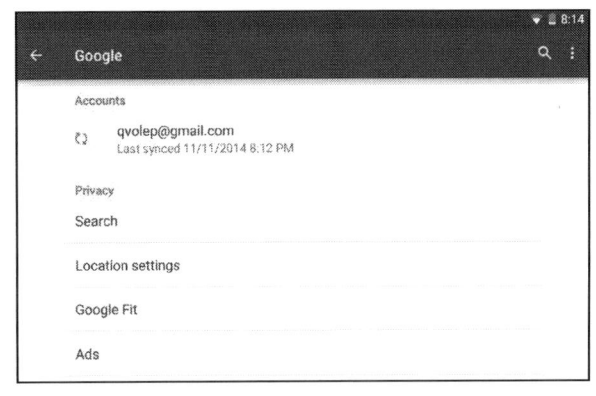

Figure 6.3 The Google Accounts screen.

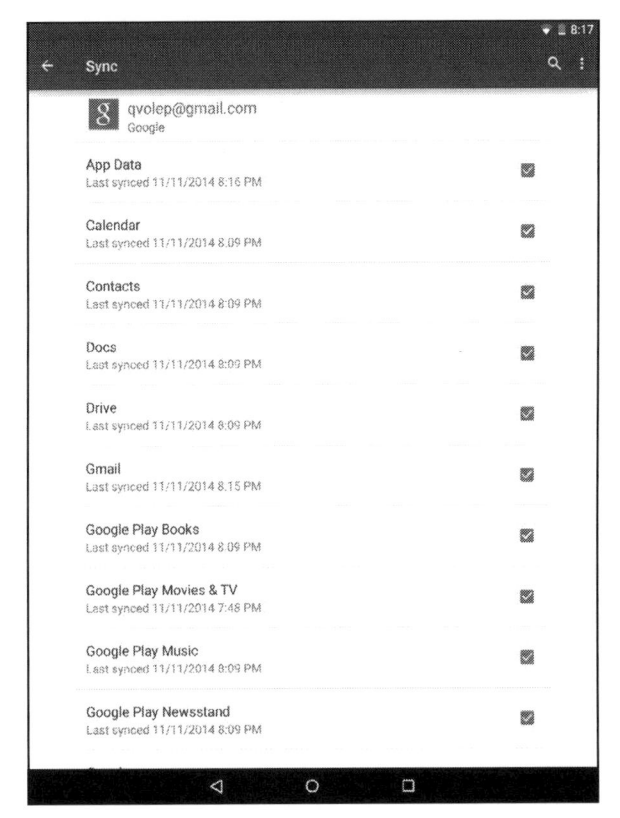

Figure 6.4 The Sync screen.

To set sync options for a Google Account:

1 Tap Settings > Accounts > Google.

   The Google screen opens (Figure 6.3). Near the top of the screen, each Google Account is listed, along with the current sync status.

2 Tap the account whose sync settings you want to change.

   The Sync screen opens (Figure 6.4).

3 Tap items to select or clear their checkboxes.

   Clearing an item doesn't remove information from your Nexus; it simply stops it from syncing with the version on the web.

To sync a Google Account manually (if auto-sync is turned off):

1 Tap Settings > Accounts > Google.

2 Tap the account whose data you want to sync.

3 Tap the items that you want to sync.

Chapter 6   Managing Your Accounts & Data   77

Backing Up or Erasing Your Data

You can back up settings and other data associated with your Google Account(s). If you replace your Nexus or get a new Android gadget, you can restore your data for any account that you previously backed up. You can also reset your Nexus to its original factory state, erasing all your personal data and settings (handy if you're selling your Nexus).

Tip: If your tablet has multiple users, only the owner can access backup and reset settings.

Tap Settings > Backup & Reset and then tap one of the following options on the Backup & Reset screen:

- **Back up my data.** Backs up a variety of your personal data, including wi-fi passwords, Chrome bookmarks, Google Play apps, personal-dictionary words, Home-screen layout, and most of your custom settings. Some third-party apps tap into this feature, so you can restore your data if you reinstall an app. If you turn off this option, your data is no longer backed up, and any existing backups are deleted from Google's servers.

- **Backup account.** Lists which Google Accounts are backed up. To back up additional accounts, tap Backup Account > Add Account.

Tip: You can restore only a backed-up account when you factory-reset or first set up your Nexus. (See "Setting Up Your Nexus" on page 16.)

- **Automatic restore.** Restores an app's data and settings when you reinstall the app, provided that the app supports the backup service.

- **Factory data reset.** Erases all your personal data and settings from your Nexus, including your Google Account; other accounts; all users; system and app settings; network settings; downloaded apps; and your locally stored media, documents, and other files. After resetting your Nexus, you must go through the setup process again (see "Setting Up Your Nexus" on page 16).

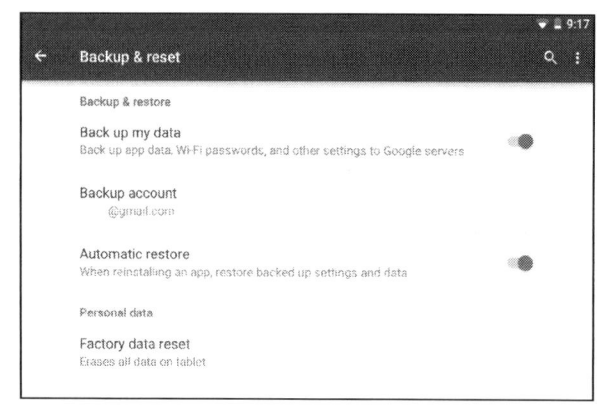

Figure 6.5 The Backup & Reset screen.

CHAPTER 7

Connecting to Computers

You can use the USB cable that came with your Nexus to transfer files to and from your Windows PC or Apple Macintosh computer.

Tip: To manage files directly on your Nexus, download a file-manager app (such as ES File Explorer or File Manager Explorer) from the Google Play store.

Connecting to a Windows PC via USB

You can use a USB cable to connect your Nexus to a Windows computer and transfer music, videos, pictures, documents, and other files between them. This connection uses Media Transfer Protocol (MTP). Windows Vista, Windows 7, Windows 8, and later support MTP. Windows XP supports MTP only if Windows Media Player 10 or later is installed. Pre-XP versions of Windows may not recognize the Nexus.

When you connect your Nexus to a USB port on your Windows computer, the Nexus's USB storage appears as a drive in the Computer folder (Figure 7.1). The notification *Connected as a media device* appears on the Nexus's notification shade.

To open the Computer folder on your PC, choose Start > Computer or press Windows logo key + E. Double-click the Nexus folder and its subfolders to navigate its internal storage (Figure 7.2). To return the previous folder, press Backspace or click the Back button in the toolbar.

You can copy files back and forth as you would using any other external storage device. If you copy a folder of photos from your computer to the Nexus's internal storage, for example, you can view it as an album in the Photos app. When you're done, disconnect the USB cable.

Tip: To change your Nexus's USB connection options, tap Settings > Storage > ⋮ > USB Computer Connection.

Figure 7.1 The Computer folder in Windows.

Figure 7.2 Double-click folders to burrow to the file or folder you want.

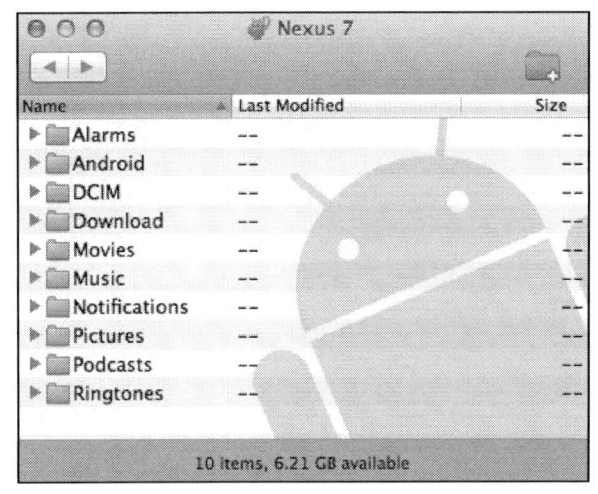

Figure 7.3 The Android File Transfer window in OS X.

Connecting to a Mac via USB

You can use a USB cable to connect your Nexus to a Macintosh computer and transfer music, videos, pictures, documents, and other files between them. This connection uses Media Transfer Protocol (MTP). Mac OS X doesn't support MTP natively, so you must first install the free **Android File Transfer** application on your Mac: go to *www.android.com/filetransfer*, and then follow the download and installation instructions.

The first time that you use Android File Transfer, double-click it to open it. Afterward, it opens automatically when you connect your Nexus to your Mac via USB cable.

When you connect your Nexus to a USB port on your computer, Android File Transfer opens a window that displays the contents of your Nexus, along with storage-space details at the bottom of the window (Figure 7.3). You work with the Android File Transfer window much as though it were a Finder window. The notification *Connected as a media device* appears on the Nexus's notification shade.

You can copy files back and forth as you would using any other external storage device. If you copy a folder of photos from your computer to the Nexus's internal storage, for example, you can view it as an album in the Photos app. When you're done, disconnect the USB cable.

Tip: To change your Nexus's USB connection options, tap Settings > Storage > ⋮ > USB Computer Connection.

CHAPTER 8

Getting Notifications

Certain apps can push notifications to you even when you're not actively using those apps. The Nexus provides a central list, called the **notification shade**, of all the apps that are trying to get your attention. You can get notifications for incoming mail and messages, calendar events, alarms, ongoing or completed downloads, system and app updates, and more. The Nexus's built-in apps, as well as third-party apps, can send notifications.

Viewing Notifications

When a notification arrives, its icon appears in the status bar at the top of the screen (Figure 8.1). To open the notification shade, swipe down from the top of the screen (Figure 8.2). To close the notification shade, tap off the shade or swipe up.

Tip: If you swipe twice in succession, or once with *two* fingers, Quick Settings opens.

Pending notifications

Figure 8.1 Status bar with notification icons.

Swipe left or right to dismiss notification

Tap to take a specific action

Tap icon to open associated app

Swipe with two fingers or spread or pinch to expand or collapse

Tap to open Google Now

Dismiss all notifications

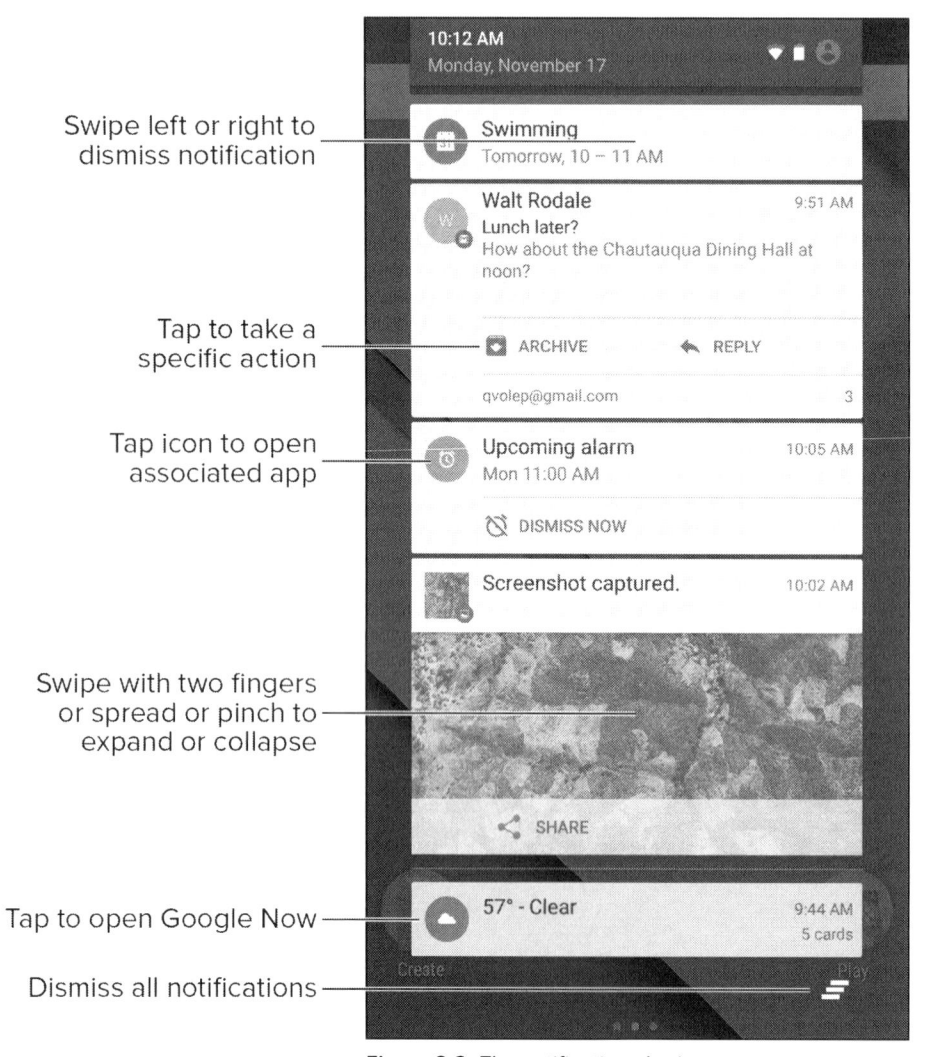

Figure 8.2 The notification shade.

84 Google Nexus 7 & 9

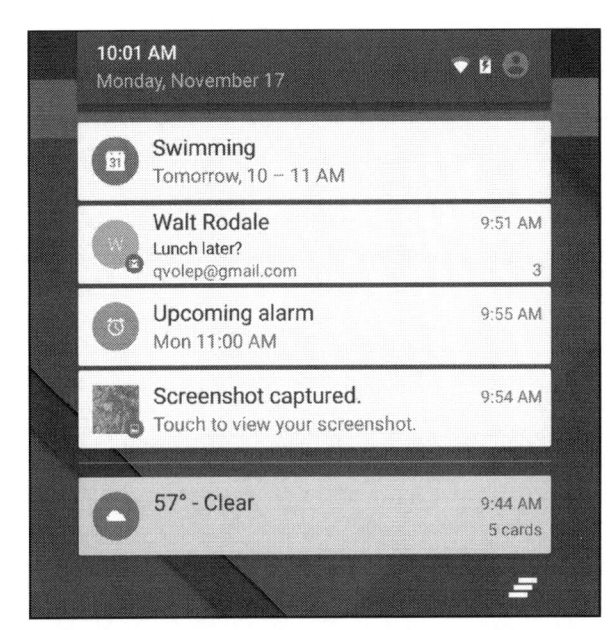

Figure 8.3 Collapsed notifications.

Figure 8.4 Notifications on the Lock screen.

- **Set app-specific preferences**. You can set notification preferences within some apps, usually by tapping ≡ or ⋮ and then Settings in the app.
- **Light up for notifications**. To slowly pulse the notification light on the Nexus 7 (2013), tap Settings > Display > Pulse Notification Light.

Managing Notifications

Here are some tips for using notifications:

- **Open an app**. To open the app that sent the notification, tap the notification icon or image on the left side of the shade. (In some cases, such as email notifications, you can tap any part of the notification.)
- **Show more info**. Some notifications can be expanded to show more information, such as email previews, pictures, and upcoming alarms. The topmost notification is always expanded, if possible. You can swipe two fingers or spread or pinch to expand or collapse a notification. Figure 8.3 shows the notifications from the preceding figure in collapsed forms.
- **Take an action**. Some expanded notifications contain icons that let you take certain actions from within the notification itself. You can snooze or dismiss alarms, for example.
- **Dismiss notifications**. When you're done with a notification, swipe it left or right to dismiss it. To dismiss all notifications, tap ≡ at the bottom of the shade. A notification will also self-dismiss when you tap it to jump to its related app.
- **Set notification preferences**. Tap Settings > Sound & Notification to:
  - ▸ Change the notification volume (separately from the main volume)
  - ▸ Stop some or all notifications indefinitely or for a fixed duration when you don't want to be interrupted (shortcut: press the Nexus's volume button and then tap None, Priority, or All on the volume overlay that appears)
  - ▸ Change the default alert sound (ringtone) for new notifications
  - ▸ Show or hide notifications on the Lock screen (Figure 8.4)
  - ▸ Block or prioritize notifications for specific apps
  - ▸ Give third-party apps ("listeners") access to your notifications

Chapter 8 Getting Notifications 85

CHAPTER 9

Google Now

Google Now is a personalized search app that recognizes your repeated actions on your tablet and displays relevant information when you summon it.

Using Google Now

Google Now (Figure 9.1) uses a wide array of personal and public data—including your current location, commonly visited places, calendar events, and search history—to provide contextually relevant information when you need it. When you have a meeting, for example, Google Now automatically offers directions to the location and travel time in current traffic conditions.

To open Google Now:

- Do any of the following:
  - ▸ Swipe up from the bottom edge of the screen.
  - ▸ Tap the Google app on the Home screen or All Apps screen.
  - ▸ Swipe to the leftmost Home screen (on the Nexus 9).

You can fine-tune your preferences and settings by tapping ≡ > Settings on the Google Now screen, but the best way to customize it is to simply be you. Commute to work. Walk around town. Search the web. Make appointments. Check the weather. Compare flights. Look up sports scores. Travel. Do the things that you normally do. Over time, Google Now learns your habits and interests, and shows you contextual information based on your calendar, recent searches, current location, or time of day, sometimes in surprising ways. If you're near a subway stop in New York City, for example, Google Now shows you what trains are coming next, when they'll arrive, and where they're headed. If you're traveling internationally, currency-exchange rates appear.

Tip: Google Now is integrated with Google Search. For details on using the search bar at the top of the Google Now screen, see Chapter 10.

Figure 9.1 Google Now.

Turning Off Google Now

You can turn off Google Now (and your location history) at any time. Open Google Now, tap ≡ > Settings, and then tap the Google Now slider.

Turning off Google Now stops the display of cards and returns Google Now settings to their defaults.

Figure 9.2 The Google Location Settings screen.

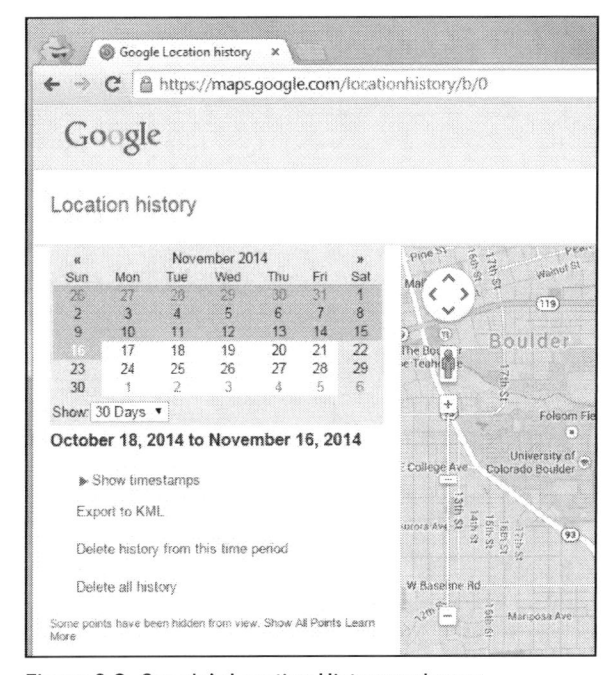

Figure 9.3 Google's Location History webpage.

Tip: If you visit a Google website from a different device or computer, make sure that you're signed in to the same Google Account that you use on your Nexus.

Controlling Location Privacy

If Google Now's location tracking feels Big Brother-ish, you can turn off location reporting and history and still use Google Now, but location and traffic information will be limited or won't appear.

Even if you turn off both location reporting and history, your previously recorded history is still available to Google Now and other Google products unless you delete it manually.

If you're feeling very private, you can turn off Google's Location services (page 180) and GPS to stop your Nexus from reporting location data to various apps, though doing so will disable many useful features on your Nexus.

To turn off location services, reporting, or history:

1 Open Google Now and then tap ≡ > Settings > Accounts & Privacy > Google Location Settings.

2 To turn off all location services and GPS, turn off the Location slider at the top of the screen.

   or

   To turn off only location reporting or history, tap Google Location Reporting (Figure 9.2).

To delete your location history:

- Open Google Now and then tap ≡ > Settings > Accounts & Privacy > Google Location Settings > Google Location Reporting > Location History > Delete Location History (at the bottom of the screen).

   or

   In a browser, go to *maps.google.com/locationhistory*, sign in to your Google Account, tap Map, and then tap Delete All History (Figure 9.3).

The Location History webpage lets you delete your location history, as well as view your history for any date. You can also delete a portion of your location history, starting from a specific date you choose in the calendar.

Displaying and Managing Cards

Google Now displays each snippet of information as a discrete card (Figure 9.4) that slides into view when Google Now thinks you're likely to need it.

When Google Now has a new update, a notification appears in the status bar at the top of the screen. You can drag the notification shade down from the top of the screen to see the card, respond to the notification, or dismiss it.

You can show more cards, browse sample cards, dismiss cards, and edit card settings.

To show more cards:

- Scroll to the bottom of the Google Now screen and then tap More.

To dismiss a card:

- Scroll the Google Now screen to the target card and then swipe the card off the screen (on the Nexus 9, swipe right).

  The card returns the next time it's relevant, which may be minutes, hours, or days from now. (To learn your preferences, Google Now may occasionally ask whether a card is useful to you.)

Tip: To bring the card back immediately after swiping it away, tap Undo at the bottom of the screen.

To turn off a card:

- Scroll the Google Now screen to the target card, tap ∎∎∎ near the top-right corner of the card, and then tap No.

  The card stops appearing in Google Now.

To edit settings for a card:

- Scroll the Google Now screen to the target card and then tap ∎∎∎ near the top-right corner of the card (Figure 9.5).

  You can fine-tune some cards by answering questions (such as whether to display Fahrenheit or Celsius on the Weather card, for example).

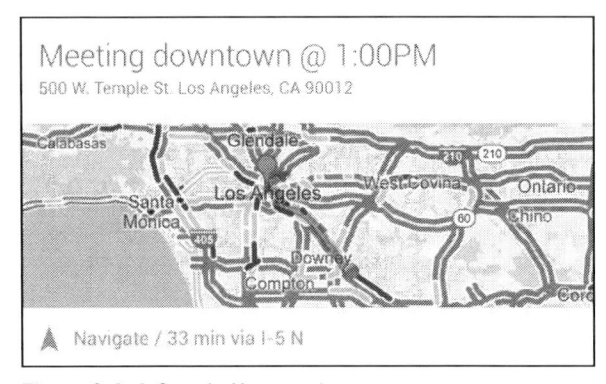

Figure 9.4 A Google Now card.

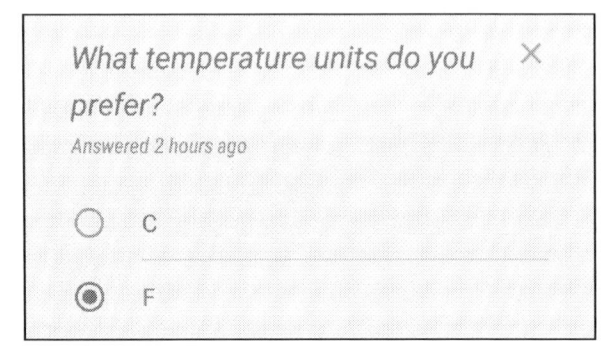

Figure 9.5 Editing a Google Now card.

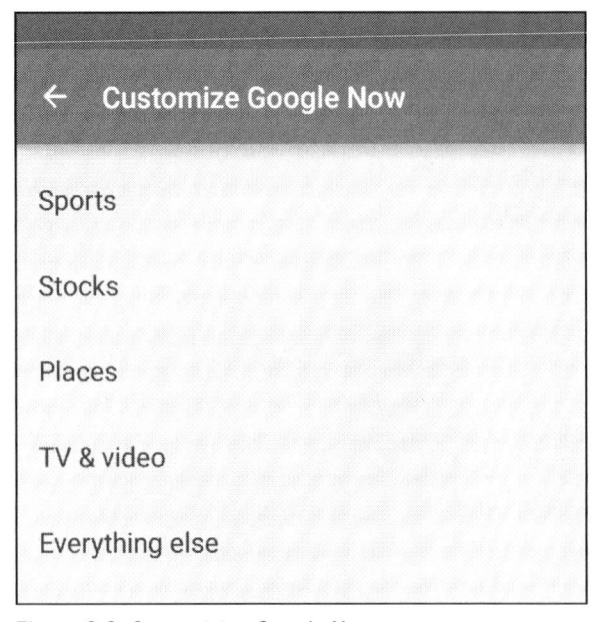

Figure 9.6 Customizing Google Now.

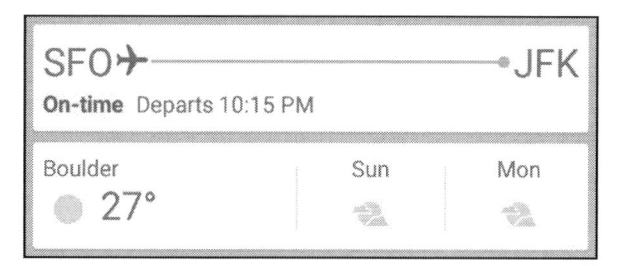

Figure 9.7 Google Now widget.

To customize Google Now:

- Open Google Now and then tap ≡ > Customize (Figure 9.6).

    To improve Google Now's results, you can specify your home and work addresses, preferred mode of transportation, the sports teams or stocks that you follow, and so on.

To set notification options for Google Now:

- Open Google Now and then tap ≡ > Settings > Notifications.

Tip: To see a summary of your Google Now cards, place the Google Now widget (Figure 9.7) on your Home screen. You can tap the widget to open Google Now. For widget details, see "Navigating and Organizing the Home Screen" on page 26.

Changing Home and Work Locations

Some Google Now cards, such as Traffic, offer traffic information and travel help. If you commute to and from work daily, Google Now usually can figure out your home and work locations, but it's surer to enter them manually. You can change your work or home address at any time: if you move or find a new job, or if Google Now guesses wrong.

To change your home and work locations manually:

- Do any of the following:
    ▸ Open Google Now and then tap ≡ > Customize > Places.
    ▸ In a browser, go to *maps.google.com/maps/myplaces*, tap My Places, and then tap Home or Work.
    ▸ In the Google Maps app (Chapter 16), tap ≡ > Settings > Edit Home or Work.

Tip: If you visit a Google website from a different device or computer, make sure that you're signed in to the same Google Account that you use on your Nexus.

Settings Reminders in Google Now

You can use Google Now to create reminders for tasks, places to visit, and events.

To set a reminder in Google Now:

1. Open Google Now, tap 🎤 in the search bar (or say "OK Google"), say "Remind me to", and then say what you want to be reminded about.

    or

    Open Google Now, tap ≡ > Reminders, and then tap +.

2. Complete the reminder card (Figure 9.8) that appears (a title is required), and then tap ✓ when you're finished. (To cancel the reminder, tap × or swipe the card off the screen.)

To acknowledge a reminder:

- When the reminder comes due, a notification appears in the status bar at the top of the screen. To view or snooze the notification, swipe down from the top of the screen.

To view or edit upcoming and past reminders:

- Open Google Now and then tap ≡ > Reminders.

To delete a reminder:

- Open Google Now, tap ≡ > Reminders, tap the target reminder, and then tap Delete.

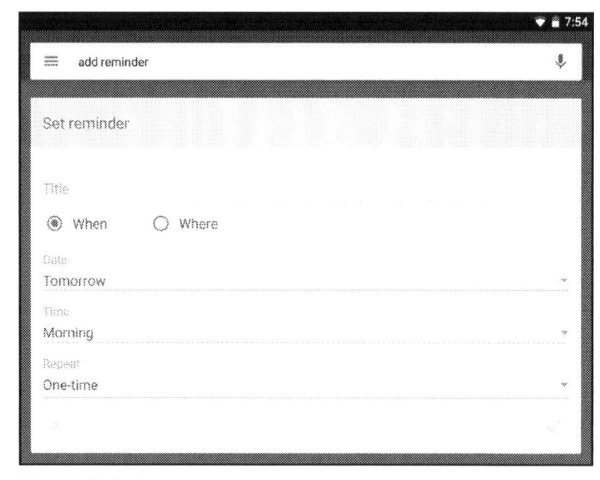

Figure 9.8 Reminder card.

Example Reminders

To set a reminder for a particular time, say, for example:

- "Remind me to go to the farmers market every Tuesday and Friday at 10am."
- "Remind me to buy eggs this evening."

To remind yourself to do something at a location the next time that you're nearby, say, for example:

- "Remind me to pay my electric bill when I get home."
- "Remind me to try the coffee at the Pearl Street Mall."

Google Now keeps track of your Google searches (Chapter 10). If you search Google for a certain event (concert, class, game, whatever) while signed in to your Google Account, a Remind Me link for that event may appear in Google Now. Tap the link to set a reminder for the event.

Tip: You can also use Google Search voice actions (page 98) and Clock (page 152) to set reminders or alarms.

CHAPTER 10

Google Search

Google Search lets you search the web, search your tablet, and issue commands, all by typing or speaking.

Using Google Search

Google Search on your Nexus offers all the features of Google.com on the web, plus extras such as voice search, audible feedback, and the ability to search your tablet. You can also use voice actions to get directions, send email, play music, and issue other Android commands.

The search bar is available at:

- The top of the Home screen (Figure 10.1).
- The top of the Google Now screen. (To open Google Now, swipe up from the bottom of the screen.)

Tip: Context-sensitive searches are available in Settings, Chrome, Gmail, Contacts, Calendar, Maps, and other apps.

To search by typing:

1. Tap the search bar.

    The onscreen keyboard appears.

2. Type your query in the search box. As you type, suggestions appear below the search box (Figure 10.2). The first few suggestions try to complete what you're typing.

3. To search for a suggestion immediately, tap it. (Tapping one of the lower results opens an app or searches your tablet instead of searching the web.)

    or

    To search for the contents of the search box (exactly as typed), tap the Search key 🔍 on the keyboard.

Figure 10.1 The search bar is available throughout Android.

Figure 10.2 Tap a suggestion to search the web by using Google, or tap one of the lower results to open an app or search your tablet.

Figure 10.3 Speak when the microphone icon appears.

Figure 10.4 Results for an example voice search.

To search (voice search) or issue commands (voice actions) by speaking:

1. Tap the microphone icon 🎤 in the search bar.

   or

   On the Home screen or Google Now screen, say "OK Google". (Don't tap anything—just speak.)

Tip: Search uses hotword detection to trigger a search or action when you say "OK Google". To turn it off or on, swipe up from the bottom of the screen to open Google Now and then tap ☰ > Settings > Voice > "OK Google" Detection.

2. Speak the terms to search for or the voice action to perform (Figure 10.3).

   For conventional web searches (voice search), results are listed and, in some cases, read aloud (Figure 10.4). Web searches show a conventional list of Google search results. Some results also show a card and produce an audible response ("It's 45 degrees and cloudy in Chicago").

   For commands (voice actions), the related app opens or a card appears that you can tap to complete the command. Voice actions (page 98) are triggered by certain phrases such as "Send email" and "Directions to".

Tip: Only spoken searches, not typed ones, produce audible responses.

Running Sample Search Queries

The best way to learn about Google Search is to experiment. Here are some sample queries to get you started:

- "Denver Broncos" (or any team name) (Figure 10.5)

- "Pictures of Maui" (or "Images of Maui") (Figure 10.6)

- "Convert 100 miles to kilometers"

   You can convert standard units of measure, including distances, temperatures, angles, areas, astronomical units, cooking measures, time periods, energy, density, pressure, speed, volume, weight/mass, power, frequency, and more.

- "Star Wars Miami" (or simply "Movie" or "*movie name*" for local movie showtimes)

- "Define schadenfreude"

- "Weather Dublin" (or simply "Weather" for the local weather)

- "Area code 808"

- "Zip code 97201" (or "Postal code 97201")

- "Time in Paris" (or simply "Time" for the local time)

- "United Airlines Flight 824"

Figure 10.5 Result card for "Denver Broncos".

Figure 10.6 Result card for "Pictures of Maui".

Figure 10.7 Result card for "Google stock price".

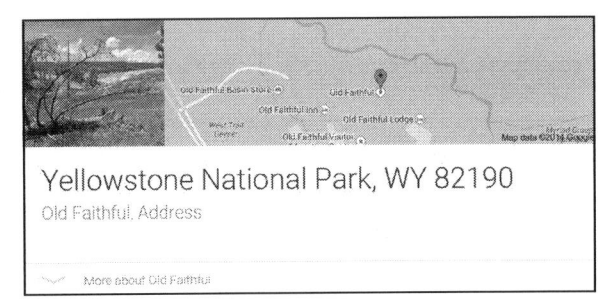

Figure 10.8 Result card for "Where is Old Faithful".

- "Translate to German A beer please"

  You can translate to many other languages.

- "80 divided by 6 plus 7"

  You can use any mathematical expression.

- "Chinese food in Ann Arbor, Michigan"

  Or you can simply say "*food name*" for the local restaurants and markets.

- "Google stock price" (Figure 10.7)
- "Who directed Fight Club"
- "Runtime of Avatar"
- "Who wrote Doctor Faustus"
- "What year was The Call of the Wild published"
- "What year was the Eiffel Tower built"
- "What is the second law of thermodynamics"
- "How many protons are in carbon"
- "What is the speed of light in parsecs per year"
- "Who invented the carburetor"
- "Where is Old Faithful" (Figure 10.8)
- "Do a barrel roll"

Chapter 10 Google Search 97

Using Voice Actions

You can use **voice actions** with Google Search to get directions, send email, and issue other common commands. Search distinguishes voice actions from conventional search terms by listening for special phrases that trigger commands, listed below. If Search doesn't understand you, it lists a set of possible meanings; tap the one you want.

Some voice actions, such as "Send email" and "Note to self", open a panel that lets you complete the action by typing or speaking. (For the latter, see "Dictating Text" on page 59.) You can tap any existing text in the panel to edit it. Tap or drag across underlined words to see a list of alternative transcriptions. (Search underlines words that it didn't hear clearly.) Buttons at the bottom of the panel let you add optional fields or complete the action.

"Open", "Turn on", "Turn off"
: Say "Open" followed by the name of an app. Say "Turn on" or "Turn off" followed by the name of a setting ("wi-fi" or "GPS", for example).

"What does my day look like tomorrow"
"Show me my schedule for tomorrow"
: View your agenda.

"Create a calendar event"
: Say "Create a calendar event" followed by an event description, day or date, and time (see "Setting Up Calendars & Events" on page 144).

"Listen to TV"
: Display TV cards relevant to the TV show that's currently being broadcast.

"Map of"
: Say "Map of" followed by an address, point of interest, landmark, business name, type of business, or other location (see Chapter 16).

"Directions to" or "Navigate to"
: Say "Directions to" or "Navigate to" followed by an address, point of interest, landmark, business name, type of business, or other location (see Chapter 16).

"Post to Google+"
: Say "Post to Google Plus" followed by what you want posted to Google+ (Google's social network).

"What's this song?"
: When you hear a song, ask "What's this song?". Your Nexus listens through its microphone for a few seconds, identifies the song and artist, and provides a link to the song in the Google Play store (if available). An internet connection is needed to identify the song.

"Remind me to"
: Say "Remind me to" followed by what you want to be reminded about (see "Settings Reminders in Google Now" on page 92).

"Go to"
: Say "Go to" followed by a web address (URL) or search string.

"Send email"
: Say "Send email" followed by one or more of the following:

  ▸ "To" and contact names

  ▸ "Cc" and contact names

  ▸ "Bcc" and contact names

  ▸ "Subject" and subject text

  ▸ "Message" and message text (speak punctuation)

"Note to self"
: Say "Note to self" followed by email message text.

"Set alarm", "Set a timer"
: Say "Set alarm" followed by "For", time, "Label" and the name of the alarm. Say "Set a timer" followed by a duration.

"Listen to"
: Say "Listen to" followed by words to search Play Music or YouTube for, such as the name of a song, artist, or album.

Sample Voice Actions

Here are some examples of voice action commands:

- "Open Gmail"
- "Turn on airplane mode"
- "What does my day look like tomorrow?"
- "Show me my schedule for the weekend."
- "Create a calendar event: Breakfast in Denver, Saturday at 8:00 AM"
- "Map of Boulder, Colorado"
- "Map of Microsoft, Redmond, Washington"
- "Map of Hyde Park, London"
- "Map of Chinese restaurants, Miami"
- "Map of Yosemite Park"
- "Map of my location"
- "Directions to Delano Hotel, Miami Beach"
- "Navigate to 1000 Fifth Avenue, New York City"
- "Navigate to home"
- "Directions to work"
- "Post to Google+ I had chili for lunch"
- "Remind me to go to the farmers market every Tuesday and Friday at 10 AM."
- "Remind me to buy eggs this evening."
- "Remind me to pay my electric bill when I get home."
- "Remind me to try the coffee at the Pearl Street Mall."
- "Go to google.com"
- "Send email to Sue Kennedy, subject, Just a reminder, message, Without me comma you're nothing period"
- "Note to self Return signed contract"
- "Set alarm for 8:30 AM"
- "Set a timer for 15 minutes"
- "Set alarm for 6 PM, label, park concert"
- "Listen to Hey Jude"

Tip: For more examples, type or speak "Google voice actions" in the search bar.

Setting Search Options

You can control aspects of speech input and output when you search by voice or use voice actions. To view Google Search settings, swipe up from the bottom of the screen to open Google Now (Chapter 9), and then tap ≡ > Settings (Figure 10.9).

Tip: Nexus 9 shortcut: touch and hold an empty area on the Home screen for a moment until icons appear near the bottom of the screen, and then tap Settings.

Tap any of the following options:

Tablet search. Select which apps on your tablet are included in Google searches of Nexus storage.

Voice. Voice settings control speech input and output when you search by voice or use voice actions:

- **Language.** Select a language for voice search input and output, which can differ from the system language (page 56) displayed by your Nexus.

- **Speech output.** Determine whether speech output is on always or on only when a headset is attached to your Nexus.

- **"OK Google" detection.** Determine whether you can say "OK Google" (rather than tap the mic icon) to initiate voice search or actions from the search bar. The Nexus can listen even when the screen is locked or (on the Nexus 9) off.

- **Block offensive words.** Determine whether search results with naughty words are blocked.

- **Audio History/Manage Audio History.** Determine whether Google saves what you say when you speak to do a search or issue a command. Google uses your audio history to learn the sound of your voice and improve speech recognition. Your audio history is private—tap Manage Audio History to view it, edit it, or delete it.

- **Bluetooth headset.** Determines whether the Nexus listens through a Bluetooth headset microphone (if available) instead of the tablet's built-in microphone.

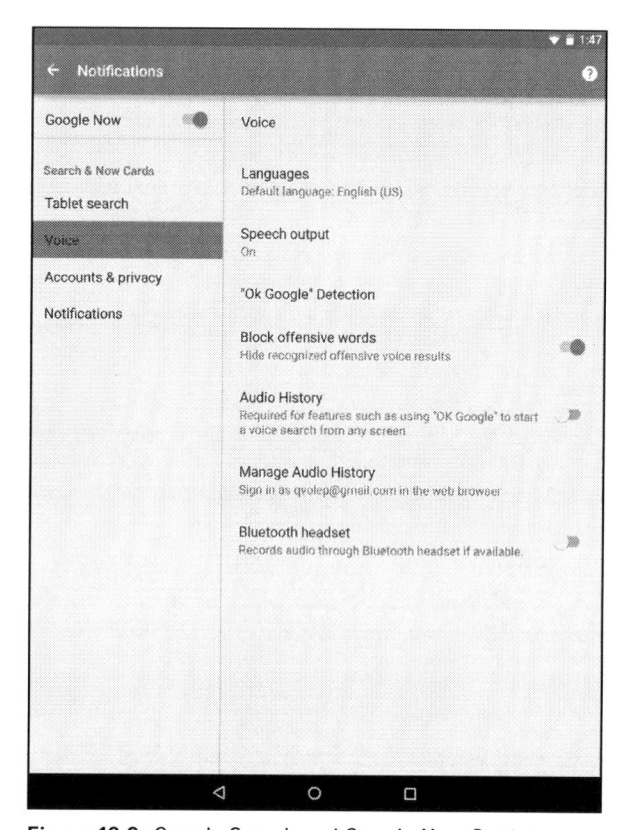

Figure 10.9 Google Search and Google Now Settings.

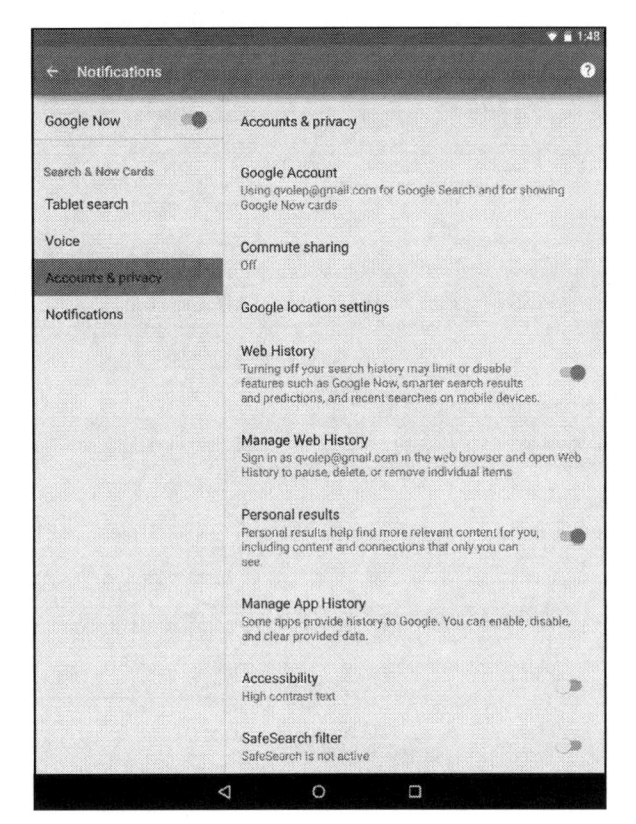

Figure 10.10 The Accounts & Privacy screen.

Accounts & privacy. Control the account for use with Google Search and search-related privacy options for that account. The Google Account used with Google Search and Google Now is shown in the Accounts & Privacy screen (Figure 10.10). You can set these options:

- **Google Account.** Choose which account to use for Google Search and Google Now.
- **Commute sharing.** Choose to share your commute (current location) with your Google+ connections.
- **Google location settings.** Opens the Location screen, where you turn location access, reporting, and history on or off. See also "Controlling Location Privacy" on page 89.
- **Web History.** Determines whether search suggestions are based on your recent searches.
- **Manage Web History.** Opens your personal Web History page in a browser, where you can pause or remove your search history. Sign in to your Google Account if necessary. (This option is relevant only if Web History is turned on.)
- **Personal results.** Returns search results biased by your search history, location history, and whatever else Google knows about you.
- **Manage App History.** Prevents certain apps from spying on you.
- **Accessibility.** Makes the screen easier to read.
- **SafeSearch filter.** Determines whether sexually explicit video and images are omitted from results.
- **Contact recognition.** Determines whether Google can scan your contacts (page 136) to respond to personal queries.
- **Search engine storage.** Lets you clear local storage caches that Google uses to accelerate searches on your tablet.
- **Help improve Google.** Don't bother.

Notifications. Set notification options (Chapter 8) for Google Now.

CHAPTER 11

Browsing the Web with Chrome

Chrome is the Nexus's native web browser. You can use it to download files and to display webpages with text, graphics, animations, sounds, video, and links—but not Adobe Flash, Microsoft Silverlight, and Java media, which aren't supported by Android.

Note that the web is a *portion* of the internet. (The terms aren't synonyms.) The internet contains not only the web, but also channels for email, instant messages, and more.

Tip: Other browsers are available in the Google Play store (Chapter 15), including Mozilla Firefox.

Using Chrome

Open Chrome from the Home screen or All Apps screen. The important part of Chrome isn't the app itself, but the access it gives you to webpages and other online resources. You'll spend most of your browsing time working within the web itself—reading, searching, scrolling, zooming, tapping links, filling out forms, downloading files, and so on—rather than using Chrome's controls (Figure 11.1).

Tip: Google also releases Chrome for Windows, OS X, Linux, iOS, and Chrome OS (*google.com/chrome*).

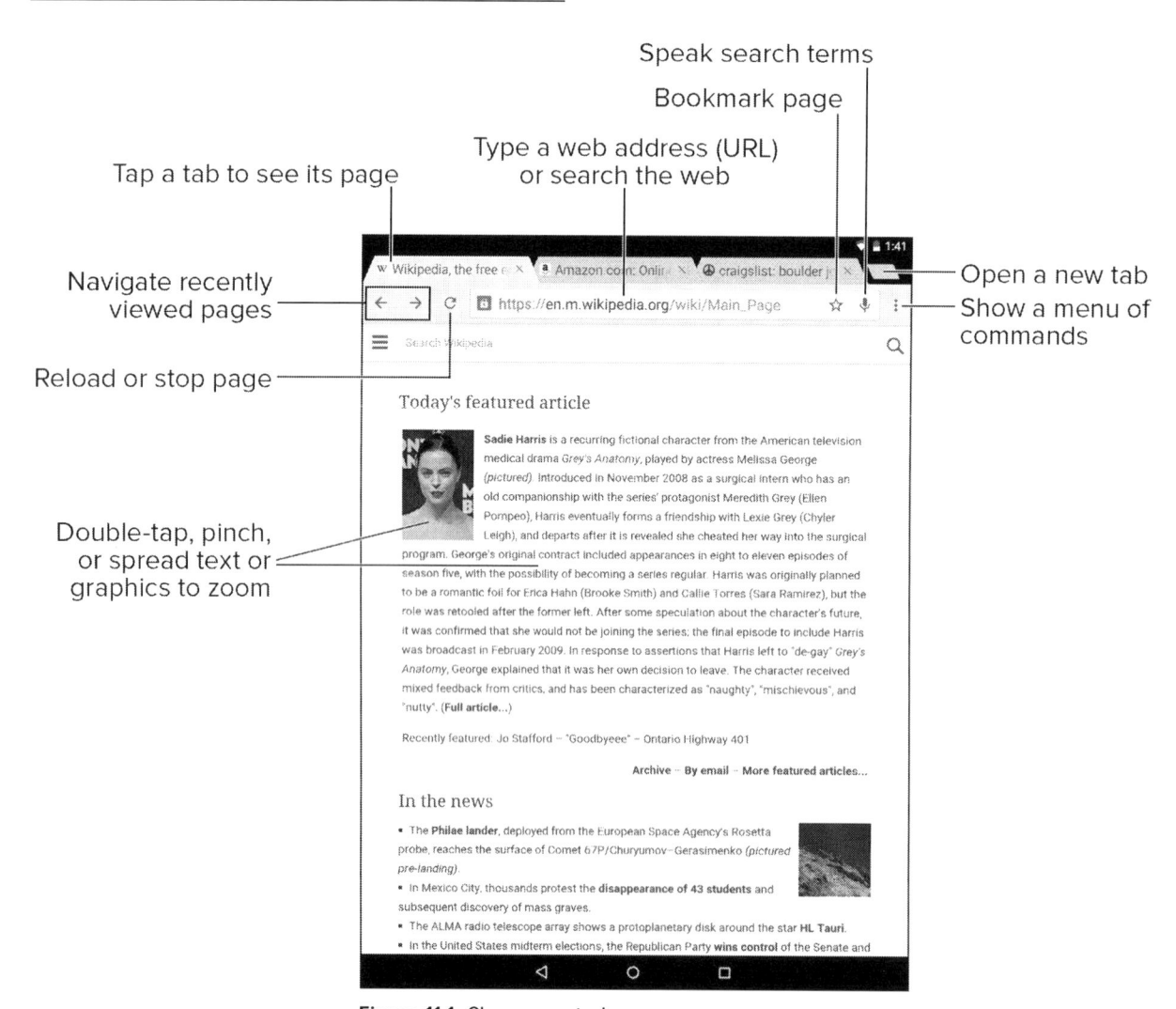

Speak search terms
Bookmark page
Type a web address (URL) or search the web
Tap a tab to see its page
Navigate recently viewed pages
Open a new tab
Show a menu of commands
Reload or stop page
Double-tap, pinch, or spread text or graphics to zoom

Figure 11.1 Chrome controls.

104   Google Nexus 7 & 9

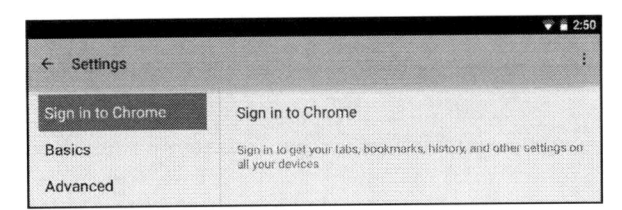

Figure 11.2 Sign in to Chrome.

Signing In to Chrome

When you sign in to Chrome with your Google Account, you can take advantage of several Google services, including syncing of bookmarks, search history, and open tabs.

Signing out of Chrome stops syncing but doesn't delete existing data stored on your Nexus and in your Google Account. All future changes within Chrome, however, won't be synced to your account.

To sign in to or out of Chrome:

1. In Chrome, tap ⋮ > Settings to open the Settings screen (Figure 11.2).

2. Tap Sign In to Chrome and then sign in.

   If you're already signed in, your account's email address appears near the top of the Settings screen.

   or

   To sign out, tap the On/Off switch next to the email address for your Google Account.

Tip: You can sync access to your Chrome bookmarks, browsing history, and open tabs from other devices where you're also signed in to Chrome. To sync open tabs, tap ⋮ > Recent Tabs > Enable Sync. To sync history and bookmarks, tap Settings > Accounts > Google > *account_name* and then turn on Chrome on the Sync screen.

Searching the Web

The **omnibox** (address bar) at the top of Chrome lets you search the web or visit a specific webpage.

To open a webpage or search the web:

1. Tap the omnibox at the top of the screen.
2. Type the address (URL) of a webpage or terms to search for (Figure 11.3).

    As you type, a list of suggestions appears. Icons in the list identify the type of match:

    ▸ The Search icon 🔍 appears next to searches.

    ▸ The Bookmark icon ☆ appears next to sites you've bookmarked.

    ▸ The History icon 🕓 appears next to sites and searches from your browsing history.

Tip: To copy a suggestion to the omnibox, tap the arrow ↖ to its right. Then you can keep typing or choose further suggestions.

---

3. To search for the contents of the omnibox or open a specific web address that it contains, tap the ➜ key on the keyboard.

    or

    To search for a suggestion or go to a suggested webpage, tap it.

    Chrome opens either the specified webpage or a list of search results.

Tip: To change the default search provider, tap ⋮ > Settings > Basics > Search Engine. To toggle suggestions for related queries and popular websites, tap ⋮ > Settings > Advanced > Privacy > Search and URL Suggestions.

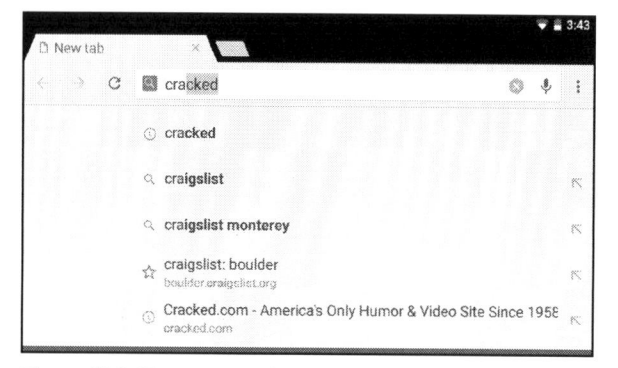

Figure 11.3 You can use the omnibox to search the web or open a specific web page.

Tips for Typing

- Press and hold the .com key to get your choice of .net, .org, .edu, and other top-level domains, depending on what country or region you've set your Nexus for.

- To erase the omnibox quickly, tap × in the right side of the box.

- To speak instead of type, tap 🎤 in the omnibox. For details, see "Dictating Text" on page 59.

- For general typing tips, see Chapter 4.

About URLs

A **URL** (Uniform Resource Locator) is a case-insensitive address that identifies a webpage uniquely. The URL for Google's home page, for example, is http://www.google.com. The transmission standard for most webpages is http://, so you don't type it; Chrome fills it in for you. Secure (banking and commerce) websites use https://. The rest of the address specifies the web server and the webpage's location on it. Some URLs don't need the www. part; others require additional dot-separated elements.

The server name's last part, called the **top-level domain** (TLD), usually tells you about the website's owner or country. The domain .com is a business, .gov is a government, .edu is a school, .uk is a United Kingdom site, .ca is a Canadian site, and so on. For a list of TLDs, see the root zone database at *www.iana.org/domains*.

Webpage files are organized in folder trees on the server, so a long URL (www.google.com/chrome/webstore/, for example) works like a path on a computer. Complicated URLs that contain ?, =, or & symbols are pages created on the fly in response to a query, such a product search on Amazon.com.

If a 404 or Not Found message appears instead of a webpage, you may have mistyped the URL, or the webpage may have been moved or removed. (Some internet providers redirect 404 errors to a page full of sleazy ads.)

Navigating Webpages

You can do any of the following things when you navigate webpages:

- **Scroll and zoom**. To scroll, swipe or drag in any direction. To zoom in or out, double-tap, spread, or pinch.

Tip: To make text bigger or smaller (without zooming), tap ⋮ > Settings > Advanced > Accessibility > Text Scaling.

- **View desktop sites**. Websites that are optimized for mobile devices typically open to a size appropriate for the device and may not permit zooming and scrolling. If you prefer to view the desktop (nonmobile) versions of sites, tap ⋮ > Request Desktop Site.

- **Rotate your Nexus**. You can view pages in either portrait (tall) or landscape (wide) view. Webpages scale automatically to the wider screen, making the text and images larger. For details, see "Changing Screen Orientation" on page 35.

- **Revisit pages**. To revisit pages that you've seen recently, tap ← (Back) or → (Forward). To choose from a list of recently visited pages, touch and hold ← or →.

- **Share a page**. To share the address of the current webpage, tap ⋮ > Share. The list of available sharing services depends on which apps you've installed.

- **Reload a page**. To reload a stale or incomplete page, tap C in the toolbar.

- **Stop downloading a page**. If you request the wrong page or tire of waiting for a slow-loading page, tap ✕ in the toolbar to stop the page from downloading any further.

- **Follow a link**. Text links typically are colored phrases. Pictures and buttons can also be links. To follow a link, tap it. If you touch and hold a link, you can see where it leads; open it in a normal or incognito tab; copy its URL or text to the clipboard to paste elsewhere; or download a file (Figure 11.4).

- **Search within a page**. To find text in the current webpage, tap ⋮ > Find in Page (Figure 11.5). The find bar appears near the top of the screen, below the omnibox. As you type in the find bar, matches are highlighted on the page, and a scrollbar on the right edge shows the relative positions of the matches. The find bar shows the total number of matches. To jump to a match, tap the up and down arrows in the find bar, or tap or drag the scroll bar.

```
http://boulder.craigslist.org/

Open in new tab

Open in incognito tab

Copy link address

Copy link text

Save link
```

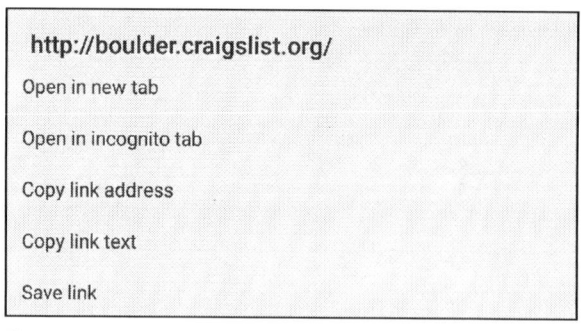

Figure 11.4 Touch and hold a link to see where it leads or to open, copy, or download it.

Find bar

Relative positions of matches on this page

Highlighted match

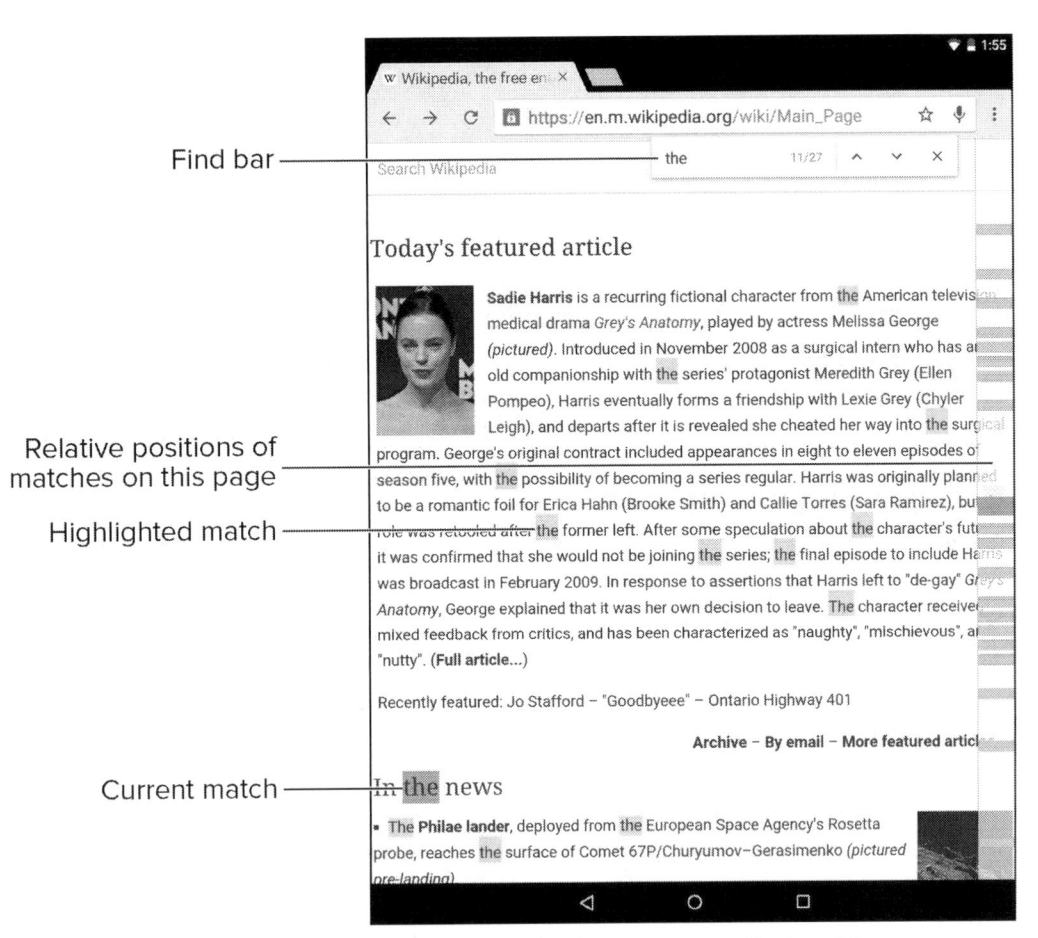

Current match

Figure 11.5 The find bar appears near the top of the screen, below the omnibox.

Working with Tabs

Like all modern browsers, Chrome features tabbed browsing, which lets you open multiple webpages on the same screen. You can open pages or links in new tabs and switch among them by tapping tabs.

To view and manage tabs, do any of the following:

- To view a different tab, tap it.

- To move to the next or previous tab quickly, swipe left or right on the omnibox (address bar).

- To open a new tab, tap ▨ or tap ⋮ > New Tab (Figure 11.6). A new tab provides quick access to web search, recently or repeatedly visited sites, bookmarked sites, and recently closed tabs.

- To open Chrome tabs that you have open on other devices, tap ⋮ > Recent Tabs (or tap Recent Tabs at the bottom of a new tab). Synced tabs are listed in the Other Devices section. You must be signed in to Chrome (page 105) to sync your open tabs across devices.

- To scroll through a long row of tabs, swipe or drag tabs left or right.

- To reorder tabs, touch and hold a tab until the other tabs dim, and then drag left or right. Alternatively, touch and hold a tab, and then drag down to the left or right.

- To close a tab, tap × on the tab.

Figure 11.6 A new tab.

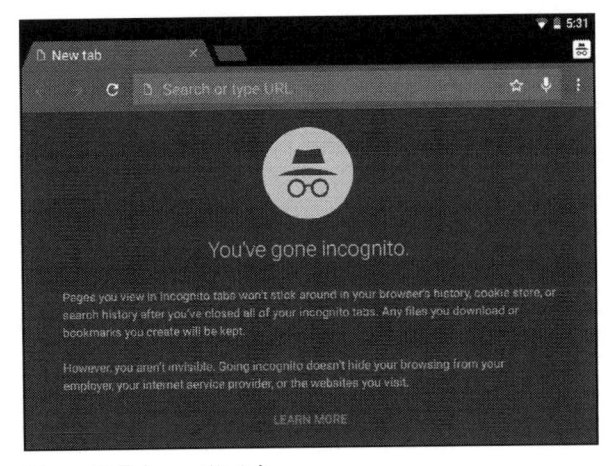

Figure 11.7 Incognito tab.

Browsing Privately

To browse privately in Chrome with **incognito tabs**, tap ⋮ > New Incognito Tab. A new tab opens with a dark background and information about going incognito (Figure 11.7). To switch in and out of incognito mode, tap 👓 in the top-right corner.

When you're browsing incognito, your browsing history, cookies, and cache are automatically cleared after you close all your incognito tabs. You can still access your normal bookmarks and omnibox suggestions. Changes that you make to bookmarks are saved.

Bookmarking Webpages

You can bookmark webpages that you like and open them quickly in the future. As your bookmarks list grows, you can organize your bookmarks in folders.

To bookmark the current page:

1. Tap ☆ in the omnibox (address bar).

   The Add Bookmark screen opens (Figure 11.8).

Tip: If a page is already bookmarked, the bookmark icon is solid ★ rather than hollow ☆.

---

2. If you like, edit the bookmark's name and address (URL).

3. Choose a folder for the bookmark.

   To create a new folder, tap the Folder menu and then tap **New Folder**.

4. Tap **Save**.

To open a bookmarked page:

1. Tap ⋮ > **Bookmarks**.

   or

   Open a new tab and then tap **Bookmarks** at the bottom of the tab (Figure 11.9).

Tip: You can navigate bookmark folders by tapping folder icons or by tapping a folder name just above the bookmark icons (below the omnibox).

---

2. Tap the bookmark you want.

   or

   Touch and hold a bookmark, and then tap **Open in New Tab** or **Open in Incognito Tab** (Figure 11.10).

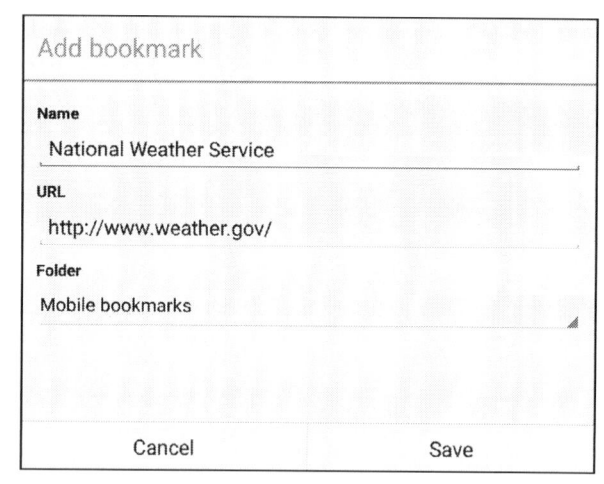

Figure 11.8 The Add Bookmark screen.

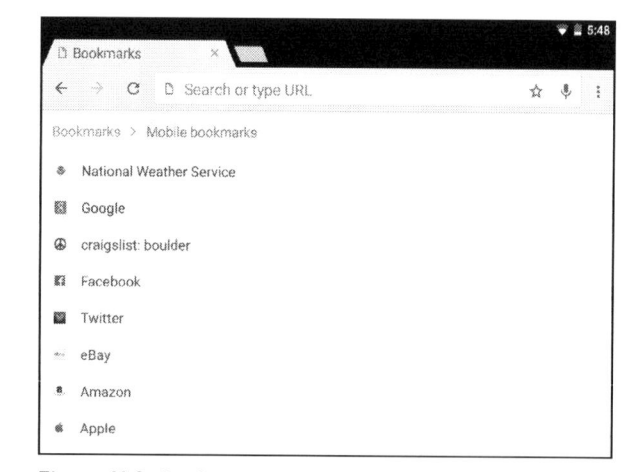

Figure 11.9 Bookmarks on a new tab.

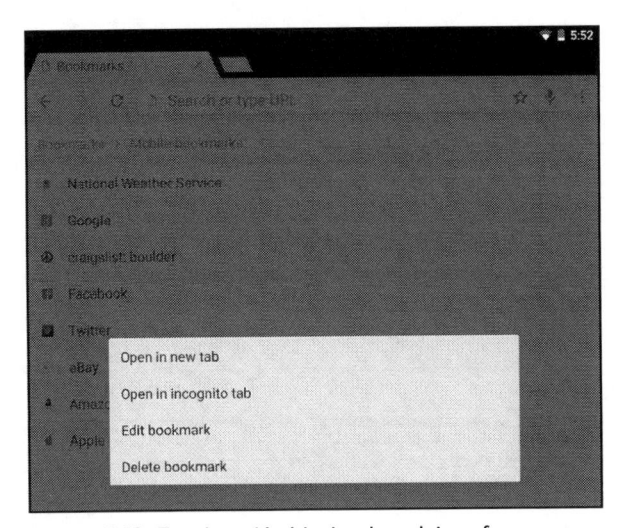

Figure 11.10 Touch and hold a bookmark icon for a menu of commands.

To edit or delete a bookmark page:

1 Tap ⋮ > Bookmarks.

   or

   Open a new tab and then tap Bookmarks at the bottom of the tab.

2 Touch and hold the target bookmark, and then tap Edit Bookmark or Delete Bookmark.

Tip: Tap ⋮ > Add to Homescreen to place a shortcut to a frequently visited webpage on your Home screen.

Downloading Files

You can download files via Chrome, Gmail, and other apps onto your Nexus and then manage them by using the Downloads app, which lists downloaded files. (Movies, music, and other media downloaded via the Google Play store don't show up in Downloads.)

Tip: To manage files directly on your Nexus, install a file-manager app (such as ES File Explorer or File Manager Explorer) from the Google Play store.

To download and manage files:

1. Touch and hold the link to the file, and then tap Save Link (or Save Image) in the window that opens (Figure 11.11).

   The download proceeds in the background. To track its progress, drag the notification shade down from the top of the screen (Figure 11.12).

Tip: To open the downloaded file quickly, tap its notification and skip the remaining steps.

2. When the download completes, open the Downloads app (Figure 11.13) from the Home screen or All Apps screen.

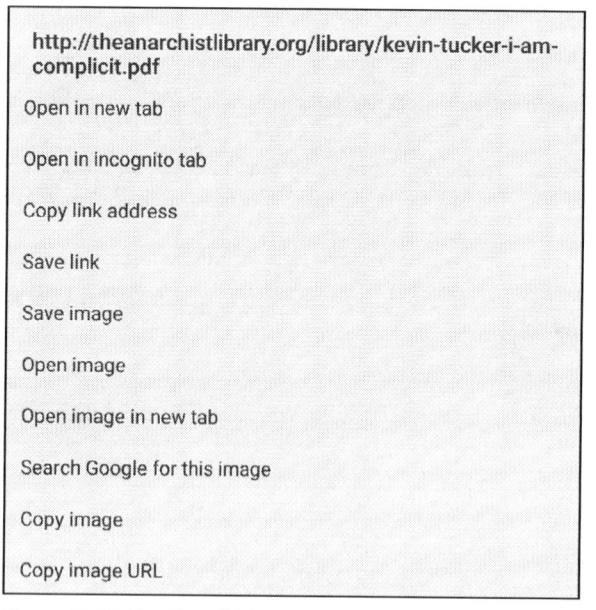

Figure 11.11 Tap Save Link to start downloading the file. To download a picture, tap Save Image.

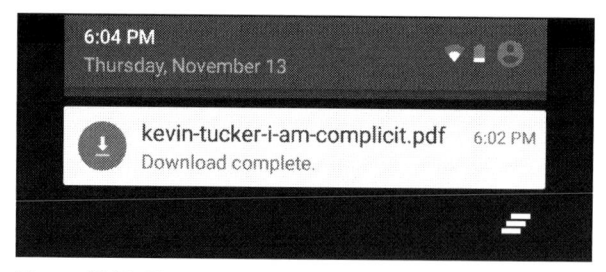

Figure 11.12 The notification shade shows the progress of each download to completion.

Figure 11.13 The Downloads app lists files downloaded via Chrome, Gmail, and other apps.

Open with

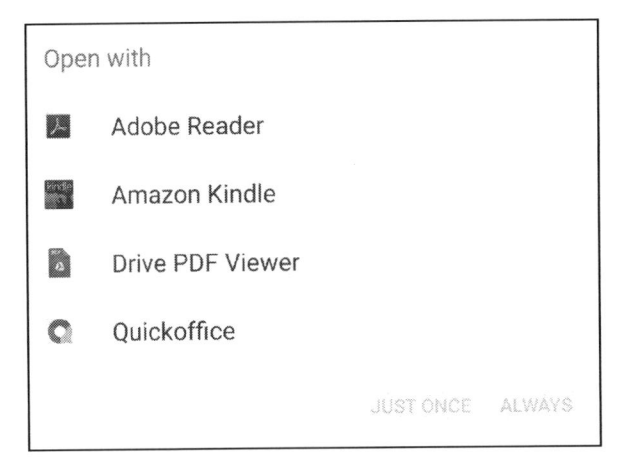

 Adobe Reader

 Amazon Kindle

 Drive PDF Viewer

 Quickoffice

JUST ONCE   ALWAYS

Figure 11.14 Choose from a list of compatible apps.

Figure 11.15 Tap to select or deselect a file. When files are selected, a toolbar appears at the top of the screen.

3. Do any of the following:

 ▶ To open a downloaded file, tap it, tap an associated app in the Open With screen that opens (Figure 11.14), and then tap Always (to always use the selected app to open this type of file) or Just Once (to use this app only this time). The list of available apps depends on which apps you've installed.

Tip: To control file-type associations, use the Launch by Default setting in an app's App Info screen. For details, see "Managing Apps and Services" on page 188.

 ▶ To sort the file list, tap ▤.
 ▶ To change the view, tap ▦.
 ▶ To delete a file, touch and hold the target file to select it, and then tap 🗑. When one or more files are selected, a toolbar appears at the top of the screen, and you can tap any file to select or deselect it (Figure 11.15).
 ▶ To share a file, touch and hold the target file to select it, and then tap ◁. The list of available sharing services depends on which apps you've installed.

Tip: Files available in the Downloads app can also be viewed in the Download folder that's visible when you connect your Nexus to a computer. You can view and copy files from this folder. For details, see Chapter 7.

Changing Chrome Settings

To change the settings in Chrome, tap ⋮ > Settings and then change any of the following settings:

- **Search engine**. Choose the default search engine for the omnibox (see "Searching the Web" on page 106).

- **Autofill forms**. This feature fills in your name, address, credit-card numbers, and other personal info on web forms, saving you from typing the same information repeatedly. (Autofill is especially useful for frequent online shoppers.) When you start filling out a form, the autofill entries that match what you're typing appear in a menu. Tap an entry to automatically complete the form with information from the entry.

- **Save passwords**. This feature memorizes and fills in user names and passwords on web forms—convenient, but a potential disaster if you ever lose a Nexus that isn't screen-locked. (For details, see "Setting the Screen Lock" on page 44.)

- **Privacy**. This option lets you control personal information (such as webpages visited) that's sent to Google when you search or browse the web.

    The most useful option is Search and URL Suggestions. When this option is turned on, Chrome uses a prediction service to show you related queries, matches from your browsing history, and popular websites as you type in the omnibox (address bar), provided that your default search engine is Google or uses Google's prediction service. Chrome sends the text you type to Google to retrieve suggested searches and sites, which are then displayed in the omnibox menu. Google anonymizes any sent text within a day.

Tip: To clear your browsing history, cookies, saved passwords, and other personal data, tap Clear Browsing Data in the top-right corner of the Privacy screen.

- **Accessibility**. This option makes Chrome easier to use and text easier to read.

- **Content settings**. This setting controls the type of content—including cookies—that websites can show and the information they can use.

- **Reduce data usage**. Experiment with this option if your data plan has a bandwidth cap (usage-based billing).

- **Developer tools**. This option (if available) offers advanced settings for software developers and website authors.

- **About Chrome**. Gives the current version of Chrome, Android, JavaScript, and more on your tablet.

About Cookies

Cookies are messages given to Chrome by websites and stored on your Nexus as small files. A cookie's main purpose is to identify you and possibly prepare customized webpages for you. When you enter shopping preferences and personal information at, say, Amazon.com, that information is stored in a cookie, which Amazon can read when you return.

Most cookies are innocuous and spare you from having to fill out forms repeatedly, but some sites and advertisers use tracking cookies to record your browsing history.

CHAPTER 12

Watching YouTube Videos

Though you can use Chrome (or any browser) to watch YouTube videos at *youtube.com*, Nexus comes with a dedicated YouTube app that makes finding, watching, and keeping track of videos easier.

Tip: Google owns YouTube, so a YouTube Account is the same as a Google Account.

Using the YouTube App

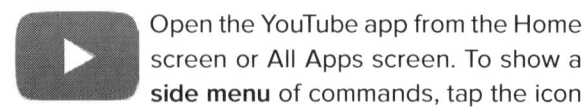

Open the YouTube app from the Home screen or All Apps screen. To show a **side menu** of commands, tap the icon in the top-left corner of the screen or swipe right from the left edge of the screen (Figure 12.1). To hide the side menu, swipe left, tap the top-left icon again, or tap off the menu.

You can browse and watch videos without a Google Account, but you must sign in if you want to comment on videos, add them to your playlists, upload videos, and use other personal features. To do so, tap Sign In in the side menu or tap ⋮ > Sign In. After you sign in, the side menu shows your account, subscriptions, uploads, favorites, history, playlists, and more.

To change your account settings, sign in and then tap ⋮ > Settings. You can resize the caption font, clear your search history, and more.

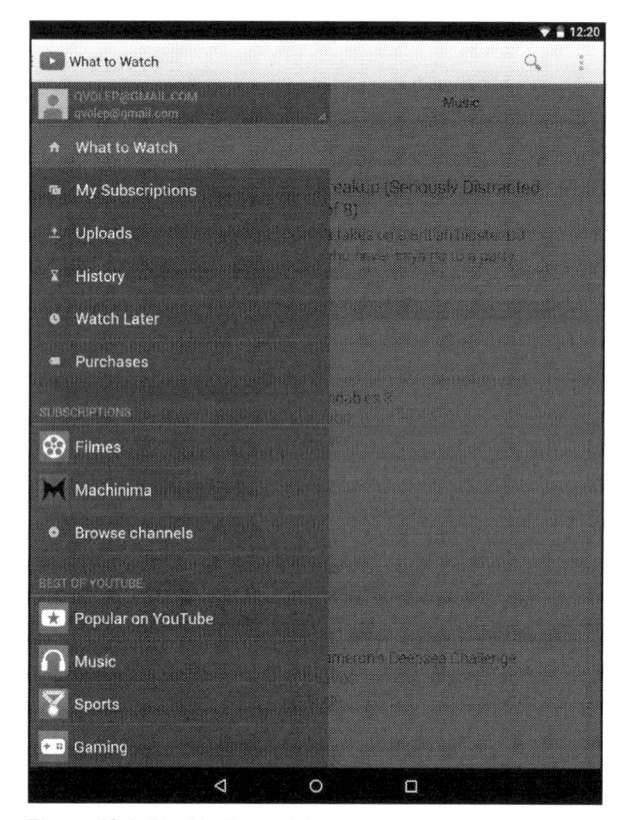

Figure 12.1 The YouTube side menu.

Figure 12.2 A YouTube Info screen for a video.

Finding and Watching Videos

Millions of YouTube videos are available, submitted by people and organizations around the world. You can watch them in full-screen view or with the video's Info page showing. The playback controls work about the same way that they do in most video apps.

To find and watch a YouTube video:

1. To browse for videos, tap a category in the side menu.

   Swipe up or down to scroll the list of categories, if necessary.

   or

   To search for videos, tap 🔍 at the top of the screen and then type search terms. To speak instead of type, tap 🎤 in the search field (for details, see "Dictating Text" on page 59).

Tip: A YouTube **channel** is a collection of a person's videos, playlists, and other YouTube information. You can open other people's channels and subscribe to them: tap Browse Channels in the side menu.

---

2. Tap a video thumbnail or title to see that video's Info screen (Figure 12.2).

   continues on next page

3. If the video doesn't start playing automatically, tap ▶ to play it.

   Tap the video at any time to show or hide playback and other controls. To watch full-screen, rotate your Nexus to landscape (wide) view (Figure 12.3).

> **Tip:** If you tap ⌄ to minimize a video to a thumbnail in the corner of the screen, you can tap the thumbnail to restore it or swipe the thumbnail left or right to dismiss it.

Minimize video and show previous screen

Tap screen to show or hide playback controls

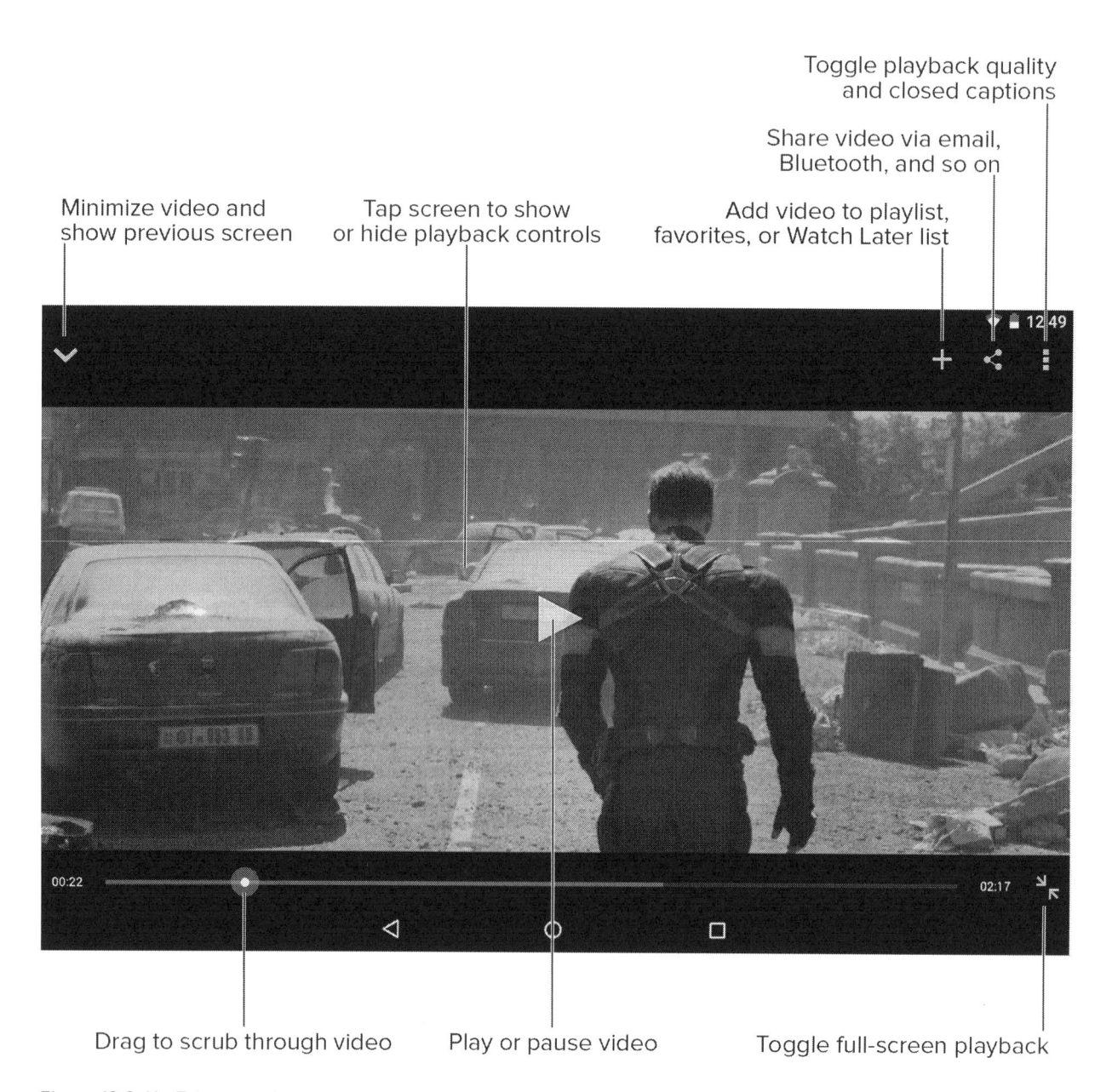

Add video to playlist, favorites, or Watch Later list

Share video via email, Bluetooth, and so on

Toggle playback quality and closed captions

Drag to scrub through video

Play or pause video

Toggle full-screen playback

Figure 12.3 YouTube controls.

CHAPTER 13

Email, Messaging & Keeping in Touch

Gmail is the Nexus's native email app for Google Accounts. Your messages are stored on Google servers, but you can read, write, and organize messages with Gmail on your Nexus or from any web browser. When you set up your Nexus with a Google account, the Gmail app is ready to go.

If you haven't set up an account yet, or if you want to set up another account, tap Settings on the Home screen or All Apps screen, tap Accounts, and then tap Add Account. For details, see Chapter 6.

You can also use the Gmail app for non-Gmail email accounts (Yahoo, Hotmail, and so on).

About Gmail

You can open Gmail from the Home screen or All Apps screen. Your most recent conversations are displayed in your inbox. Because Google stores your Gmail messages on its servers, you can search your entire message history at any time. The servers also sync your actions across devices. If you read a message in Gmail on your Nexus, for example, it's marked as read at *gmail.com* in a web browser.

Each Gmail message and all its replies are grouped in your inbox as a single **conversation** that's easy to follow. Old email apps, by contrast, spread an original message and its replies across your inbox, typically sorted by date received and separated by other messages.

You can tag Gmail conversations with multiple standard or custom **labels** to organize them in different ways. In old email apps, each message lives in only one folder.

Non-Gmail Email Accounts

You can use the Gmail app with email accounts other than Gmail, such as Yahoo, Hotmail, AOL, Apple, Microsoft, and Microsoft Exchange Server. (The old Email app for non-Gmail accounts is gone.) To set up an account, in Gmail, tap ≡ > Settings > Add Account. For Exchange accounts, ask your IT department or system administrator for help. For personal accounts, IMAP and POP3 are available:

- **IMAP** (Internet Message Access Protocol) servers keep all your mail online, letting you get the same mail on any computer or device you use. IMAP servers track which messages you've read and sent. If you run out of mailbox space on the IMAP server, you must delete old messages to prevent any new incoming mail from bouncing back to the senders. Most popular web-based providers (Gmail, Yahoo, and so on) and modern organizations use IMAP.

- **POP3** (Post Office Protocol) accounts use an older messaging protocol that wasn't designed to check mail from multiple computers. Unless your provider saves copies of your mail on its server, a POP3 server transfers incoming mail to your computer (or Nexus) before you read it. You won't get copies of messages when you log in from another computer because you've already downloaded them.

Non-Gmail mail isn't stored on Google's servers. When you set up a non-Gmail account, use the account settings provided by your internet service provider (ISP), account administrator, or employer. These settings include your email address, your password, and the addresses of your provider's incoming and outgoing mail servers (which look like *mail.servername.com* and *smtp.servername.com*, respectively).

Touring Your Inbox

The first time you open Gmail, it shows a scrolling list of your most recent conversations, placing the one with the most recent messages at the top (Figure 13.1).

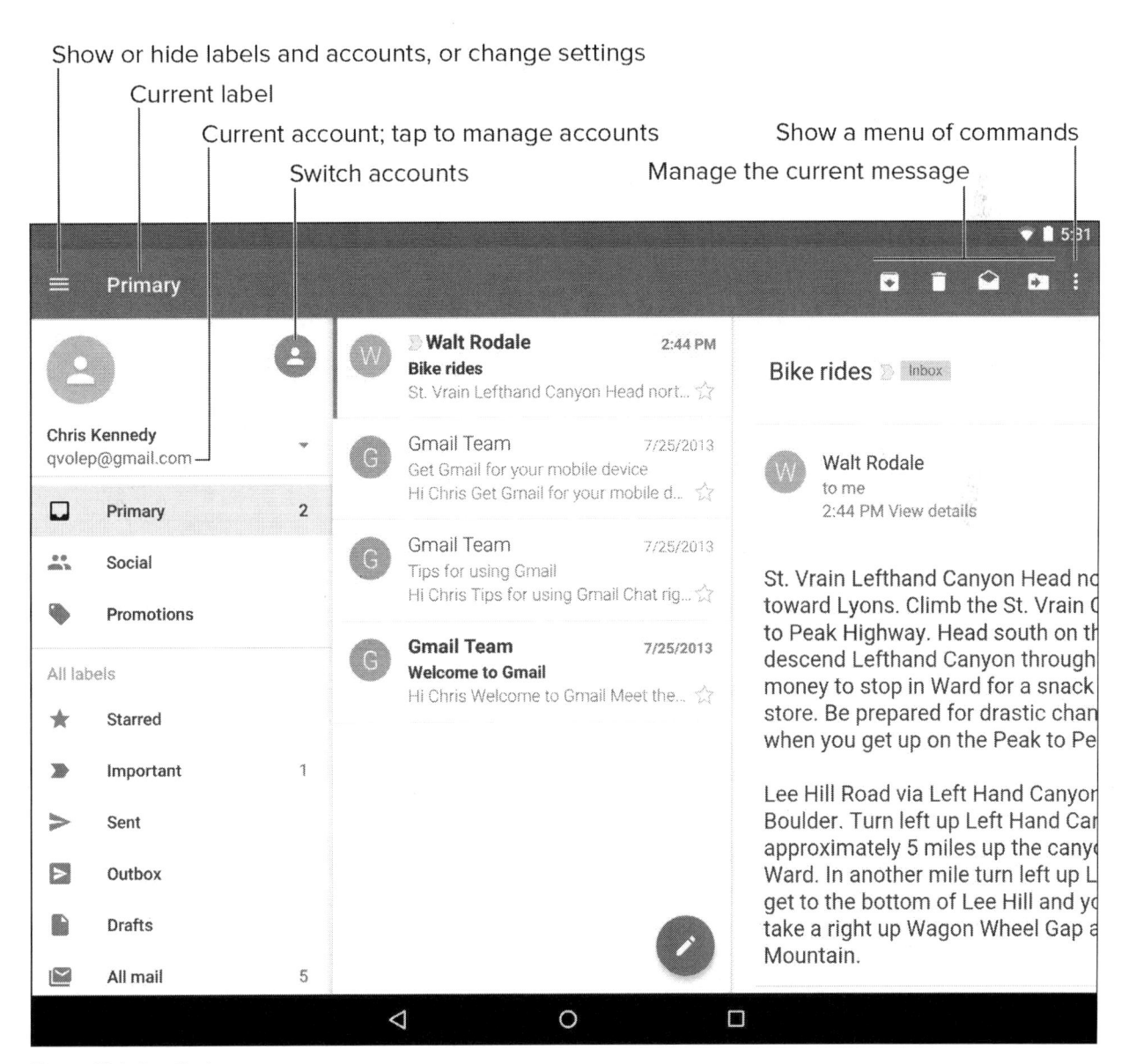

Show or hide labels and accounts, or change settings

Current label

Current account; tap to manage accounts

Switch accounts

Show a menu of commands

Manage the current message

Figure 13.1 Gmail inbox.

All your conversations are shown in your inbox unless you delete, archive, or filter them (Figure 13.2). You can also tap Priority Inbox or any other label in the list in the side menu. Conversations with new messages are bolded in conversation lists. Small icons tell you about the message:

- 〉〉 means the message was sent directly to you, and 〉 means you were copied.

- If you mark a conversation message as important (tap ⋮ > Mark Important), or if you're using Priority Inbox, messages are flagged with 〉〉 or 〉.

- If a message was sent to you as part of a group, it has no icon or is marked with 〉.

Tap a label to see its conversations
Number of unread messages
Tap icon (sender image) to select conversation
Current message

Tap to read message
View new message (bold conversation)
Compose a new message
Swipe down to fetch latest mail
Tap to star a conversation

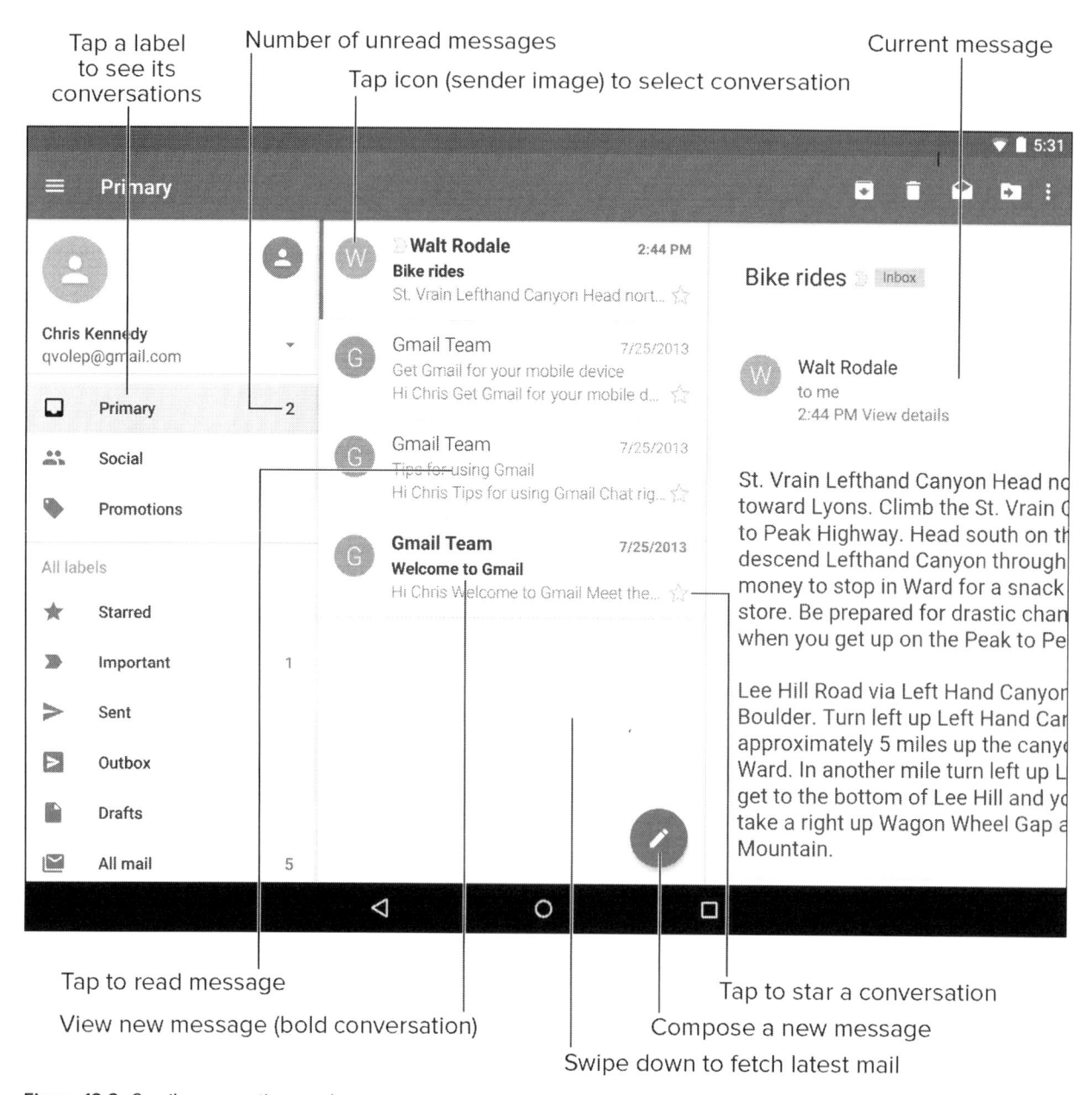

Figure 13.2 Gmail conversations and messages.

124 Google Nexus 7 & 9

By tapping items in the side menu, you can view all conversations that you've starred or that have the same label. To control how labeled conversations are synced, tap ≡ > Settings > *account_name* > Manage Labels.

If you're offline, you can read messages synced to your Nexus. You can also compose and send messages, which are stored on your Nexus with the Outbox label until you're back online, when they're sent automatically. By default, Gmail syncs (downloads) the previous 30 days of messages.

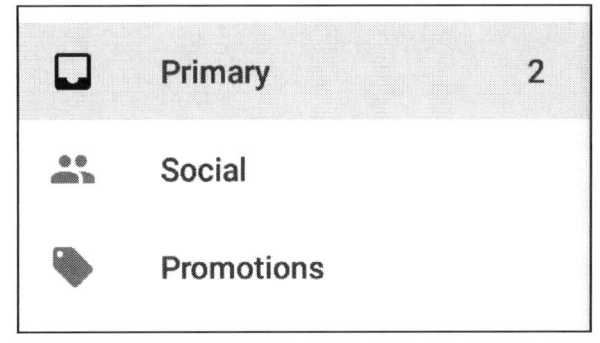

Figure 13.3 Gmail inbox categories.

Inbox categories

By default, your inbox messages are classified into categories such as Promotions, Social, and Updates (Figure 13.3). You can choose to use categories as inbox tabs, and as labels. These categories let you focus on only important messages and easily read all messages of the same type.

Gmail categorizes your messages automatically into the following optional tabs:

- **Primary**. Messages from friends and family, as well as any other messages that don't appear in other tabs.

- **Promotions**. Your deals, offers, and other promotional emails.

- **Social**. Messages from social networks, media-sharing sites, online dating services, gaming platforms, and other social websites.

- **Updates**. Notifications such as confirmations, receipts, bills, and statements.

- **Forums**. Messages from online groups, discussion boards, and mailing lists.

To choose which categories (if any) to show, tap ≡ > Settings > *account_name* > Inbox Categories.

Priority Inbox

If you get a lot of mail, you may want to use Priority Inbox to separate the wheat from the chaff. If you configure Gmail on the web (at *gmail.com*) to show Priority Inbox, Gmail on your Nexus will show it as well.

Gmail labels a message important and sticks it in Priority Inbox based on your past treatment of similar messages, how directly the message is addressed to you (To or Cc), and other factors.

To add or remove Priority Inbox conversations manually, you can mark them as important or not important. In any conversation list, select the target conversations and then tap ⋮ > Mark Important or Mark Not Important. Over time, Gmail learns what kinds of messages are important to you.

To set Priority Inbox as your default inbox, tap ≡ > Settings > *account_name* > Inbox Type > Priority Inbox.

Reading Mail

Gmail pushes new messages to your Nexus automatically as they arrive. (You don't need to tap anything to retrieve them.) When you get a new message, a notification appears in the status bar at the top of the screen. You can drag down from the top of the screen to show the notification shade and a brief summary of the message.

Tip: To toggle notifications for Gmail messages, tap ≡ > Settings > *account_name* > Notifications.

To read a conversation's messages, tap the conversation (Figure 13.4). A conversation opens to the first new (unread) message or to the first starred message. To reread messages in a multiple-message conversation, tap one of the earlier messages to expand it.

To move to the previous or next conversation, swipe the message left or right. For details on copying and pasting message text, see "Selecting and Editing Text" on page 58.

Tip: When you tap 🔍 to find messages, you can search by using terms that appear in message contents, addresses, subjects, labels, and so on.

Archive, Delete, and Mute

Archiving a conversation moves it out of your inbox without deleting it. Archived conversations are included in search results and are available under the All Mail label and any other labels you've assigned to them. If someone replies to a message that you've archived, its conversation reappears in your inbox.

When you **delete** a conversation, it's moved under the Trash label, where it's deleted automatically after about 30 days.

If an ongoing conversation wearies you, then you can **mute** it to remove it from your inbox. In your inbox, select the conversations you want to mute and then tap ⋮ > Mute, or when you're reading a message, tap ⋮ > Mute. New messages addressed to the group members of a muted conversation bypass your inbox and are archived automatically. (New messages with your address in the To or Cc field still appear in your inbox.) To view muted conversations, tap the All Mail label.

Tap to collapse or expand message

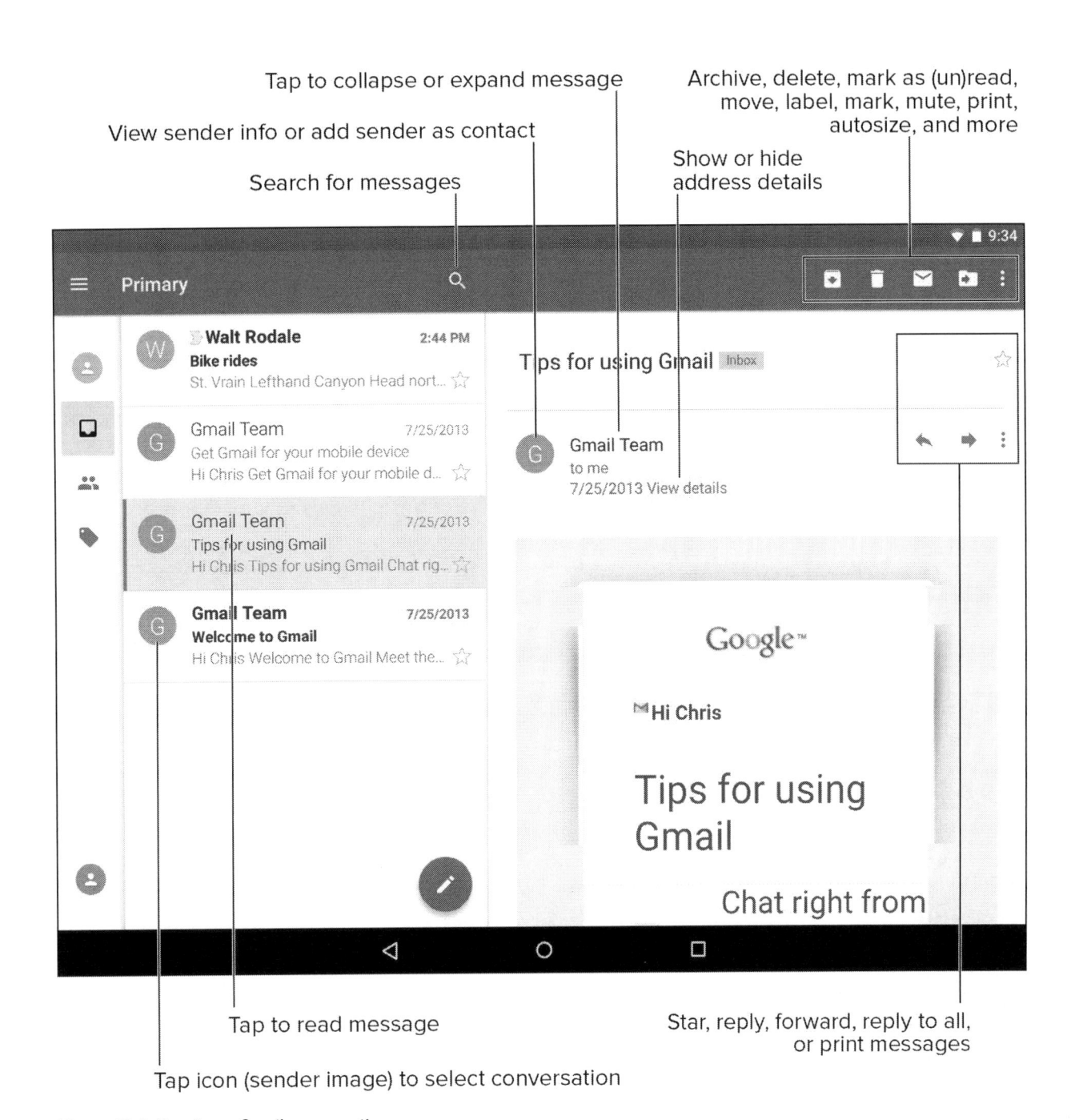

View sender info or add sender as contact

Search for messages

Show or hide address details

Archive, delete, mark as (un)read, move, label, mark, mute, print, autosize, and more

Tap to read message

Tap icon (sender image) to select conversation

Star, reply, forward, reply to all, or print messages

Figure 13.4 Reading a Gmail conversation.

Chapter 13 Email, Messaging & Keeping in Touch 127

Working with Attachments

When a message has an attached file, a paper-clip icon 📎 appears near the sender's name in the message list, and information about the attachment appears at the bottom of the message (Figure 13.5).

Depending on the type of attachment, your installed apps, and your settings, Gmail may display a thumbnail image or a menu ⋮ of options.

Download or Play. Download the attachment (if it hasn't already been downloaded) and then view or play it by using a related app.

Preview. Partially download the attachment and view it in a separate window. For multiple-page documents, Preview downloads only the first few pages to view, which is faster and less space-consuming than Download, which downloads the entire attachment.

Info. Show information about the attachment, if no installed app can open it.

Tip: You can download apps that open different kinds of files from the Google Play store.

Save. Download the attachment and save it on your Nexus or to Google Drive (cloud storage).

Downloaded files are available from the Downloads app (see "Downloading Files" on page 114) or in the Download folder when you attach your Nexus to your computer (see Chapter 7).

Tip: To download attachments automatically, tap ☰ > Settings > *account_name* > Download Attachments.

Figure 13.5 Attachment information in a message.

Managing Conversations in Bulk

You can archive, label, delete, and perform other actions on multiple conversations at the same time, in your inbox or another conversation list. In a conversation list, tap the icons (sender images) of the conversations that you want to work with as a group and then choose an action (Figure 13.6). A selected conversation is marked with a ✓ icon.

Tip: To show or hide sender images in conversation lists, tap ☰ > Settings > General Settings > Sender Image.

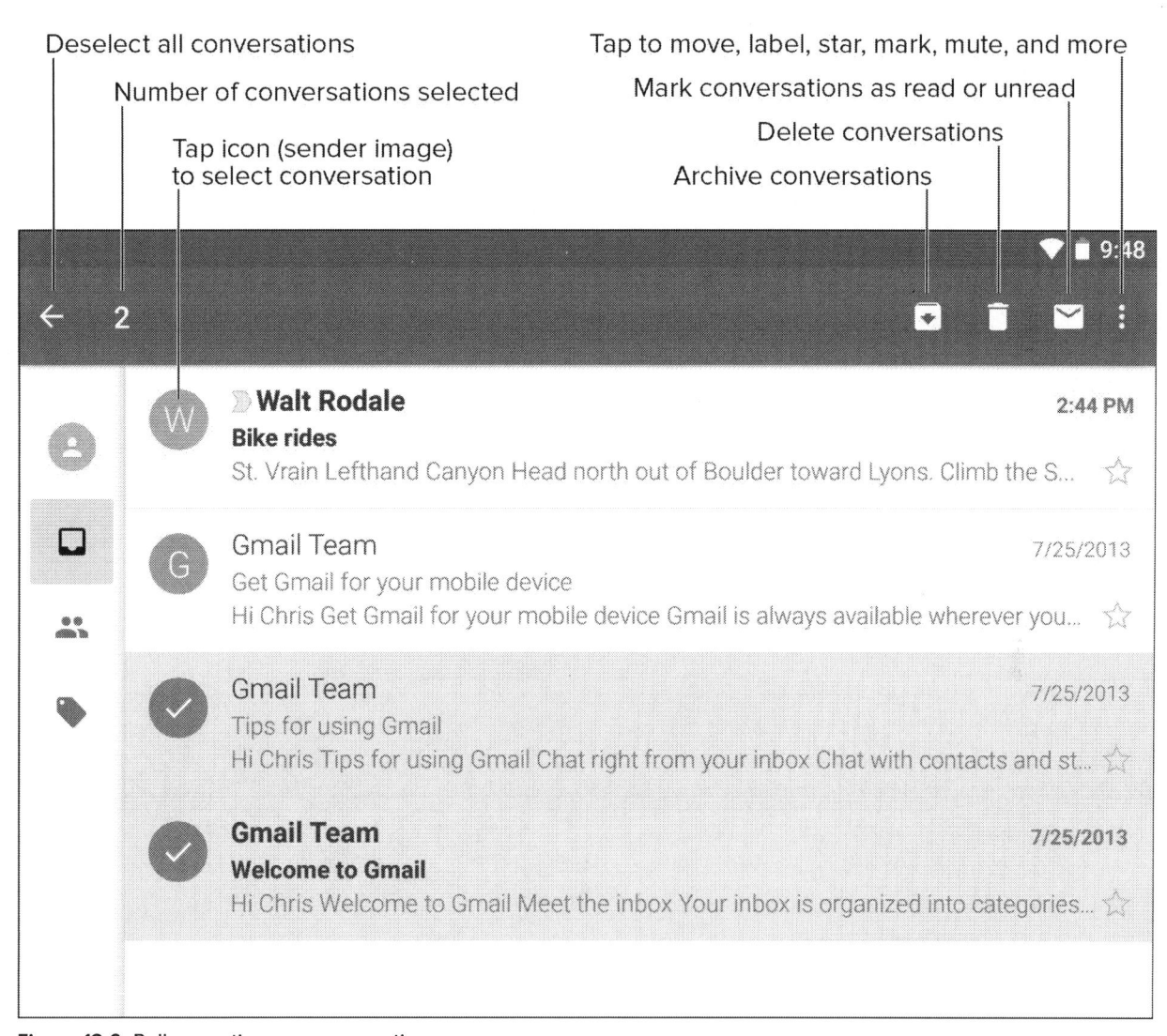

Figure 13.6 Bulk operations on conversations.

Writing and Sending Mail

You can use Gmail to write (compose) a message and send it to anyone who has an email address.

To write and send a message:

1. View a list of conversations or a message.

2. To start from scratch, tap ⊘.

   or

   To continue a conversation by replying to or forwarding one of its messages, tap Reply ↩, Forward ➡, or ⋮ > Reply All in the message header or at the bottom of the message.

   Whatever you do, Gmail creates a new message (Figure 13.7).

3. If you have multiple Google accounts, tap the From field at the top of the message and then choose the account to send from. (You can't change the From field if you're replying to or forwarding a message.)

4. To add a recipient, tap the To field and then type the recipient's email address or contact name.

   If the recipient is in Contacts, Gmail autosuggests addresses as you type (which you can tap or ignore).

Tip: To remove a recipient, backspace over it or tap it and then tap the × that appears next to it.

---

5. If you want to send copies of the message to other people, tap ∨ to the right of the To field; then tap the Cc (carbon copy) or Bcc (blind carbon copy) field, and fill it out as you did the To field.

Tip: Bcc recipients aren't disclosed to the message's other recipients. It's common to use Bcc when you're addressing many recipients or recipients who don't necessarily know one another (members of a mailing list, for example).

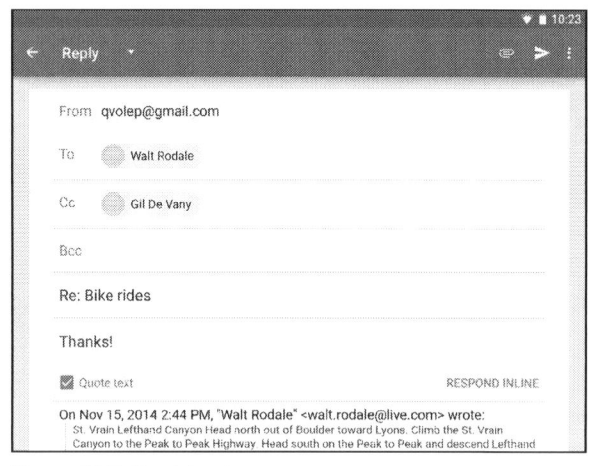

Figure 13.7 Replying to a message.

Replying and Forwarding

If you reply to a message, files or photos attached to the original message aren't sent back. To include attachments, forward instead of reply.

In replies and forwards, you can tap Respond Inline to interleave your message with the text of the old one.

In replies, you can turn off Quote Text to exclude the message you're replying to from the text of the new message (also removing any attachments or formatting in the original message).

Replying to or forwarding messages without changing the subject adds your reply to the current conversation. Changing the subject starts a new conversation.

All the messages in the conversation, up to the one you're replying to or forwarding, are included in the new message; any messages that follow the message you're responding to are omitted.

6   Tap the Subject field and then type whatever this message is about.

    If you're replying to or forwarding a message, you can edit the existing subject (which starts a new conversation).

7   To attach a photo or file, tap 📎 at the top of the message.

Tip: To remove an attachment, tap × to the right of the attachment's name.

---

8   Tap the Compose Email area and then type your main text.

Tip: For tips on typing on the onscreen keyboard, see Chapter 4.

---

9   When you're done, tap ▶ at the top of the message to send it, or tap ⋮ to discard the message or to save it as a draft for later.

Tip: If you're not online, sent messages are stored with the Outbox label until you're online again. Outbox messages are sent automatically.

Changing Gmail Settings

You can change general or account-specific settings in Gmail.

General settings

To change general settings, tap ≡ > Settings > General Settings (Figure 13.8) and then change any of the following settings:

- **Gmail default action**. Determines whether swiping in a conversation list archives or deletes messages.

- **Swipe actions**. Determines whether you can swipe in a conversation list to archive or delete messages.

- **Sender image**. Determines whether the sender's image (or a color-coded icon) appears next to each message in a conversation list.

- **Reply all**. Determines whether Reply or Reply All is the default action in message replies and notifications.

- **Auto-fit messages**. Determines whether message text is automatically resized to fit the available space.

- **Auto-advance**. Lets you choose which screen opens when you delete or archive a conversation whose messages you're viewing.

- **Confirm before deleting**. Determines whether you must confirm that you want to delete a message.

- **Confirm before archiving**. Determines whether you must confirm that you want to archive a message.

- **Confirm before sending**. Determines whether you must confirm that you want to send a message.

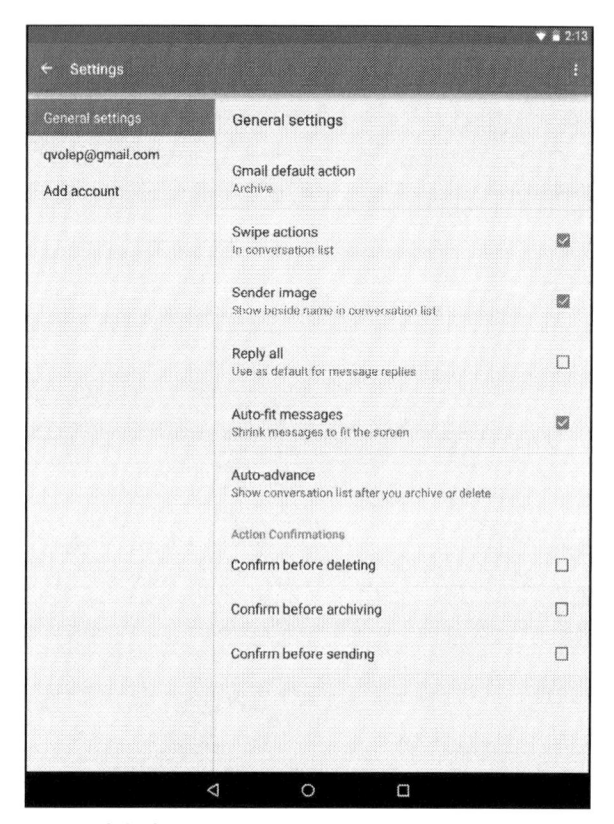

Figure 13.8 Gmail general settings.

Figure 13.9 Gmail account settings.

Account settings

To change account-specific settings, tap ≡ > Settings > *account_name* (Figure 13.9) and then change any of the following settings:

- **Inbox type**. Determines whether Priority Inbox is your default inbox, so it (instead of the default inbox) opens when you start Gmail and have new messages. You receive notifications only for new messages that are part of important conversations (rather than for every new message).

- **Inbox categories**. Lets you choose which categories are used to classify inbox messages.

- **Notifications**. Determines whether you receive a notification when you get a new message.

- **Inbox sound & vibrate**. Fine-tunes notifications on a per-label basis. This setting is available only if Notifications is turned on.

- **Signature**. Adds an optional personalized tag to the bottom of each outgoing message. Typically, a signature is your name, title, contact info, or—if you must—a favorite quote or legal disclaimer.

- **Vacation responder**. Send a custom reply automatically to let all senders (or only your contacts) know that you won't be able to get back to them right away. Use this feature if you're going on vacation or will have no internet access.

- **Sync Gmail**. Determines whether Gmail syncing (page 76) is turned on or off for this account.

- **Days of mail to sync**. Sets the number of days' worth of email messages that you want to sync (download) automatically.

- **Manage labels**. Manages which conversations are synced.

- **Download attachments**. Determines whether message attachments are downloaded automatically when you receive them, rather than requiring you to download them explicitly.

- **Images**. Determines whether Gmail asks you before showing photos and images in emails. (For security, Gmail serves all images through Google's secure proxy servers.).

Hangouts

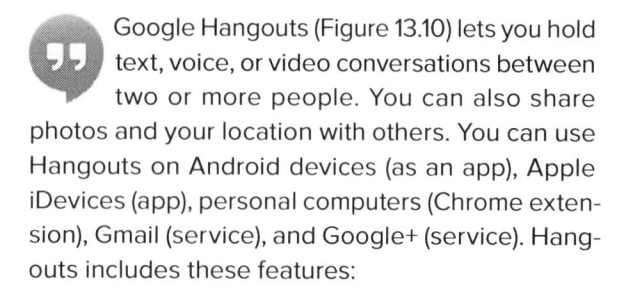

Google Hangouts (Figure 13.10) lets you hold text, voice, or video conversations between two or more people. You can also share photos and your location with others. You can use Hangouts on Android devices (as an app), Apple iDevices (app), personal computers (Chrome extension), Gmail (service), and Google+ (service). Hangouts includes these features:

- **Works with multiple devices**. Hangouts conversations are synced automatically across devices, so you can start a hangout on your Nexus and continue on your computer or phone.

- **Make video calls**. Have video conversations with up to nine other people.

- **Send SMS/MMS and Hangouts messages**. You can start a hangout with just one person or multiple people. You can also send text messages by using Hangouts and your mobile phone number.

- **Make phone calls**. Almost all calls in and to the U.S. and Canada, for example, are free. A few U.S. and Canadian destinations cost USD $0.01 per minute depending on the specific phone number. The one-cent rate may vary depending on the local currency. Calls to destinations outside of the U.S. are at low rates, but calling isn't available to all locations. If you don't see the option to make calls, it's probably because you're in a country where this feature isn't available. For example, calling isn't available in Mexico, China, Russia, India, Argentina, Thailand, Myanmar, Vietnam, and various Middle East and African countries.

Hangouts replaces the Google Talk and Messenger apps from early Android versions.

For more information, go to *google.com/hangouts*.

Figure 13.10 Hangouts.

Tip: For video chat, the popular Skype app is also available from the Google Play store.

CHAPTER 14

Organizing Your Life

This chapter covers apps that help you manage your day-to-day activities.

Maintaining Contacts

Contacts (formerly named People), an electronic address book, stores names, addresses, telephone numbers, email addresses, birthdays, anniversaries, and other contact information. Your contacts are available in Gmail, Hangouts, Calendar, Maps, Google Search and Now, auto-correction, Android Beam, and other apps and services that tap into Contacts.

When you first set up your Nexus and sign into your Google Account, that account's existing contacts are downloaded to your tablet. After that, any changes that you make to your contacts on your Nexus, on the web, or on another device or smartphone are synced online in the background. Microsoft Exchange contacts can also be synced in this way.

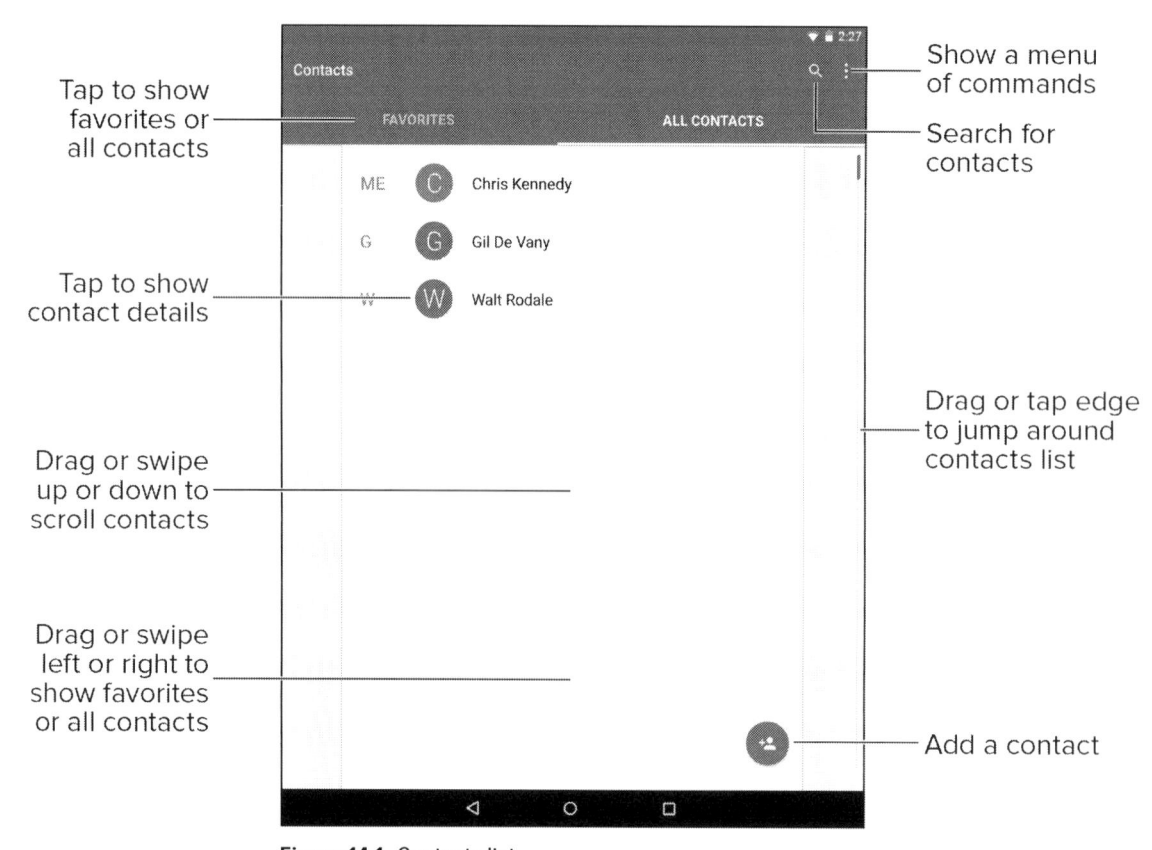

Figure 14.1 Contacts list.

Using Contacts

Open Contacts from the Home screen or All Apps screen. In the contacts list, browse contacts by tapping, dragging, or swiping (Figure 14.1). Tap a contact in the list to see its details (Figure 14.2). You can scroll contact info, or tap a field or icon to call, email, send a message, video-chat, share a vCard (.vcf) file, show an address in Maps, open a home page, and more.

Tip: Tap ⋮ > Place on Home Screen to place a shortcut to a frequent contact on your Home screen.

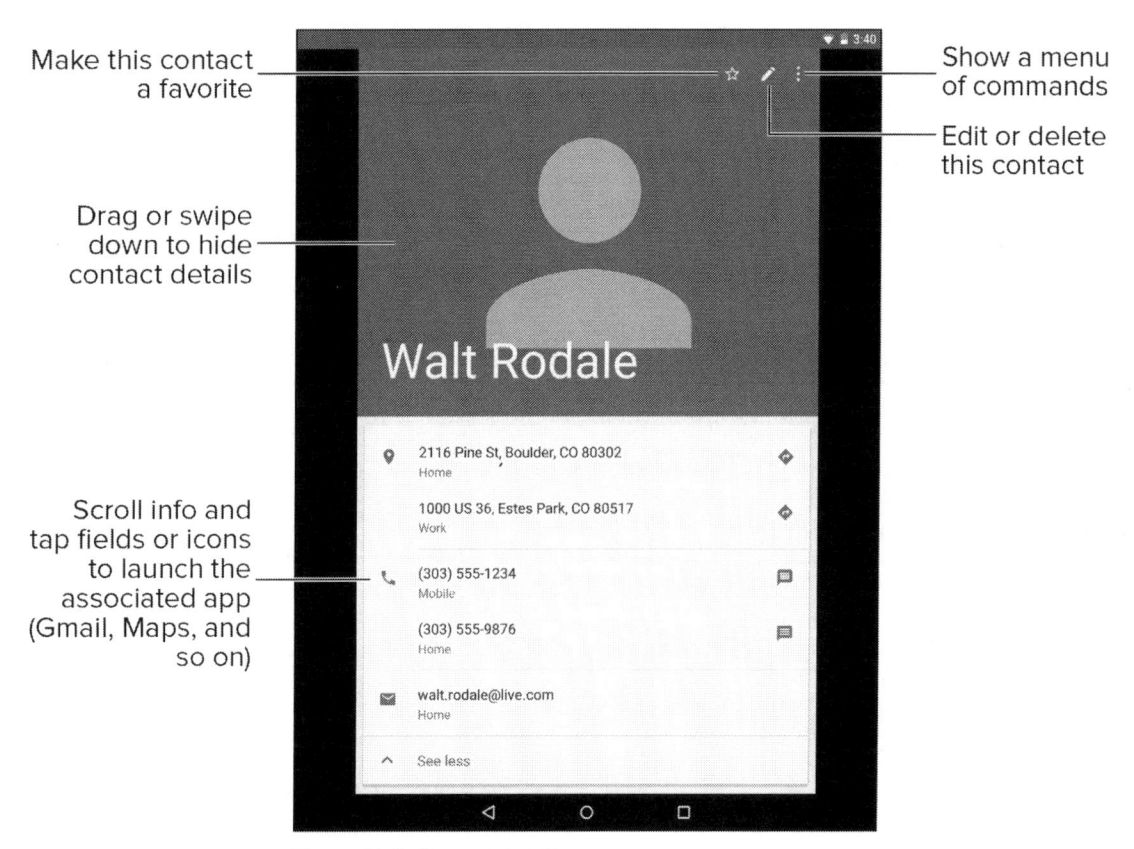

Make this contact a favorite

Show a menu of commands

Edit or delete this contact

Drag or swipe down to hide contact details

Scroll info and tap fields or icons to launch the associated app (Gmail, Maps, and so on)

Figure 14.2 Contact details.

Viewing specific contacts

By default, Contacts shows all the contacts from all your accounts, but you can filter the view to see only contacts from one account, from one group, or a custom set of contacts. You can designate contacts as **favorites** and then view only your favorites and frequent contacts.

To view only favorite contacts:

- Above the contacts list, tap Favorites. To view everyone again, tap All Contacts.

To designate a contact as a favorite:

- Tap the contact to view its details and then tap the star ☆.

  A filled-in star ★ indicates a favorite. You can tap again to unfavorite the contact.

To change which contacts are displayed:

1. Above the contacts list, tap All Contacts.
2. Tap ⋮ > Contacts to Display.

   The Contacts to Display screen opens (Figure 14.3).
3. Tap All Contacts, tap a specific account, or tap Customize to set up a fine-grained selection.

   If you tap Customize, the Define Custom View screen opens. Tap an account to open or close a list of its groups and other categories, and then select those that you want. You can make selections within multiple accounts. Categories within accounts can include contacts that you've starred as favorites. When you're done, tap OK.

To change how contacts are displayed:

- Above the contacts list, tap ⋮ > Settings and then tap a display option.

  You can sort contacts by first or last name, or display last name or first name initially for each contact (for example, Tim Orlov or Orlov, Tim).

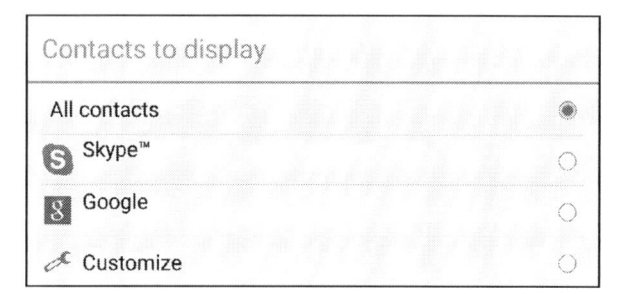

Figure 14.3 You can specify which contacts from which accounts are displayed.

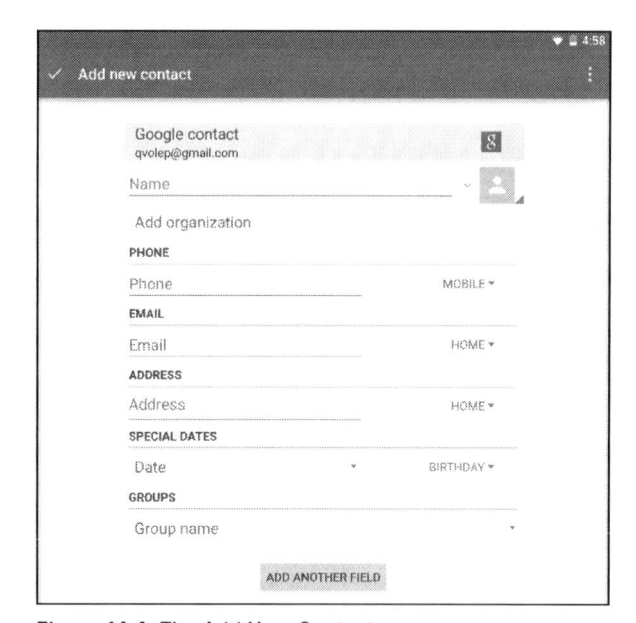

Figure 14.4 The Add New Contact screen.

Adding contacts

You can add contacts on your Nexus and then sync them with the contacts in your Google Account, your Microsoft Exchange account, or other accounts that support syncing.

To add a new contact:

1. Above the contacts list, tap All Contacts.

2. Tap +👤.

   The Add New Contact screen opens (Figure 14.4).

3. If you have more than one account with contacts, tap the one to use.

4. Type the contact's name and other information.

   Tap a field to type or choose a value. Swipe up or down to scroll the categories.

5. To add multiple entries for a category, tap Add New for that field.

   You can add a work address after typing a home address, for example.

6. To open a menu with preset labels, such as Mobile or Work for a phone number, tap the label to the right of the item of contact information.

   or

   To create your own label, tap Custom in the drop-down menu.

7. To add the contact to one or more contacts groups, tap the Groups field.

   or

   Tap Create New Group in the drop-down menu to add the contact to a new group.

Tip: Groups are synced between Contacts on your Nexus and Contacts on the web. To view or edit contacts on a computer or other device, go to *google.com/contacts* and then sign in.

8. To add other types of contact information, tap Add Another Field (Figure 14.5).

   You can add a variety of contact information. To keep track of birthdays or anniversaries, for example, tap Special Dates in the Add Another Field menu.

9. When you're finished, tap ✓ Add New Contact.

   To cancel your edits, tap ⋮ > Discard Changes.

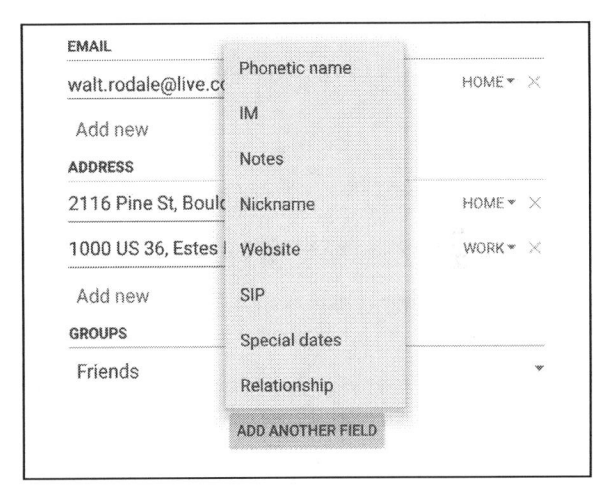

Figure 14.5 The Add Another Field menu.

Importing and exporting contacts

If you copy contacts stored in vCard (.vcf) format to your Nexus, you can import them into Contacts. You can also export all your contacts in vCard format to internal storage and later copy them to a computer or other device.

You need to import your contacts only once. Contacts for your Google Account stay in sync across your Nexus, the web, and your computers and devices (including new devices that you sign in to).

To import contacts to your Google Account on the web:

1 Export your contacts from a web-based email account (Yahoo or Hotmail, for example) or an address-book or email program (Microsoft Outlook or Mac OS X Contacts for example) as a file.

 The most common file formats used for export/import are CSV (.csv) and vCard (.vcf).

2 In a browser, go to *google.com/contacts*, sign in to your Google Account, choose More > Import, and then import the file.

Tip: You can view or edit your Google Account's contacts at *google.com/contacts* on any computer.

To import contacts to your Nexus's internal storage:

1 Connect your Nexus to your computer via USB cable.

2 Copy one or more contacts in vCard (.vcf) format to your Nexus's internal storage.

 For details, see Chapter 7.

3 In Contacts on your Nexus, tap ⋮ > Import/Export.

 The Import/Export Contacts screen opens (Figure 14.6).

4 Tap Import from Storage.

5 If you have more than one account on your Nexus, tap the target account.

6 If you have more than one vCard file in storage, choose whether to import a single file, multiple files, or all files.

 A message appears on your Nexus until all the contacts are imported. If you don't see them in Contacts, make sure that they're not filtered from view; see "Viewing specific contacts" on page 138.

To export contacts to your Nexus's internal storage:

1 In Contacts on your Nexus, tap ⋮ > Import/Export.

 The Import/Export Contacts screen opens.

2 Tap Export to Storage.

3 Tap OK.

 Contacts creates a vCard (.vcf) file containing all your contacts in your Nexus's internal storage. You can connect your Nexus to your computer via USB cable (see Chapter 7) and then copy this file for use with any application that can work with vCard files, such as email and address-book programs.

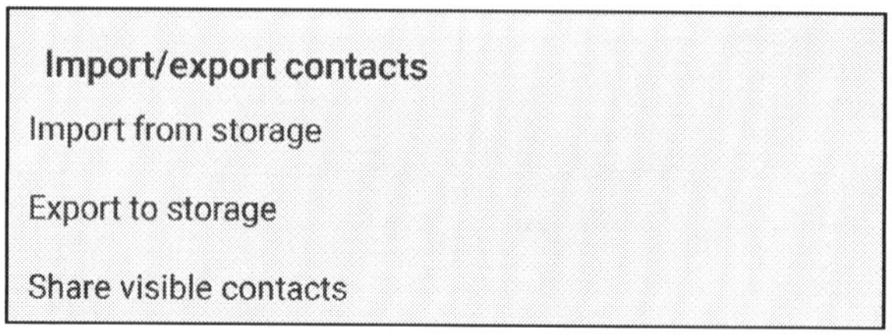

Import/export contacts

Import from storage

Export to storage

Share visible contacts

Figure 14.6 The Import/Export Contacts screen.

Share contact via

M   Gmail

S   Skype

●   Android Beam

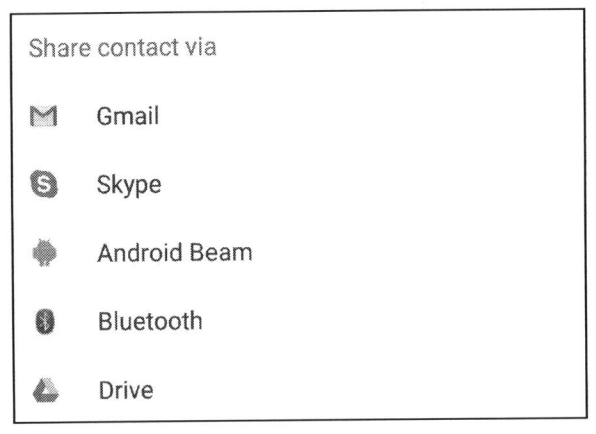

●   Bluetooth

▲   Drive

Figure 14.7 The Share Contact Via screen.

Sharing contacts

You can share contacts in vCard (.vcf) format by using Gmail, Android Beam, or other apps and services.

To share a contact from Contacts:

1. In the contacts list, tap the contact that you want to share.

2. Tap ⋮ > Share.

    The Share Contact Via screen opens (Figure 14.7). The available sharing methods depend on the apps you've installed.

3. Tap a method for sharing the vCard: Gmail, Android Beam, and so on.

4. Use the app or service that you chose to finish sharing the .vcf file.

    If you choose Gmail, for example, the contact is shared as an email attachment.

Editing contacts

The screen for editing a contact is the same as the screen for adding a contact.

To edit a contact:

1. In the contacts list, tap the contact that you want to edit.
2. Tap ✎.
3. Edit the contact information.

    For editing details, see "Adding contacts" on page 139.

4. When you're finished, tap ✓ Edit Contact.

    To cancel your edits, tap ⋮ > Discard Changes.

Deleting contacts

If you delete a contact from a Google Account (or any account with editable contacts), the contact is also deleted from Contacts on the web at *google.com/contacts* when you next sync your Nexus.

To delete a contact:

1. In the contacts list, tap the contact that you want to delete.
2. Tap ✎.
3. Tap ⋮ > Delete.
4. Tap OK to confirm the deletion.

Multiply Sourced Contacts

If you edit a contact that contains information from multiple sources, changes made to info from one source don't affect the info from other sources. Instead, the info from each source is grouped in its own labeled section in the contact details. If you have information about the same contact from a Google Account and a Microsoft Exchange account, for example, and both accounts are configured to sync contacts, edits to the information from the Google Account are synced to that account on the web, whereas the contact's info in the Exchange account remains unchanged. See also "Joining or separating contacts" on page 143.

Read-Only Accounts

If you try to delete a contact from a read-only account such as a Skype or Twitter account, Contacts only *hides* that contact and displays a message to that effect. To restore any hidden contacts, you must delete the pertinent account from your Nexus and then add it again (see Chapter 6). If the contact contains information from an editable account *and* from a read-only account, a message tells you that the information from the read-only account will be hidden, not deleted.

Joining or separating contacts

When you add a new account, Contacts automatically tries to merge duplicate contacts into a single entry. If Contacts guesses wrong, you can join or separate contacts manually. After you do, however, automatic merging no longer works for that contact.

To join contacts:

1. In the contacts list, tap the contact that you want to join with one or more other contacts.

    This contact is the one that you'll see in Contacts after the join.

2. Tap ✏.

3. Tap ⋮ > Join.

    The Join Contacts screen opens.

4. Tap the contact whose information you want to join with the first contact. You can scroll to a contact or search for contacts by tapping 🔍.

    The information from the second contact is added to the first contact, and the second contact disappears from the contacts list.

5. Tap ✓ Edit Contact.

6. To join another contact to the main contact, repeat the preceding steps.

To separate contacts:

1. In the contacts list, tap the contact that you want to separate.

2. Tap ✏.

3. Tap ⋮ > Separate.

    The Separate command is available only if the contact information comes from at least two sources.

4. Tap OK to confirm the separation.

    The contact information separates into individual contacts.

Tip: The web-based version of Google Contacts also offers a tool to eliminate duplicate contacts. Go to *google.com/contacts*, sign in to your account, and then choose More > Find & Merge Duplicates.

Setting Up Calendars & Events

Calendar keeps you on schedule and lets you track your life's important events. You can view individual calendars or a single combined calendar, which makes it easy to manage work and personal appointments at the same time.

Tip: Schedule view presents a scrollable list of your events in chronological order. A thin blue line indicates the current time.

Using Calendar

Open Calendar (Figure 14.8) from the Home screen or All Apps screen. Calendar displays events from each of your accounts that synchronizes its calendars with your Nexus. Each account can have multiple calendars available for display, based on the way you've set up that account's calendars in a browser. For Google Accounts, you can set up calendars at *google.com/calendar*.

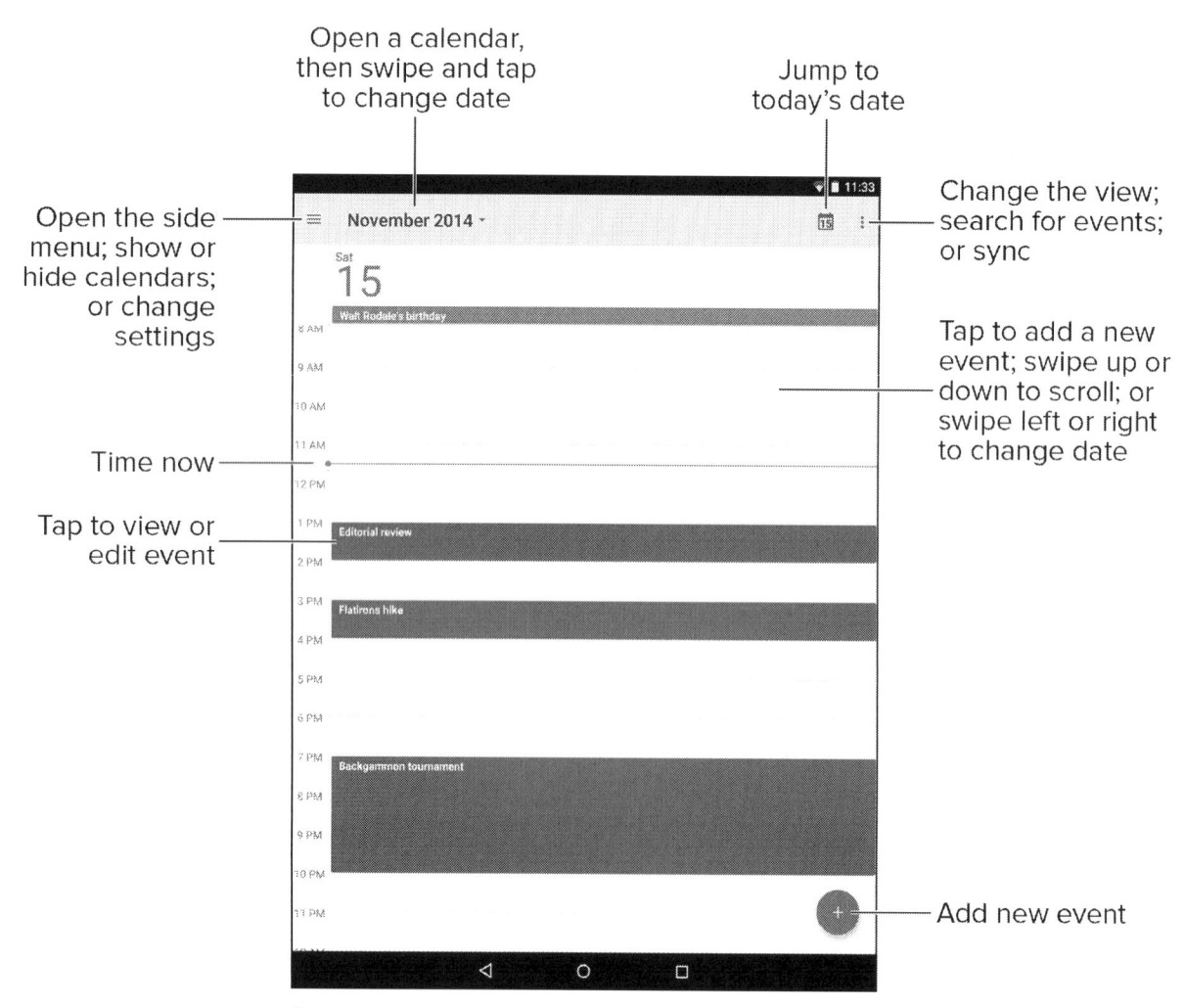

Figure 14.8 Calendar controls.

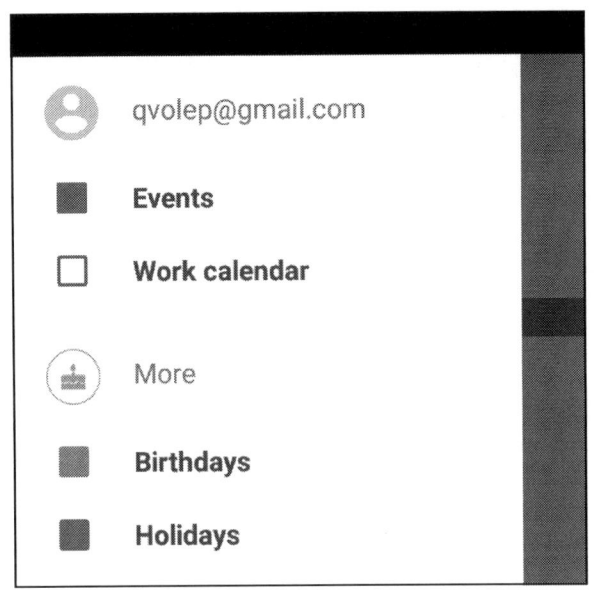

Figure 14.9 The Calendar side menu.

Syncing and viewing calendars

Calendar offers various settings that let you determine how calendars are synchronized and displayed.

To show or hide an account's calendars:

1. Tap ☰ to open the side menu and then tap the account (Figure 14.9).
2. Select or clear the color box for each calendar that you want to show or hide.

   Events from each calendar are displayed in that calendar's color.

Tip: Hiding a calendar doesn't stop it from syncing.

To sync all your calendars manually:

- Tap ⋮ > Refresh.

Tip: Refresh (as well as automatic sync) requires an internet connection.

To declutter the screen:

- Tap ☰ > Settings > General > turn on Show More Events (this setting hides the seasonal illustrations).

Setting Up Accounts

The Accounts screen (covered in Chapter 6) lets you view or change which of your accounts are synced with Calendar. To sync a Google Account calendar, for example, tap Settings > Accounts > Google, tap the account whose calendar you want to sync, and then select Calendar. When you first set up Calendar for a Google Account or Microsoft Exchange account, all the calendars that are displayed when you view that account's calendar in a browser are also displayed in Calendar. You can change which calendars are shown.

Adding, editing, and searching events

You can add, update, delete, and search for events on any of your calendars, and set Calendar to alert you to upcoming events. If you're traveling, you can make Calendar display event dates and times in a specific time zone.

Tip: For Google Accounts, events that you create or edit in the Calendar app appear both on your Nexus and in Google Calendar on the web at *google.com/calendar*.

To add an event:

1 Tap ⊕.

   or

   In Day or Week view, tap a spot at the desired date and time, and then tap it again.

   The New Event screen opens (Figure 14.10).

2 Enter details about the event, such as the event name, time, location, invitees (contact names or email addresses), event color, and reminders.

3 When you're finished, tap Save.

   The event is added to your calendar, and invitees receive an email invitation.

To edit an event:

1 Tap the event that you want to edit and then tap ✏.

   The Edit Event screen opens; it's the same as the New Event screen.

2 Make your changes to the event.

3 When you're finished, tap Save.

   The changes are saved, and updates are emailed to any invitees.

To delete an event:

1 Tap the event that you want to delete, tap ✏, and then tap Delete (at the bottom of the Edit Event screen).

2 Tap OK to confirm the deletion.

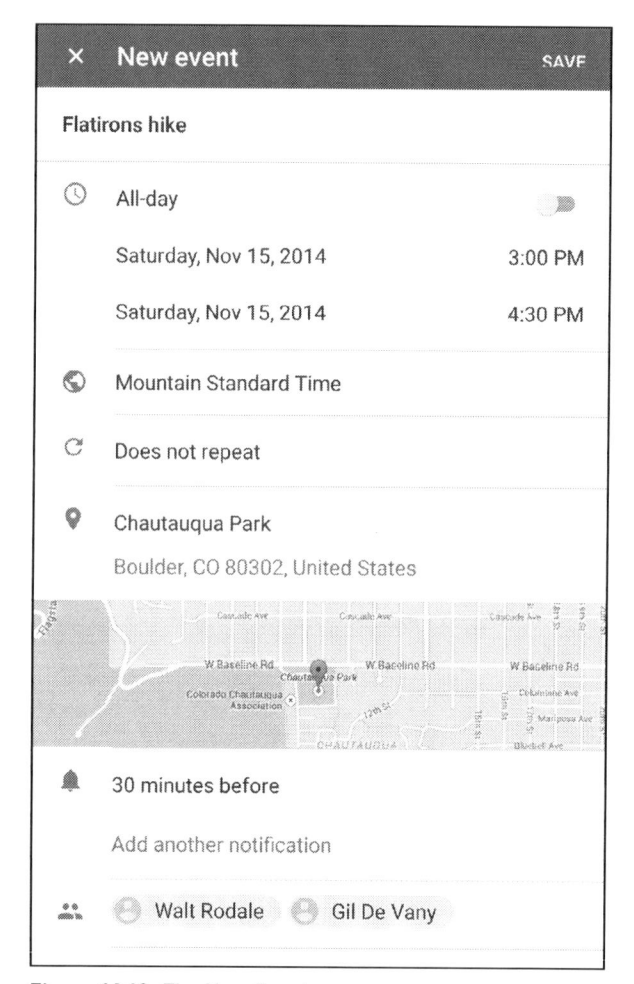

Figure 14.10 The New Event screen.

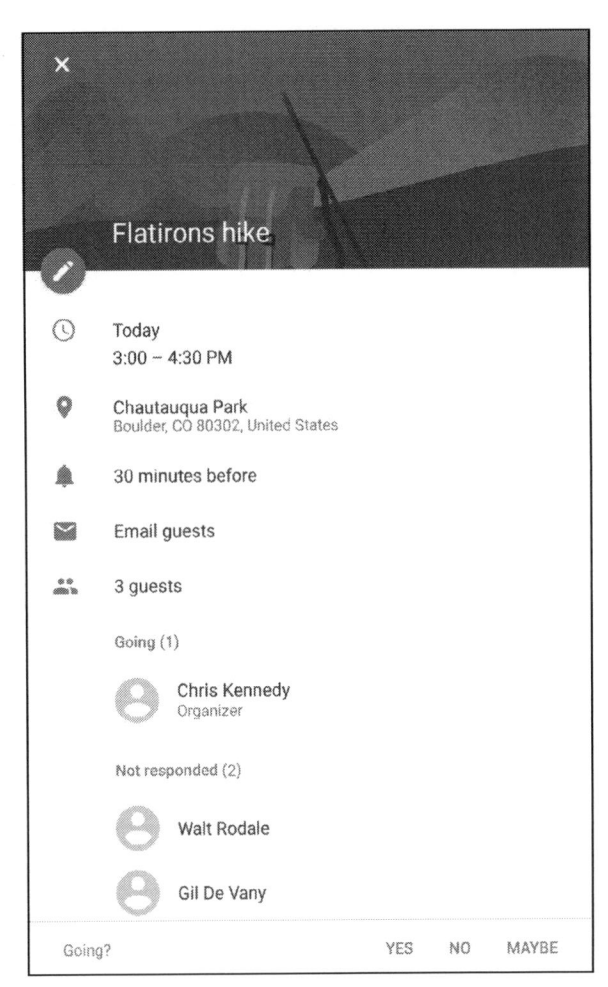

Figure 14.11 Tap an invitation in your calendar to respond to it.

To search for events:

1. Tap ⋮ > Search.

2. Type search terms, or tap 🎤 to speak them.

   Calendar lists matching events for the calendars that you're currently viewing.

To show event times in a specific time zone:

1. Tap ☰ > Settings > General.

2. Turn off Use Device Time Zone.

3. Tap Time Zone and then select a time zone.

Responding to invitations

If you have a Google, Microsoft Exchange, iCloud, or CalDAV account (such as Yahoo Calendar), you can send and receive invitations.

To invite others to an event, tap Invite People or the invitee list while you're adding or editing an event and then type an email address or a name to select invitees from Contacts (page 136).

If you receive an invitation, it lands in the scheduled slot on your calendar with a border around the event. To respond, tap the event. You can accept or decline, view the event organizer's contact info, see or email other invitees, or set reminders (Figure 14.11).

Tip: You can also respond by dragging the notification shade down from the top of the screen and then tapping the event's notification.

Chapter 14 Organizing Your Life 147

Changing Calendar settings

To change the settings in Calendar, tap ☰ > Settings > General (Figure 14.12) and then change any of the following settings:

- **Start of the week.** Lets you choose the first day of the week: Saturday, Sunday, or Monday.

- **Use device time zone.** Determines whether Calendar displays event dates and times using a specific time zone when you're traveling.

- **Time zone.** Lets you choose a specific time zone. This option is available only when Use Home Time Zone is turned off.

- **Show declined events.** Determines whether declined invitations appear on your calendars.

- **Show more events.** Determines whether the seasonal artwork appears atop the calendar.

- **Default event duration.** Sets the default duration for newly added events.

- **Notify on this device.** Determines whether you receive event notifications.

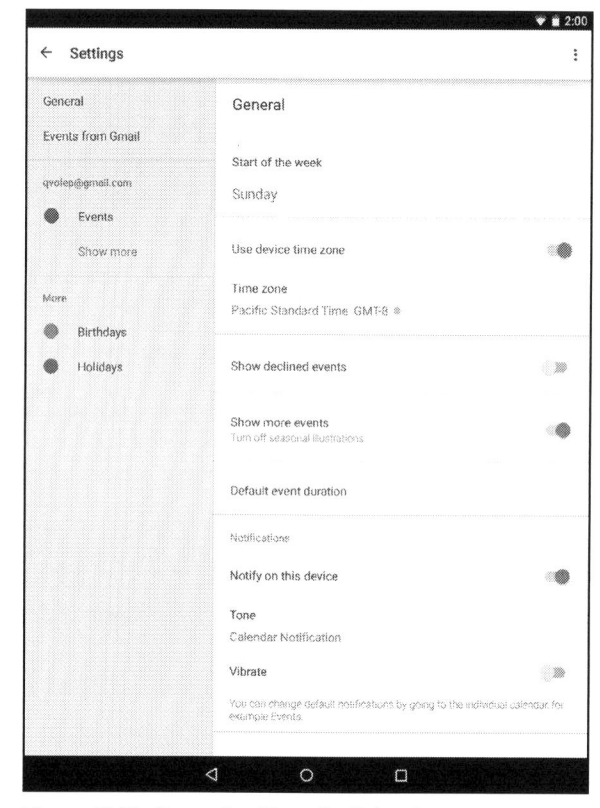

Figure 14.12 General settings for Calendar.

Tip: You can tap a specific calendar in Calendar Settings to change its default notifications, color, and more.

- **Tone.** Sets an alert sound for event notifications.

- **Vibrate.** Determines whether event notifications vibrate the tablet.

- **Quick responses.** Lets you edit default responses that you can use to respond to invitations quickly.

Tip: If Events From Gmail is turned on in Calendar Settings, then, when you get an email about an event such as a flight, concert, or restaurant reservation, it's added to your calendar automatically—no need to copy the details to your calendar.

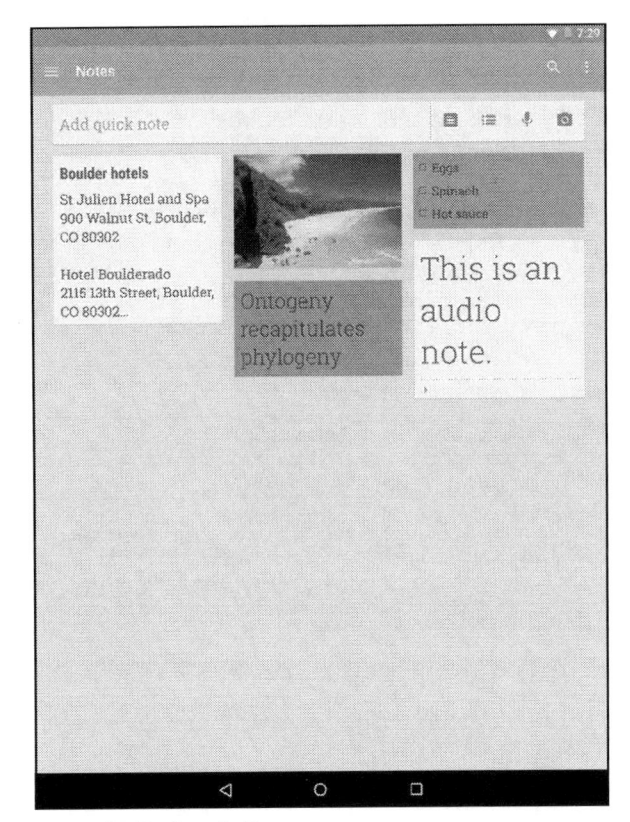

Figure 14.13 Google Keep.

Taking Notes

Google Keep is a note-taking app that lets you create notes and sync them across your Nexus, other Android devices, through a Chrome app, and on the web. With Keep, you can:

- Use text, voice, or photos to create notes, and add multi-purpose checklists
- Drag notes and lists to rearrange them, and archive or delete them when you no longer need them
- Browse and search notes
- Use widgets for quick note-taking and viewing
- Set reminders

Using Keep

When you open Keep (Figure 14.13), all the notes that you've created are displayed. You can rearrange your notes or view them in a single column or in multiple columns. Text in the notes reflows automatically to fit the view. If you don't want certain notes to show up on the main Keep screen, you can archive them.

To view your (unarchived) notes:

- On the main Keep screen, tap ≡ > Notes.

To rearrange notes:

- Touch and hold a note, and then drag it.

To switch views:

- Tap ⋮ > Single-Column View or Multi-Column View.

Chapter 14 Organizing Your Life   149

To add a quick note:

1 Tap Add Quick Note and then type the note.

   To expand the note, tap ⌞ ⌝. To change the note color, tap 🎨.

2 When you're finished, tap the ✓ key.

To create a note:

1 Tap 📄 at the top of the screen.
2 To add an optional title, tap the Title field.
3 To add text, tap the Note field.
4 When you're finished, tap ← to save.

To add checkboxes to a note to make it a list:

- While editing a note, tap ⋮ > Show Checkboxes.

To change the color of a note:

1 While editing a note, tap 🎨 at the top of the screen.
2 Tap a color.

To add a photo to a note:

1 While editing a note, tap 📷 at the top of the screen.
2 Take a photo or choose an existing photo.

To create or edit a list:

1 Tap ☰ at the top of the screen.
2 Do any of the following:

   ▸ To enter an optional title, tap the Title field.

   ▸ To add an item to the list, tap List Item and then type.

   ▸ To add more items, tap Return on the keyboard to move to the next item.

   ▸ To remove an item, tap it, and then tap × to the right of it.

   ▸ To check (tick off) items on your list, tap the box next to the item.

   ▸ To hide the checkboxes, tap ⋮ > Hide Checkboxes.

   ▸ To reorder list items, touch and hold the grab handle on the left side of an item, and then drag to reposition the item.

3 When you're finished, tap ← to save.

To create an audio note:

1 Tap 🎤 at the top of the screen.
2 Speak your note.
3 When you're finished, tap 🎤 or stop speaking.

   An audio snippet and the spoken text are added to the note.

4 To add an optional title, tap the Title field.
5 To edit the transcribed text, tap the text above the audio snippet.
6 When you're finished, tap ← to save.

Tip: To remove the audio snippet (but not the note itself), tap × to the right of the snippet.

To create a photo note:

1 Tap 📷 at the top of the screen.
2 Take a photo or choose an existing photo.
3 To add an optional title, tap the Title field.
4 To add text, tap below the image.
5 When you're finished, tap ← to save.

Tip: To remove the photo (but not the note itself), tap the photo and then tap × on the photo.

To send a note:

- Open the note and then tap ⋮ > Send.

  or

  On the main Keep screen, touch and hold the note and then tap ⋮ > Send.

  The available sharing methods depend on the apps you've installed.

Tip: To share existing photos to Keep, select the photos in the Photos app (Chapter 17) and then tap ◁.

To edit a note:

- Tap the note, make your changes, and then tap ← to save.

To archive a note:

- Open the note and then tap 🗄.

  or

  On the main Keep screen, swipe the note, or touch and hold a note and then tap 🗄.

To view archived notes:

- On the main Keep screen, tap ☰ > Archive.

To unarchive a note:

- Open the note and then tap 🗄.

  or

  On the Archived Notes screen, touch and hold the note and then tap 🗄.

To delete a note:

- Open the note and then tap 🗑.

  or

  On the main Keep screen, touch and hold a note and then tap ⋮ > Delete Note.

To search for notes:

- On the main Keep screen, tap 🔍.

  As you type, the matching notes are displayed.

Tip: Two Google Keep widgets are available: one that shows your existing notes and lets you create new notes quickly, and another that lets you create new notes from the Home screen.

Setting reminders in Google Keep

You can use Google Keep to create time and location reminders:

- When creating or editing a note, tap 👆 Remind Me at the bottom of the note, and then edit the reminder details.

- On the main Keep screen, touch and hold a note, and then tap 👆 at the top of the screen.

You can add only one reminder per note. To see all your Keep reminders, tap ☰ > Reminders. In Google Now (Chapter 9), a card appears for Keep reminders. See also "Settings Reminders in Google Now" on page 92.

Using the Clock

The Clock app (Figure 14.14) has an alarm clock, a world clock, a countdown timer, and a stopwatch.

To set an alarm:

1. Tap the Alarm Clock icon at the top-left corner of the screen, or swipe to the alarms screen.

Tip: The alarms screen shows any existing alarms. To turn one on or off, tap the switch.

2. Tap + to add a new alarm.
3. Select the time you want, and then tap OK.

Tip: You can also add a label to an alarm, change its ringtone (alert sound), or repeat it periodically. To change these options for a single alarm, tap the small arrow below the alarm switch.

To view the current date and time:

- Tap the Clock icon at the top of the screen, or swipe to the clock screen. The screen background changes color depending on the time of day.

Tip: You can touch and hold the clock screen to dim the Nexus screen before bed.

To add world clocks:

1. Tap the Clock icon at the top of the screen, or swipe to the clock screen.
2. Tap the Globe icon at the bottom-center of the screen.

   The Cities screen opens.

3. Scroll or search the list, tapping cities to show or hide their clocks.

Tip: The clock widgets (page 26) can display analog or digital clocks on the Home screen. Tapping a clock widget opens the Clock app.

Figure 14.14 The Clock app.

To set a timer:

1. Tap the Timer icon at the top of the screen, or swipe to the timer screen.

2. Enter the time you want, and then tap the Start button.

3. The timer beeps when the time is up, and keeps beeping until you tap the Stop button.

   You can create multiple, saved timers and label them. Indicators on the right edge of the screen glow to show you which timer is active. Swipe up or down to see the different timers. When a timer is running, you can pause it, reset it, add an additional minute, or delete it.

To use the stopwatch:

1. Tap the Stopwatch icon at the top-right corner of the screen, or swipe to the stopwatch screen.

2. Do any of the following:

   ▶ To start the stopwatch, tap the Start button.

   ▶ To add laps, tap the bottom-left icon while the stopwatch is running.

   ▶ To pause the stopwatch, tap the Pause button.

   ▶ To reset the stopwatch to zero, tap the bottom-left icon while the stopwatch is paused.

   ▶ To share your results, tap .

Changing Clock settings

To change the settings in Clock, tap ⋮ > Settings on the alarm or time screen, and then change any of the following settings:

- **Style**. Choose whether to display an analog or digital clock face.
- **Automatic home clock**. Determines whether a home clock is added while you're traveling.
- **Home time zone**. Set your home time zone.
- **Silence after**. Set when you want your alarm to stop ringing.
- **Snooze length**. Set how long your alarm will snooze if you tap Snooze when the alarm goes off.
- **Alarm volume**. Adjust the alarm volume independently of the main volume setting.
- **Volume buttons**. Choose whether you want your Volume buttons to snooze, dismiss, or do nothing.

Tip: If you're using your Nexus as a bedside alarm clock, tap ⋮ > Night Mode.

CHAPTER 15

Shopping for Apps, Games & Media

Google Play is Google's digital app and media distribution service. It includes an online store for music, movies, TV shows, books, magazines, and Android apps and games. You can access Google Play on the web at *play.google.com/store* or use the Play Store app on your Nexus. Your purchases are available across your computers and Android devices. Your Nexus comes with dedicated apps for playing music, watching video, and reading books and magazines that you get from the Google Play store.

Accessing the Google Play Store

To access the Google Play store, open the Play Store app from the Home screen or All Apps screen (Figure 15.1).

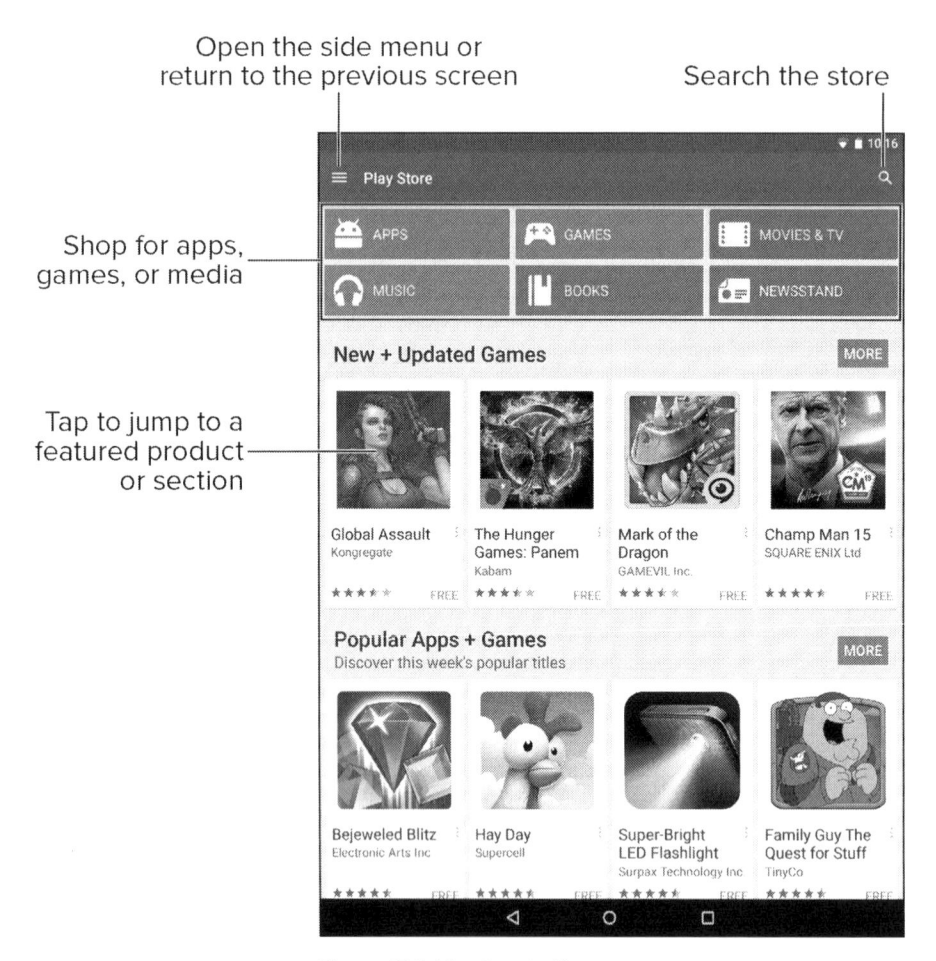

Open the side menu or return to the previous screen

Search the store

Shop for apps, games, or media

Tap to jump to a featured product or section

Figure 15.1 The Google Play store.

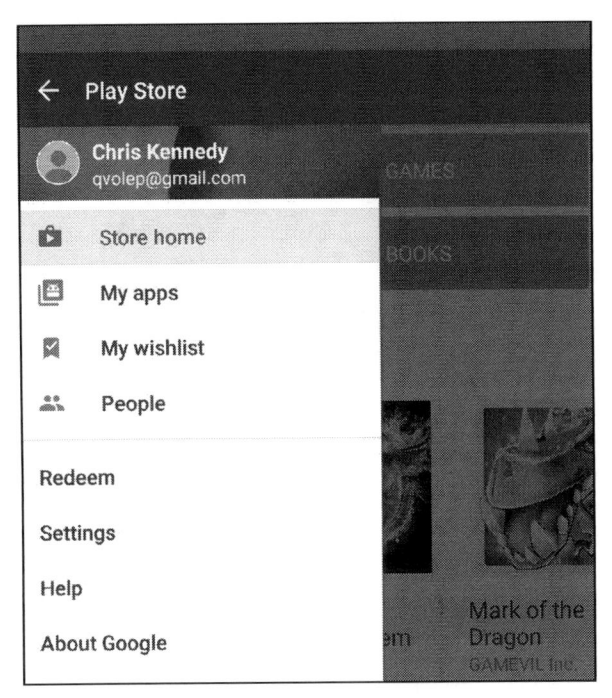

Figure 15.2 The Google Play Store side menu.

You can use the **side menu** on the left side of the screen to return to the store's home screen, list your store purchases, redeem gift cards, and more. To show to the side menu, tap the icon in the top-left corner of the screen (repeatedly, if necessary) or swipe right from the left edge of the screen (Figure 15.2).

To shop in the store, you must have a Google Account, which is linked to your Google Play downloads and purchases. You have several ways to pay for store purchases:

- **Google Wallet**. You can connect your Google Account with Google Wallet to pay for purchases from Google Play (and other online stores). Google Wallet is a secure mobile payment system (similar to PayPal) that lets you store debit cards, credit cards, loyalty cards, gift cards, and more. To set up or sign in to Google Wallet, go to *google.com/wallet*.

- **Gift cards**. Google Play gift cards are available in various cash denominations. To find a retailer, go to *play.google.com/about/giftcards*. To redeem a gift card, tap Redeem in the Play Store side menu, or go to *play.google.com/redeem*. Redeemed cards appear in your Google Account as part of your Google Play balance. Availability of Google Play gift cards varies by country.

- **Store credits**. In some cases, Google awards free Google Play credit to people who buy Google products or sign up for Google Wallet or other services. Credits appear in your Google Account as part of your Google Play balance.

Getting Apps and Games

To get apps or games from the Google Play store, open the Play Store app from the Home screen or All Apps screen, tap Apps, and then do any of the following:

- **Browse for apps.** Swipe left or right to browse by category or see featured, top, or trending apps (Figure 15.3).

- **Search for apps.** Tap 🔍 at the top of the screen and then type keywords such as the name of the app or developer. Initially, your history of recent searches appears. As you type, Google Play autosuggests terms (Figure 15.4). To find free apps, include the word *free* in your search. Tap a suggestion or tap the 🔍 key to see a list of matching apps. To speak instead of type, tap 🎤 in the search field or on the onscreen keyboard (for details, see "Dictating Text" on page 59).

Tip: To clear your search history, open the side menu and then tap Settings > Clear Local Search History.

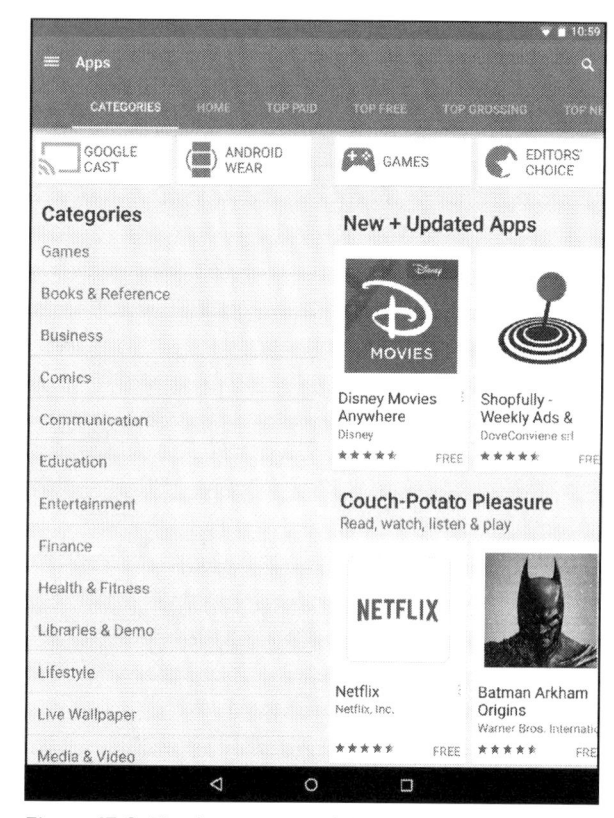

Figure 15.3 The Apps screen of the Google Play store.

Can't Find an App?

If you can't find an app, try different search terms, in case the app's name has changed. Also, an app may not appear if it doesn't run on your Nexus because the developer targeted it for a different screen size, Android version, country, or whatever. It's also possible that a publisher removed the app from the store.

The store is curated, meaning that Google can yank an app from the store if it crashes too much, violates store policy, is complained about excessively, or whatever. Yanked apps disappear from the store but not from your Nexus; after you download an app and back it up, it's yours.

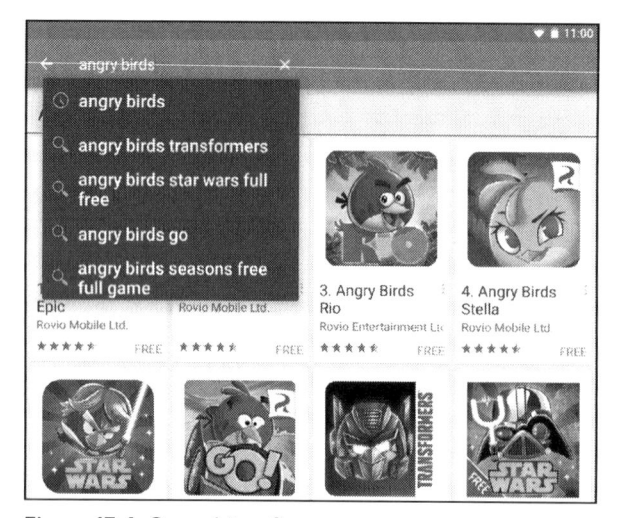

Figure 15.4 Searching for apps.

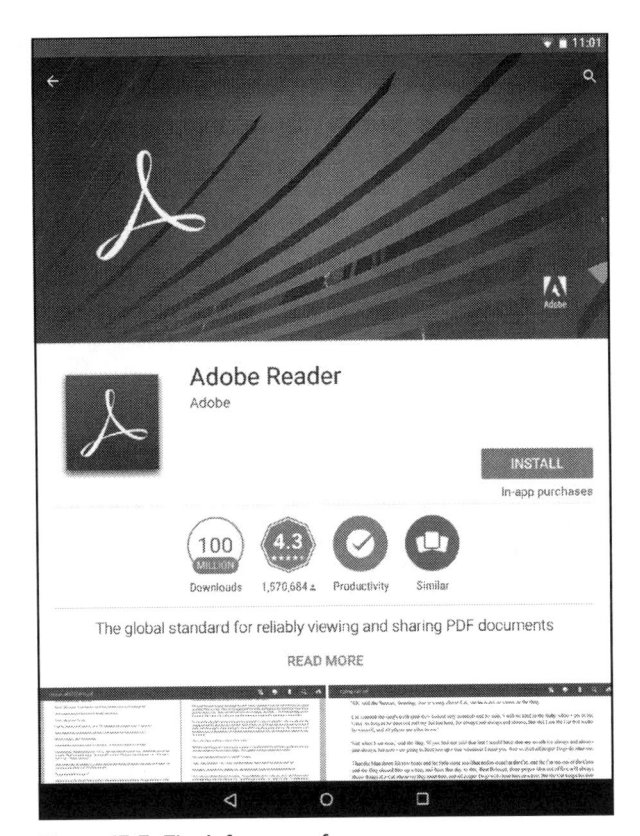

Figure 15.5 The Info screen for an app.

- **Install an app.** Browse to or search for the app that you want. Tap the app's icon to see its **Info screen** (Figure 15.5), where you can read a description, see screenshots, read customer ratings and reviews, and more. To install the app, tap the app's price (or tap Install). In the window that opens, tap Accept to accept the permissions for the app (or tap off the window if you don't want to download). The app starts downloading immediately and lands on your Home screen and All Apps screen. To prevent new icons from landing on your Home screen, open the side menu, tap Settings, and then clear Add Icon to Home Screen.

Tip: If you've already downloaded the app, Uninstall and Open appear instead of a price or Install. If an update is available for an installed app, Update appears.

Most apps download in less than a minute, but you can check progress on the app's Info screen or by dragging the notification shade down from the top of the screen (for details, see Chapter 8).

- **Share an app.** To send a link to an app's Play Store page via email or another sharing app, tap ◁ on the app's Info screen.
- **Return an app for a refund.** You have two hours from the time of download to return a purchased app for a full refund. To return an app, open the side menu, tap My Apps, tap the app you want to return, and then tap Refund. If you paid by using a debit card, refunds may take a few days. If Uninstall appears instead of Refund, then the two-hour deadline has passed; to get a refund, try contacting the developer directly. (Contact info is in the Developer section of the app's Info screen.)

Tip: You can return a given app only once. If you buy the same app again, you can't return it a second time.

Play Games

The Play Games app lets you play games on Google's online multi-player social gaming network. You can get Play Games-compatible games from the Google Play store to play against friends or strangers on Android tablets and phones.

Play Games offers features common to most gaming networks. You can add people to your friends list, see what your friends are playing, get game recommendations, join multiplayer games, track your achievements (bonus points earned for completing certain tasks), and view game leaderboards ranking the best players.

- **Uninstall an app**. To remove an app from your Nexus, open the side menu, tap My Apps, tap the app to uninstall, and then tap Uninstall (Figure 15.6). Uninstalling an app also deletes the data, settings, and documents associated with that app.

Tip: To uninstall an app quickly without opening Play Store, tap ⊕ in the Favorites tray on the Home screen, touch and hold the icon of the target app, and then drag it to the word *Uninstall* at the top of the screen.

- **Update apps**. Developers occasionally update their apps with new features, bug fixes, security patches, and other improvements, and then release the new version through the store. If any updates are available, a notification icon appears in the status bar at the top of the screen. You can drag the notification shade down from the top of the screen to see how many updates are available.

  To update apps, open the side menu and then tap My Apps. Available updates are listed on the My Apps screen (Figure 15.7).

  To update all your apps, tap the Update All button near the top-right corner of the screen. To update any single app (or learn more about an update), tap the app to show its Info screen and then tap Update. If you want this app to auto-update in the future, tap ⋮ > Auto-Update in the app's Info screen. To make *all* apps autoupdate, open the side menu and then select Settings > Auto-Update Apps.

Figure 15.6 Tap Uninstall to remove an app from your Nexus.

Figure 15.7 Any available updates are listed near the top of the My Apps screen.

Tips for Apps

- To change notification settings for app updates, open the side menu and then tap Settings > Notifications.

- To manage installed apps, see "Managing Apps and Services" on page 188 and "Optimizing Data Usage" on page 191.

- To protect against rogue apps, viruses, and malware, see "Verifying Apps" on page 48.

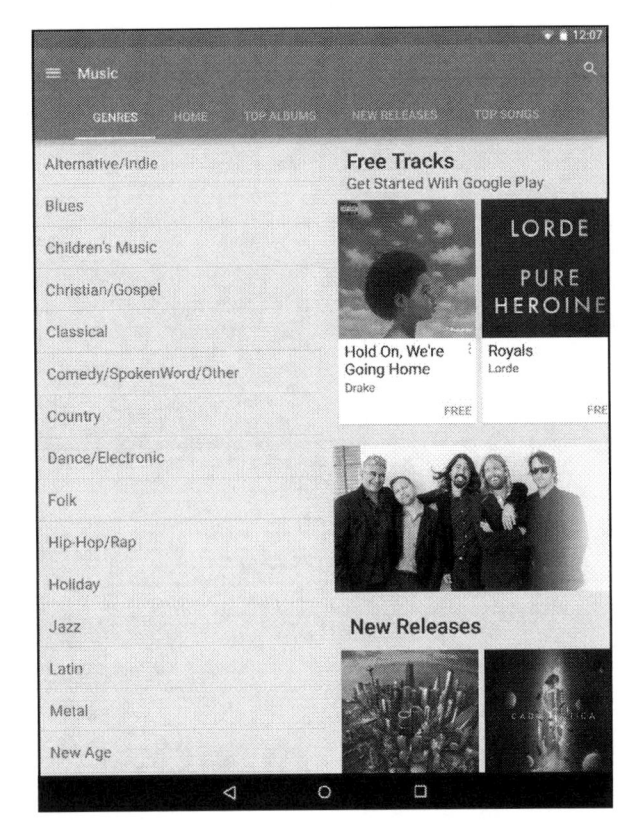

Figure 15.8 The Music screen of the Google Play store.

Playing Music

To get music from the Google Play store, open the Play Store app from the Home screen or All Apps screen and then tap Music. The store's Music screen opens (Figure 15.8). Swipe left or right to browse by genre or to see featured or top songs and albums. Or tap 🔍 at the top of the screen to search for music. Availability varies by country. When you find what you want, tap to sample or buy it.

To listen to your music, use the Play Music app, which you can open from the Home screen or All Apps screen. Music purchases from Google Play appear in the app automatically, and you can add more songs from your personal music collection on your computer. Play Music can do the things common to most digital music players: create playlists, queue songs, adjust equalization, manage your music library, share songs, stream online music, and so on.

Tip: To manage your music collection on your computer, go to *play.google.com/music* and install the Google Play Music Manager.

Chapter 15   Shopping for Apps, Games & Media   161

Playing Movies and TV Shows

To get movies and TV episodes from the Google Play store, open the Play Store app from the Home screen or All Apps screen and then tap Movies & TV. The store's Movies & TV screen opens (Figure 15.9). Swipe left or right to browse by category or to see featured or top movies and TV shows. Or tap 🔍 at the top of the screen to search for videos. Availability varies by country. When you find what you want, tap to preview, rent, or buy it. Some videos, labeled HD, are in high-definition format.

To watch movies or TV shows, use the Play Movies & TV app, which you can open from the Home screen or All Apps screen. Movie and TV purchases from Google Play appear in the app automatically. You can use Google Chromecast (page 41) to stream shows to your HDTV.

Tip: To play personal videos and movies that you copy to your Nexus, use a third-party media player from the Google Play store. MX Player, for example, can play MP4, MKV, AVI, and other popular video formats.

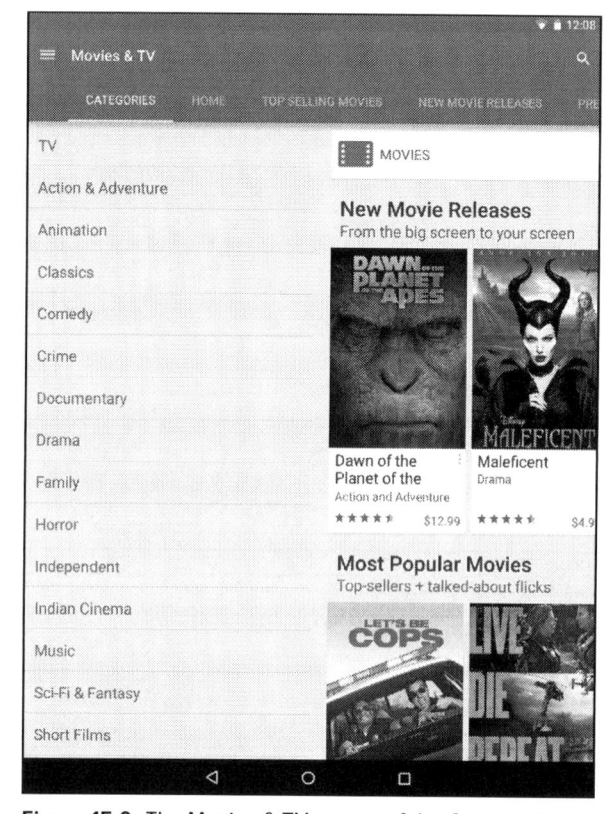

Figure 15.9 The Movies & TV screen of the Google Play store.

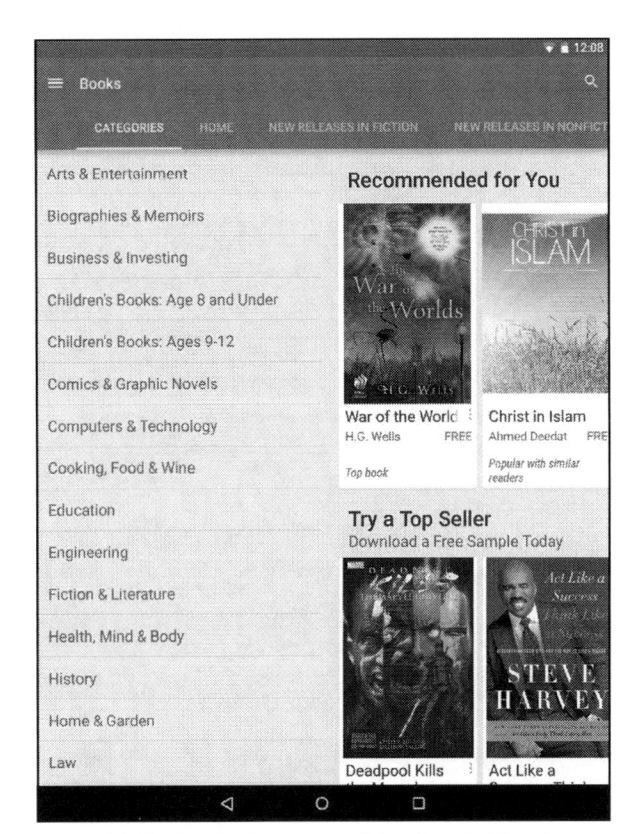

Figure 15.10 The Books screen of the Google Play store.

Reading Books

To get books from the Google Play store, open the Play Store app from the Home screen or All Apps screen and then tap Books. The store's Books screen opens (Figure 15.10). Swipe left or right to browse by category or to see featured, new, or top books. Or tap 🔍 at the top of the screen to search for books. Availability varies by country. When you find what you want, tap to sample or buy it (or download a free book).

To read books, use the Play Books app, which you can open from the Home screen or All Apps screen. Books purchases from Google Play appear in the app automatically. Play Books supports books in EPUB or PDF format. To read your own EPUB or PDF files on Play Books, read the Google support article "Upload & read documents" at *https://support.google.com/googleplay/answer/3097151?hl=en*.

Tip: Plenty of other readers—such Adobe Reader, Aldiko Book Reader, and FBReader—are available in the Google Play store, as well as bookstore apps like Amazon Kindle and Barnes & Noble Nook.

Reading Magazines and News

To get magazines and news from the Google Play store, open the Play Store app from the Home screen or All Apps screen and then tap Newsstand. The store's Newsstand screen opens (Figure 15.11). Swipe left or right to browse by category or to see featured, top, or new magazines and news. Or tap 🔍 at the top of the screen to search for periodicals. Availability varies by country. When you find what you want, tap to subscribe, buy, or read.

To read magazines and news, use the Play Newsstand app, which you can open from the Home or All Apps screen. Magazine and news purchases from Google Play appear in the app automatically. Subscriptions auto-renew when your current term expires. You can cancel your subscription before the end of the subscription term in the Play Newsstand app or at *play.google.com/newsstand*.

Tip: Your Google Currents subscriptions (from earlier versions of Android) transfer into Play Newsstand automatically.

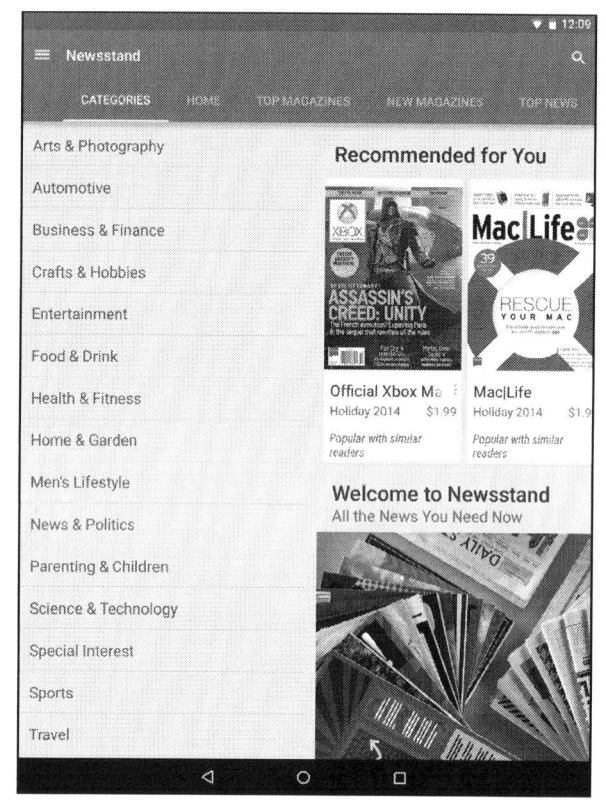

Figure 15.11 The Newsstand screen of the Google Play store.

Free Trials

When you subscribe to a periodical with a free trial, you get the current issue plus any new issues published within the trial period. All trials last at least 14 days. You must enter payment information, but you won't be charged until after the trial period. If you cancel your subscription during the trial, you won't be charged, but you can still read the issues that you got as part of the trial. You can get one free-trial period per periodical.

CHAPTER 16

Maps & Navigation

Google Maps is one of the crown jewels of the Nexus. With it, you can:

- See your location on a map
- Move, pan, and zoom the map
- Search for locations
- Get details about businesses and points of interest
- Use a compass
- View street-level images
- Get directions to travel via car, public transit, bicycle, or foot
- See real-time traffic information
- Browse local places

Using Google Maps

Open the Maps app from the Home screen or All Apps screen. A map appears, color-coded and labeled with streets, points of interest, borders, parks, bodies of water, geographic features, and much more (Figure 16.1).

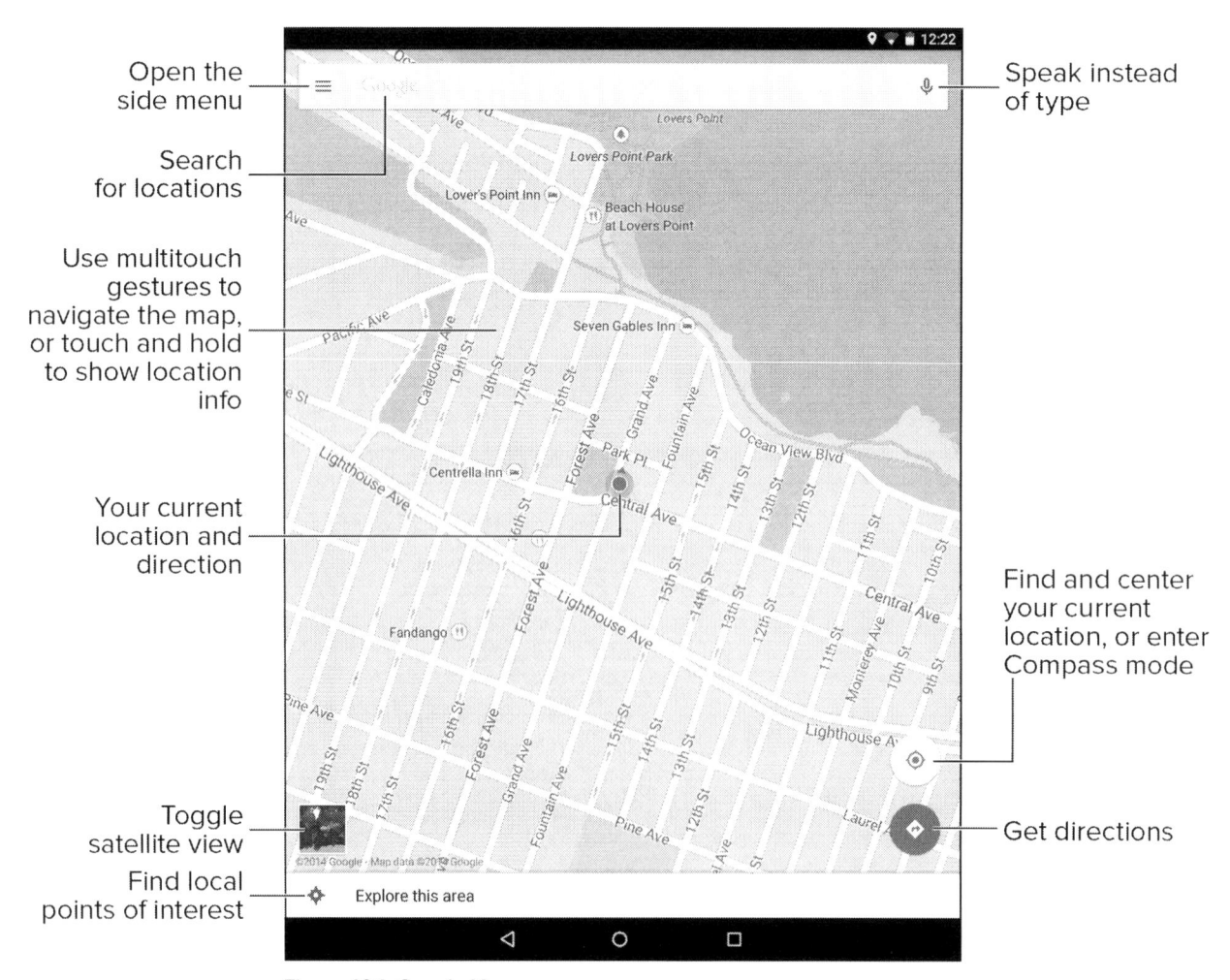

- Open the side menu
- Search for locations
- Use multitouch gestures to navigate the map, or touch and hold to show location info
- Your current location and direction
- Toggle satellite view
- Find local points of interest
- Speak instead of type
- Find and center your current location, or enter Compass mode
- Get directions

Figure 16.1 Google Maps.

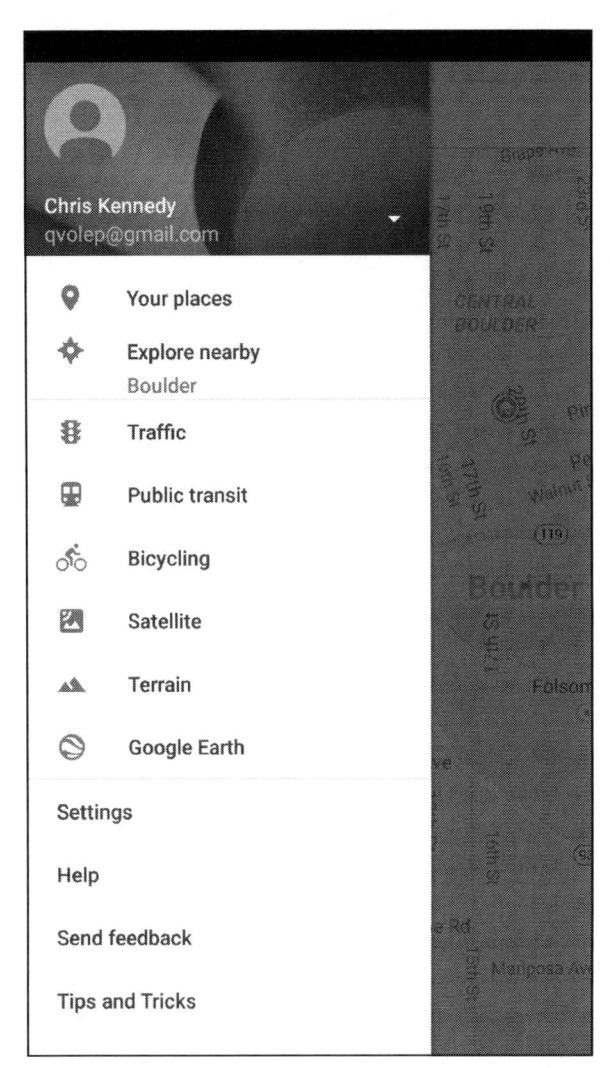

Figure 16.2 The Google Maps side menu.

The side menu

To show a **side menu** of commands (Figure 16.2), tap ☰ in the top-left corner of the screen or swipe right from the left edge of the screen. To hide the side menu, swipe left or tap the map.

> **Tips for Maps**
>
> - Unless you're viewing an offline map (see "Saving Offline Maps" on page 177), Maps needs a continuous internet connection to update its cartographic and point-of-interest data, so don't rely on it for emergency directions or wilderness hikes.
>
> - Certain Maps features, such as your reviews, saved places, and home and work addresses, use your Google Account. If you're not already signed in to your account, then you can sign in from within Maps: tap ☰ > Sign In. (To sign out, tap ☰ > Settings > Sign Out of Google Maps.)
>
> - Location access must be turned on to view your location in Maps and use your location to find nearby places: tap ☰ > Settings > Google Location Settings > Location > On. See also "Using Location Services" on page 180.
>
> - A location icon appears in the status bar at the top of the screen when Maps (or any app) is finding your location.
>
> - To change the units in which distances are measured, tap ☰ > Settings > Distance Units.
>
> - To change your home or work address, tap ☰ > Settings > Edit Home or Work.
>
> - Ads may appear at various places on the map.

Navigating the Map

You can move, zoom, rotate, and tilt the map. A zoomed-in map can show a surprising amount of detail, including points of interest; one-way-street indicators; businesses; transit stops; and even indoor floor plans for some airports, rail stations, museums, malls, hospitals, convention centers, stores, and casinos.

To move the map:

- Drag the map.

To rotate the map:

- Spread your thumb and index finger, and touch them to the map; then rotate them clockwise or counterclockwise. Or keep your fingers steady and rotate the Nexus itself.

To zoom the map:

- Do any of the following:

    ▸ To zoom in, double-tap a map location with one finger—repeatedly, if necessary (Figure 16.3).

    ▸ To zoom out, tap once with two fingers—repeatedly, if necessary.

    ▸ Touch the map with two fingers and then spread them to zoom in or pinch them to zoom out.

    ▸ Double-tap a map location with one finger, keep your finger on the screen, and then drag down (to zoom in) or up (to zoom out).

To tilt the map:

- Drag two fingers from top to bottom on the map.

    At lower zoom levels, a tilted (angled) map shows 3D buildings for some cities (Figure 16.4).

    To return to overhead view, drag two fingers from bottom to top. To return to overhead, north-up view, tap the compass icon at the top of the screen.

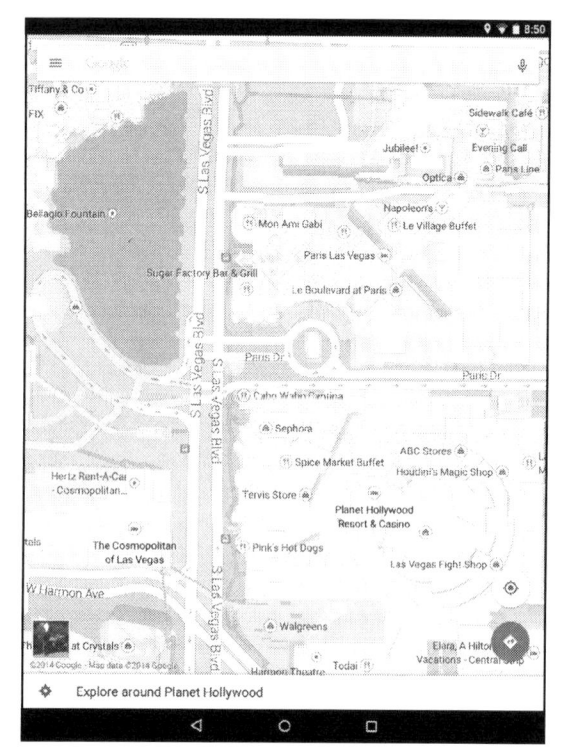

Figure 16.3 A zoomed-in map.

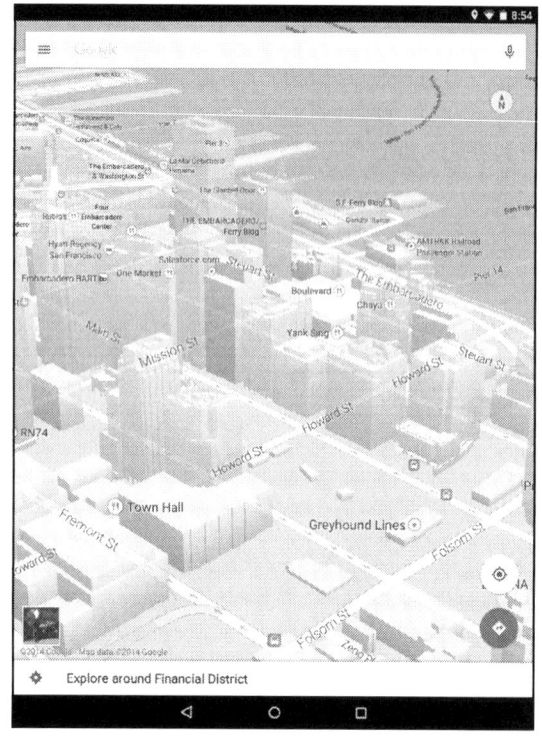

Figure 16.4 A tilted 3D map.

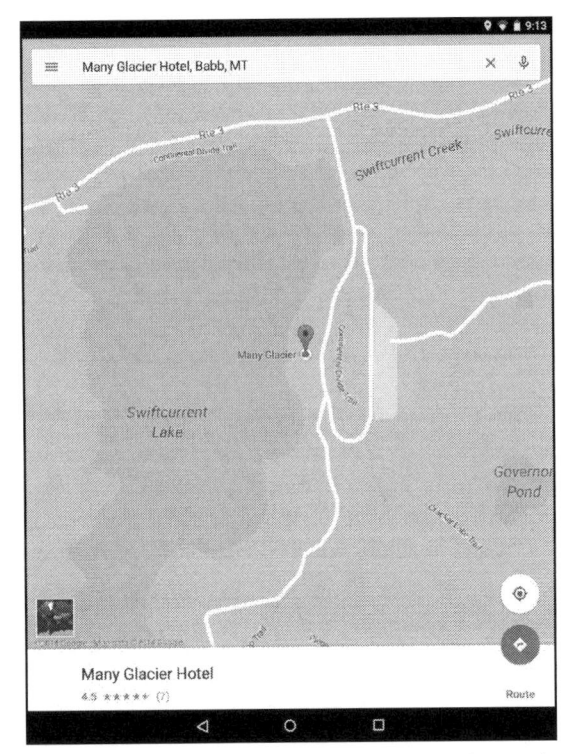

Figure 16.5 A location's info sheet (bottom of screen).

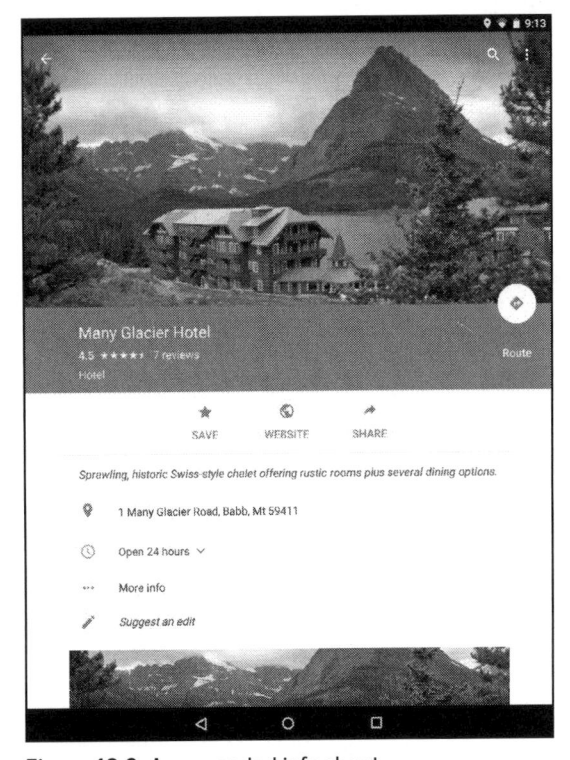

Figure 16.6 An expanded info sheet.

Viewing Location Details

You can get the address and other information about an area or point on the map.

To view location details:

1. Touch and hold a location or tap a star, symbol, or search result.

   An info sheet for the location opens (Figure 16.5).

2. Tap the info sheet to expand it (Figure 16.6).

   From the info sheet, you can save the location as a favorite place, share the location, get directions, explore Street View (page 172), see public photos, write or read reviews, open the location's website, and more. The amount of information depends on the location.

Chapter 16   Maps & Navigation   169

Finding Your Location

The location feature centers the map on your approximate current location by using a variety of methods to determine your location.

To see your location on the map:

- Tap the location icon ⊚ at the bottom of the screen.

    The location icon turns blue and the map centers on a blue dot ● that marks your location. A small arrowhead on the dot's edge indicates the direction that you're facing (Figure 16.7).

Tip: The diameter of the circle around the arrow (visible when you zoom in) indicates the location's precision. For details, see "Using Location Services" on page 180.

Your current location and direction

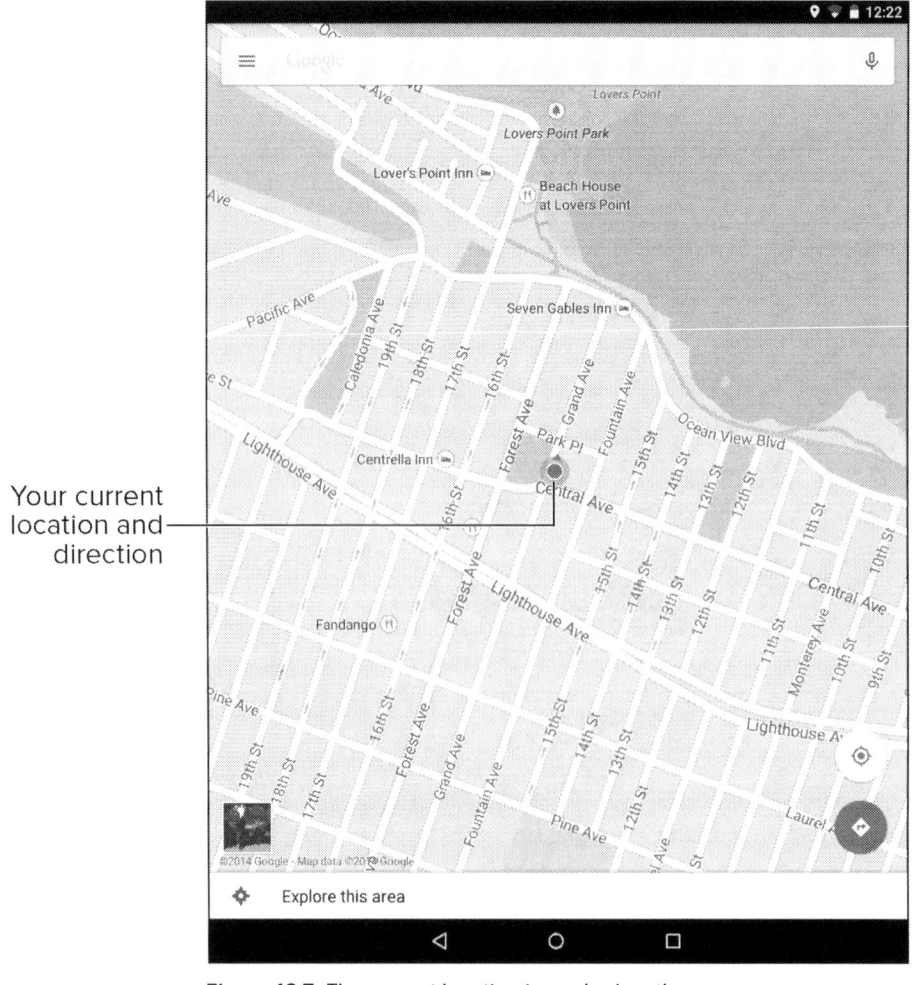

Figure 16.7 The current location is marked on the map.

Using Compass Mode

Compass mode shows an angled view of the area around you, oriented in the direction in which you're facing or moving.

Tip: The Nexus's built-in magnetometer serves as a compass.

To start Compass mode:

1. Tap the location icon ⊚ at the bottom of the screen.

   The location icon turns blue and the map centers on a blue dot ● that marks your location.

2. Tap the location icon ⊚ again.

   The location icon turns into a compass icon 🧭. The map orients in the direction that you're facing and shifts from overhead view to an angled view. The map reorients automatically when you turn or move the Nexus (Figure 16.8).

To exit Compass mode:

- Tap the compass icon 🧭, or pan or zoom the map.

Tip: Compass mode is also available in Street View (page 172).

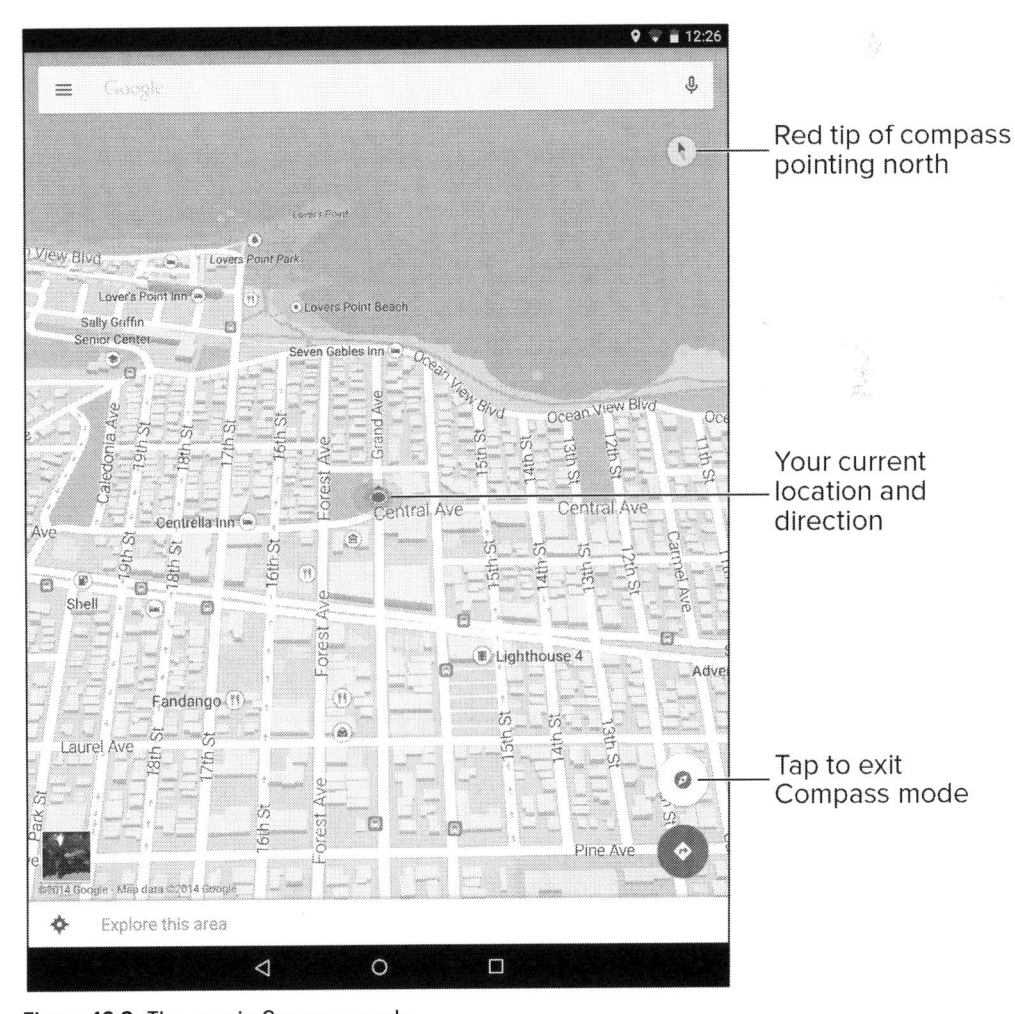

Figure 16.8 The map in Compass mode.

Exploring Street View

Street View shows ground-level photos merged into a 360-degree panoramic view. Street View isn't available for all locations.

To show Street View:

1 Touch and hold a location or tap a star, symbol, or search result.

   An info sheet for the location opens.

2 Tap the Info sheet to expand it (Figure 16.9).

3 In the info sheet, tap Street View (if available).

   Street View opens (Figure 16.10).

4 Do any of the following:

   ▸ To move down a street, double-tap in the direction that you want to move in, or tap the white arrows at the bottom of the screen.

   ▸ To pan the view, swipe or drag.

   ▸ To zoom, pinch or spread.

   ▸ To share a location, tap the screen to show the controls, and then tap ⁞ > Share. The available sharing methods depend on the apps you've installed.

   ▸ To tilt, pan, or turn the Nexus to change the view (Compass mode), tap the screen to show the controls, and then tap ⇄. Tap ⇄ again to exit Compass mode.

Tip: The Nexus's built-in accelerometer and magnetometer sense how you're holding the Nexus in physical space.

   ▸ To exit Street View, tap the screen to show the controls, and then tap ←. Alternatively, tap ◁ at the bottom of the screen.

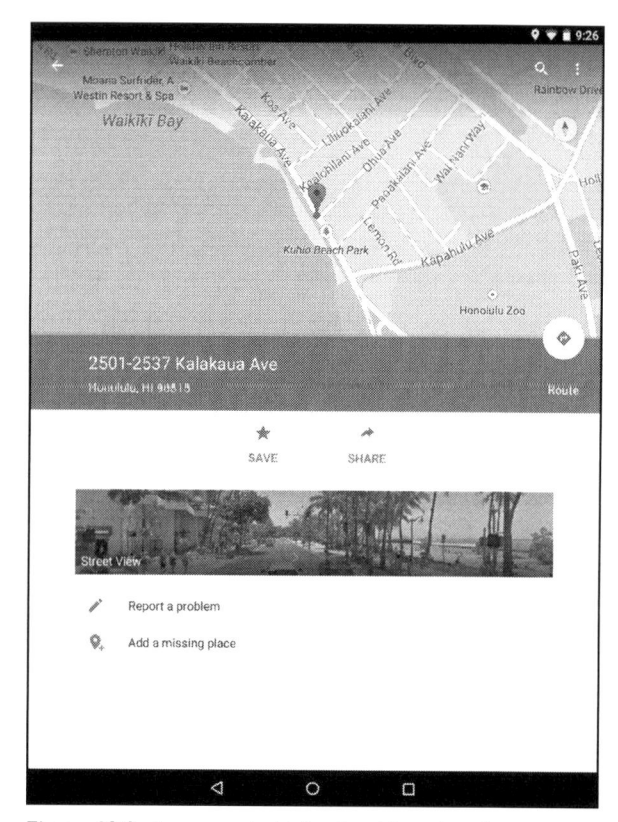

Figure 16.9 An expanded info sheet for a location.

172   Google Nexus 7 & 9

Figure 16.10 Street View.

Searching for a Location

You can search for bodies of water, geographic features, latitude–longitude coordinates, continents, countries, regions, provinces, states, cities, towns, neighborhoods, street addresses, postal or zip codes, roads, intersections, airports (names or three-letter codes), landmarks, parks, schools, businesses, and other points of interest. Partial words and misspellings sometimes work.

To search for a location:

1. If you're going to search for local, nonspecific locations, such as *coffee shops* or *movies*, scroll and zoom the map to narrow the area of interest, or tap ◉ to zoom to your current location.

2. Tap the search field at the top of the screen.

    The Search screen opens, showing recent searches, saved places, mapping services, and more (Figure 16.11).

3. Do any of the following:

    ▶ Type a location. As you type, Maps autosuggests places. You can tap a suggestion, or finish typing and then tap the 🔍 key (Figure 16.12). To see all the matches, scroll the results list or tap List Results (if it appears).

    ▶ To list nearby places to eat, drink, shop, stay, and so on, tap Explore Nearby.

    ▶ To list nearby services (gas stations, groceries, pharmacies, ATMs, and so on), tap a Services icon.

    ▶ Tap a previously saved place or a recently found location.

Tip: To speak instead of type, tap 🎤 in the search field or the onscreen keyboard (for details, see "Dictating Text" on page 59).

Figure 16.11 The search screen in Maps.

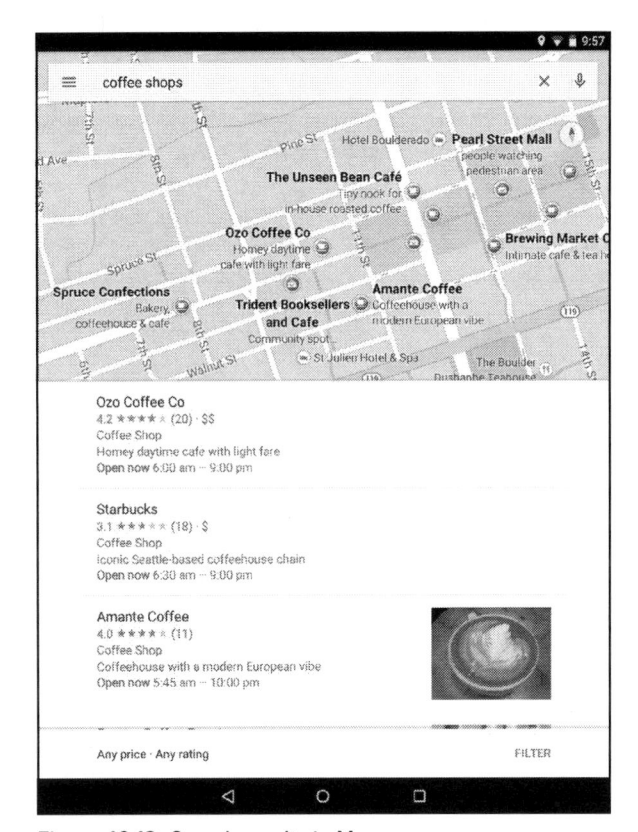

Figure 16.12 Search results in Maps.

To view your recent search and maps history:

- Tap ≡ > Settings > Maps History.

To manage your search history:

- Tap ≡ > Settings > About, Terms & Privacy > Terms & Privacy > Web History. Sign in to your Google Account and then tap Maps.

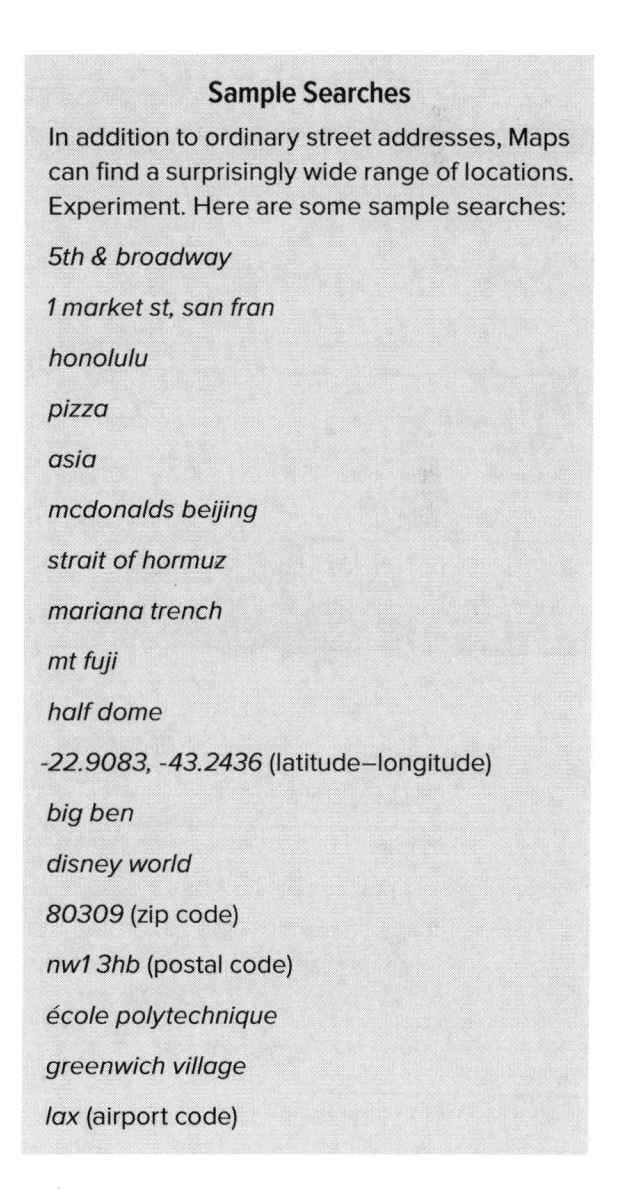

Sample Searches

In addition to ordinary street addresses, Maps can find a surprisingly wide range of locations. Experiment. Here are some sample searches:

5th & broadway

1 market st, san fran

honolulu

pizza

asia

mcdonalds beijing

strait of hormuz

mariana trench

mt fuji

half dome

-22.9083, -43.2436 (latitude–longitude)

big ben

disney world

80309 (zip code)

nw1 3hb (postal code)

école polytechnique

greenwich village

lax (airport code)

Exploring Map Views

You can view locations that have additional information overlaid on the map. You can toggle individual views to show or hide traffic conditions, public-transit lines and stations, bicycle lanes and paths, satellite imagery, and topographic information.

To show or hide map views:

1 Tap ≡ to open the side menu.

2 Tap Traffic, Public Transit, and so on to toggle the views on or off (Figure 16.13).

Tip: Tapping the Google Earth shortcut in the side menu switches to the Google Earth app (page 179).

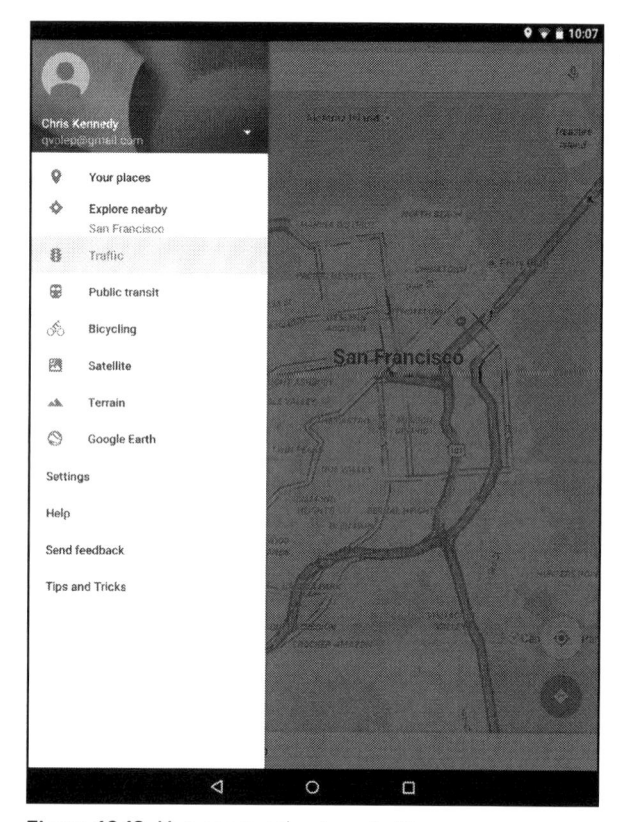

Figure 16.13 You can toggle views in Maps.

Traffic View

Where traffic information is available, the traffic view shows current, color-coded traffic conditions on highways and roads:

- **Green**: More than 50 miles per hour or 80 kilometers per hour
- **Yellow**: 25–50 mph or 40–80 kph
- **Red**: Less than 25 mph or 40 kph
- **Red/black**: Stop-and-go traffic
- **Gray**: No data available now

These speeds don't apply to traffic on smaller roads and city streets. The colors for roads with low speed limits instead denote traffic severity: green = good, yellow = fair, and red or red/black = bad.

Small icons along roadways indicate real-time accidents, construction, road closures, and other incidents. Tap an icon for more information.

Saving Offline Maps

Offline maps let you select and download certain areas of the map to view even when you're not connected to the internet. Offline maps are handy when you're traveling outside wi-fi or cellular coverage.

You can save (cache) maps provided that you have sufficient storage space on your Nexus. Each map itself also has a maximum size, so you may have to split maps of large or dense areas into several smaller saved maps. If you exceed the storage allocated for offline maps, then old saved maps are overwritten with newly saved ones. To check your storage space, on the Home screen or All Apps screen, tap Settings > Storage.

Features that need an internet connection—such as directions and navigation—aren't available offline.

To save an offline map:

1. Pan and zoom the map to the area that you want to save.
2. Tap the search field at the top of the screen.

    The Search screen opens.

3. Scroll down the Search screen and then tap Save Map to Use Offline.
4. Adjust the map by panning and zooming it, as needed, and then tap Save.
5. Name the offline map and then tap Save.
6. To view and manage offline maps, tap ≡ > Your Places.

Getting Directions

Maps can get you from Point A to Point B whether you're driving, walking, bicycling, or taking public transit (bus, train, or ferry). Depending on the route, not every mode of transportation may be available.

To get directions:

1   Tap [icon] at the bottom of the screen.

2   Choose a starting point and destination (see "Searching for a Location" on page 174) and tap a transportation method (drive, take public transit, walk, or bicycle). To avoid certain types of roads, tap Options.

   Potential routes appear with travel time, distance, and other travel information.

3   Tap your preferred route.

   The map shows your chosen route in blue or in traffic colors (Figure 16.14). Alternate routes, if available, are shown in gray. To choose an alternate route, tap it on the map.

Tip: If you chose public transit, you can schedule your trip by using the real-time transit options sourced from public transportation agencies (where available).

---

4   Do any of the following:

   ▶ To see a scrollable list of directions for your selected route, swipe the info sheet up on the map.

   ▶ To start navigation, tap ».

   ▶ To edit your directions or choose a different mode of transportation, tap the search bar.

   ▶ To exit the route map, tap × on the search bar or tap ◁ at the bottom of the screen.

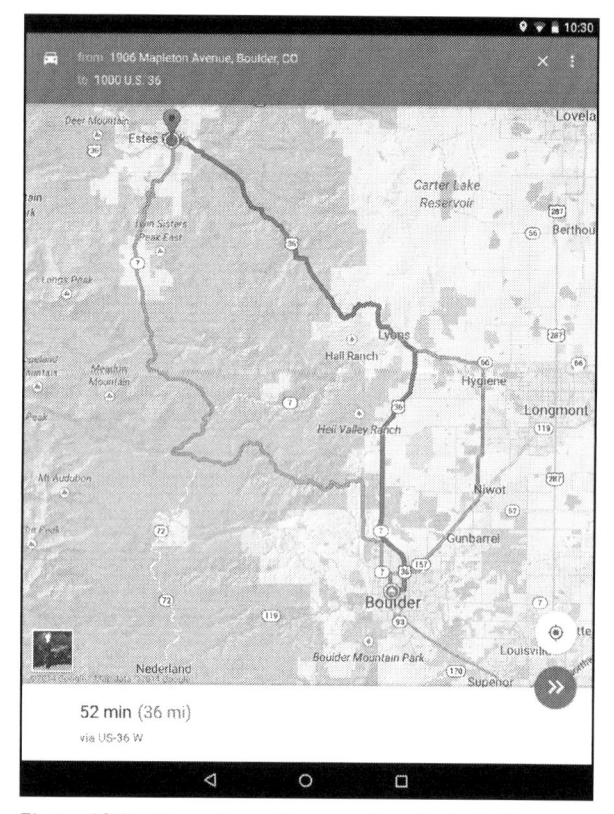

Figure 16.14 Maps shows the overall route, including any alternate routes.

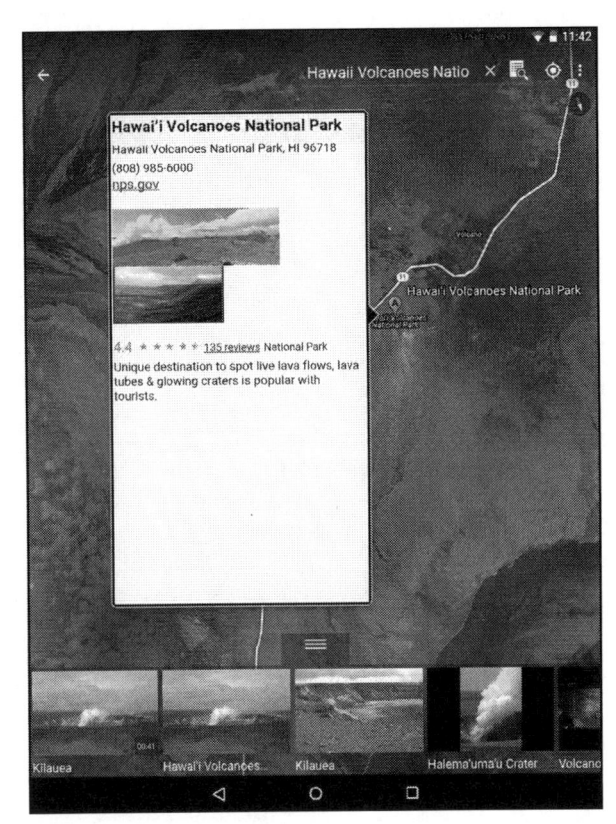

Figure 16.15 Google Earth.

Using Other Mapping Apps and Services

The Nexus comes with other mapping apps and services that you can launch from the Home screen or All Apps screen or from inside Maps.

Google Earth. Google Earth (Figure 16.15) features satellite images and aerial photos merged into a virtual globe. You can "fly" to any place around the world and toggle various layers to superimpose place names, businesses, shared photos, Wikipedia articles, borders, roads, 3D buildings, and more. You can pan, zoom, rotate, and tilt the maps. The Maps Gallery offers additional layers—such as country tours, earthquake maps, surfing spots, and hurricane paths—shared by people around the world. Tap the icon in the top-left corner to set options.

Google Maps Navigation. Navigation offers turn-by-turn GPS navigation with voice guidance, similar to that of handheld GPS navigators like those from Garmin and TomTom. Navigation's features include time to destination, directions listing, traffic conditions, satellite view, alternative routes, compass heading, automatic rerouting, volume controls, background navigation, notifications, and voice actions (page 98) such as "Navigate to...".

To work optimally, Navigation needs a continuous internet connection, which is possible on the road if you're using a cellular (LTE/HSPA+) Nexus or if you share a cellular internet connection from your smartphone or personal hotspot with your Nexus. Without an internet connection, Navigation can still provide voice guidance as long as you don't deviate from your original route, though the underlying map tiles may not update. When you're navigating, a navigation icon ▲ appears in the status bar at the top of the screen. To start navigating, tap Start on a directions info sheet. To stop navigating, tap × at the bottom of the screen.

Using Location Services

Location services let apps use your physical whereabouts via the Nexus's built-in positioning service. Built-in apps such as Maps, Chrome, and Contacts use Location services, as do many third-party apps—particularly weather, travel, search, movie-time, real-estate, and social-networking apps.

Location services determine your location by combining readings from the Nexus's built-in GPS (Global Positioning System), readings from its digital compass (magnetometer), and data from nearby wi-fi hotspots and cell towers.

Depending on data quality and other factors (such as interference from your surroundings), your location may be unavailable or inaccurate. Apps that show your location onscreen, including Maps, indicate your current location as a blue arrow or dot surrounded by a circle (visible when zoomed in) that indicates how precisely your location can be determined. The smaller the circle, the greater the precision.

To open the Location screen, tap Settings > Location (Figure 16.16). If you don't want to be found, turn off Location. To conserve battery power, tap Mode and then tap a location method (the different modes trade off location accuracy for power consumption). To toggle location reporting and history, tap Google Location Reporting. The Location screen also lists apps that have requested your location recently.

To determine whether an installed app is using Location services, tap Settings > Apps, swipe to the All list, and then tap the target app to open its App Info screen. If your precise or approximate location is listed below Permissions, then the app uses Location services.

When you download an app from the Google Play store, the app's App Permissions screen tells you whether the app uses your location.

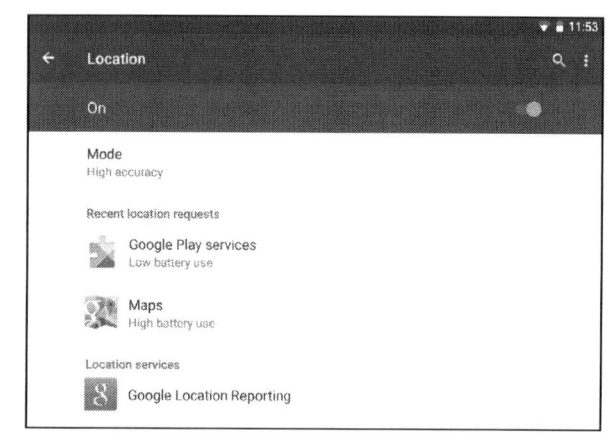

Figure 16.16 The Location screen.

CHAPTER 17

Shooting, Viewing & Managing Photos

Photos is the central app for viewing and managing photos that you've taken with your Nexus's camera; copied from your computer; or saved from email, text messages, or the web. Photos can display photos and graphics in JPEG, GIF, PNG, BMP, or WEBP format.

You can also use Photos to view and manage videos that you take with the built-in camera or copy from your computer. Photos can play videos in H.263, H.264/AVC, MPEG-4 (MP4), or VP8 format.

Tip: The Photography category of the Google Play store lists scores of full-featured alternatives to Photos.

Getting Photos onto Your Nexus

By default, the Photos app displays your photo collections grouped into albums by source, type, or folder (Figure 17.1).

Tip: To set account, sync, and other options for your pictures, tap ⋮ > Settings.

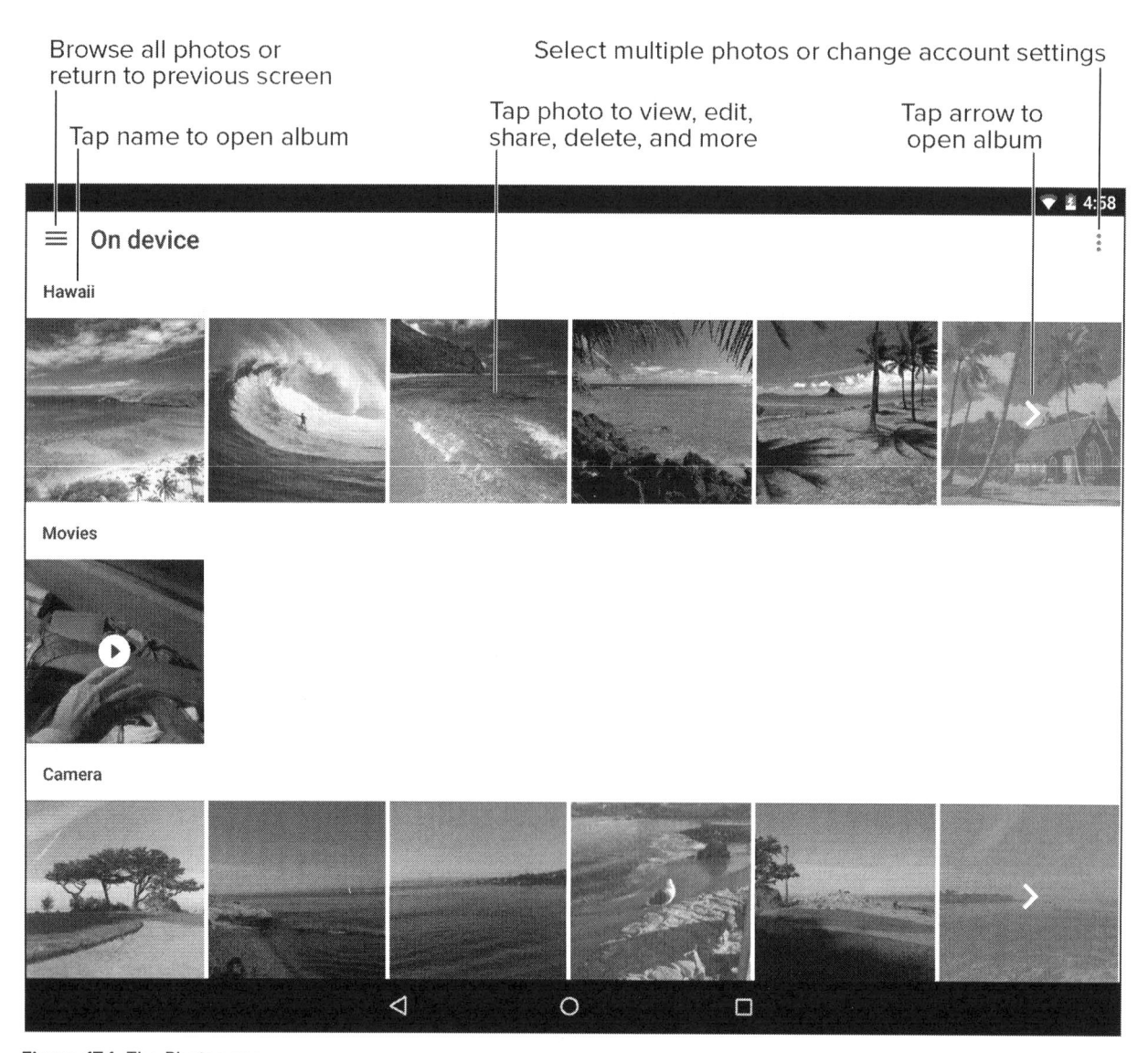

Browse all photos or return to previous screen

Tap name to open album

Tap photo to view, edit, share, delete, and more

Select multiple photos or change account settings

Tap arrow to open album

≡ On device

Hawaii

Movies

Camera

Figure 17.1 The Photos app.

182 Google Nexus 7 & 9

You can get photos onto your Nexus in the following ways.

Built-in camera. Photos and videos taken with the Nexus's built-in camera appear automatically in the Camera album in Photos. You can open Camera (Figure 17.2) from the Lock screen, Home screen, or All Apps screen. (The Nexus 7 (2012) has no rear camera or built-in Camera app.)

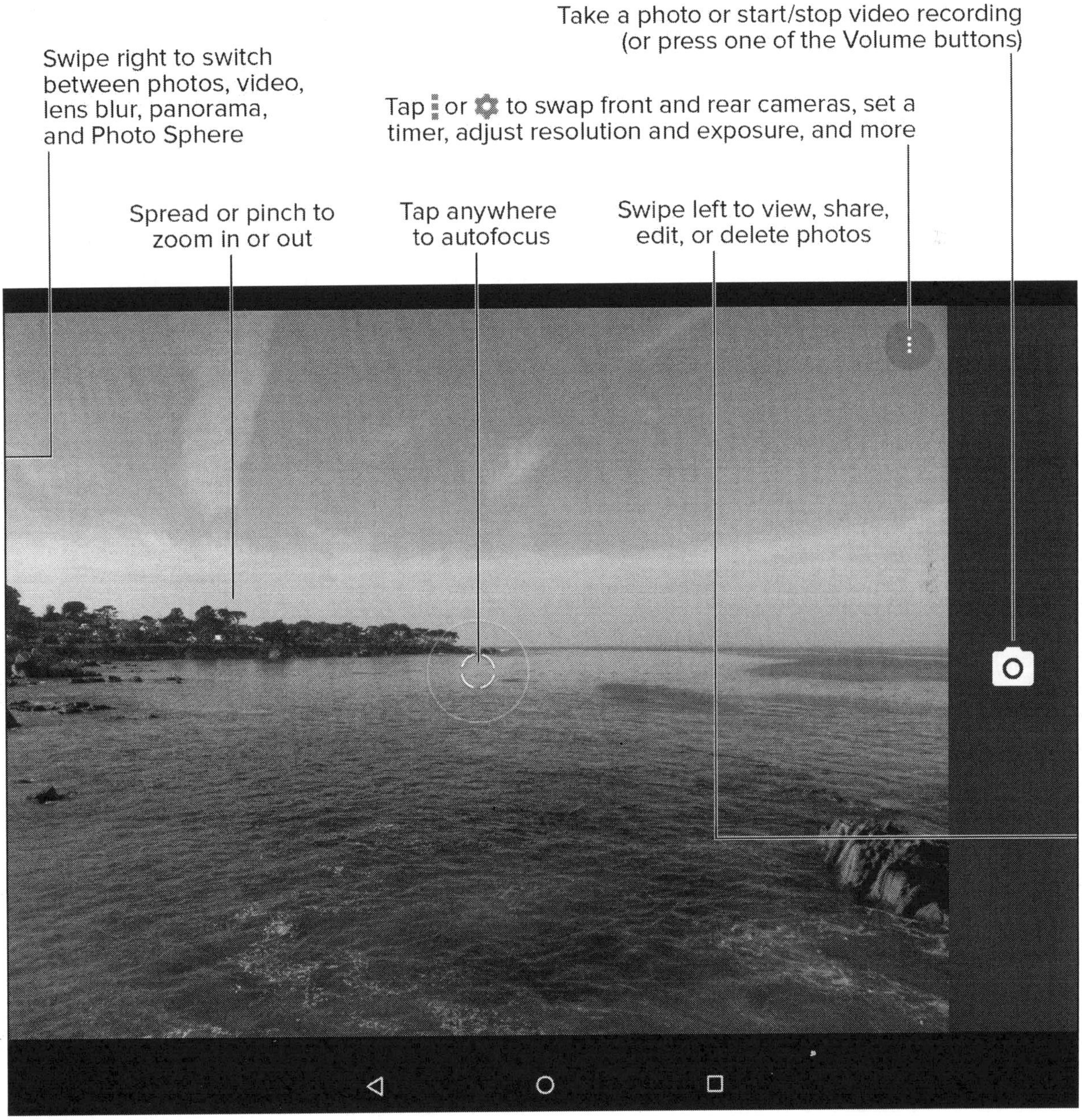

Swipe right to switch between photos, video, lens blur, panorama, and Photo Sphere

Tap ⋮ or ✿ to swap front and rear cameras, set a timer, adjust resolution and exposure, and more

Take a photo or start/stop video recording (or press one of the Volume buttons)

Spread or pinch to zoom in or out

Tap anywhere to autofocus

Swipe left to view, share, edit, or delete photos

Figure 17.2 Camera controls.

Chapter 17   Shooting, Viewing & Managing Photos   183

Downloaded images. To save an attached image from an email message, tap Save or Download in the attachment's menu (Figure 17.3); for details, see "Working with Attachments" on page 128. To save an image from a webpage, touch and hold the image, and then tap Save Image in the window that opens. You can similarly save an image from an instant message. Saved images land in the Download album in Photos. You can manage downloads by using the Downloads app (for details, see "Downloading Files" on page 114).

Copied from computer. Connect your Nexus to your Windows PC or Mac via USB cable and then copy image or video files to your Nexus's internal storage (for details, see Chapter 7). You can copy files to anywhere in the Nexus's internal storage and Photos will find them, but it's more sensible to organize your photo and video collection in the Nexus's Pictures folder. If you copy a folder of photos to your Nexus, that folder becomes an album in Photos. You can also transfer files wirelessly via Bluetooth (page 68).

Screenshots. To capture an image of whatever is on your Nexus's screen (like the figures in this book), press and hold the Power/Lock button and the Volume Down button at the same time for a second. The shot lands in the Screenshot album in Photos. When you take a screenshot, a notification icon appears in the status bar at the top of the screen. You can jump to the screenshot quickly in Photos by dragging the notification shade down from the top of the screen and then tapping the screenshot notification.

Tip: When you're not using a docked or charging Nexus, you can have it display a slideshow of photos (or other screensaver): tap Settings > Display > Daydream.

Figure 17.3 The attachments menu of an email message.

Tips for Working with Photos

- You can browse all photos, including recently deleted ones. In thumbnail view, swipe right from the left edge of the screen to open the side menu, and then tap a location.

- Tap a thumbnail to view the photo full-screen. Rotate your Nexus for the best view. Pinch, spread, or double-tap to zoom the photo. Drag to pan a zoomed photo. Swipe to view other photos. Tap to show or hide controls to edit, share, delete, show details, play a slideshow, and more.

- In thumbnail view, you can touch and hold a photo to select it and then use the controls that appear at the top of the screen. You can also tap ⋮ > Select to select photos. In select mode, you can tap the bottom-right corner of a thumbnail to view it full-screen, and then swipe to select other full-screen photos.

- After selecting a photo, you can tap others to select multiple photos for bulk operations. To deselect a selected photo, tap it. Deselecting all photos exits select mode.

- With a photo in full-screen view, tapping the pencil icon accesses editing tools. You can adjust exposure, apply artistic effects, change colors, crop, straighten, rotate, frame, and more. Tap the buttons at the top of the screen to cancel or accept your changes, or tap ⋮ to revert to the original image. When you edit a photo, a copy is created, and the original is left untouched.

CHAPTER 18

Nexus Care & Troubleshooting

This chapter shows you how to take care of your Nexus and (possibly) fix it when things go wrong.

Getting Information About Your Nexus

The About Tablet screen gives hardware, software, and status information about your Nexus and Android.

To get system information:

- Tap Settings > About Tablet (Figure 18.1).

Tip: You can touch and hold a value on the Status screen (such as the IP address) to copy it to the clipboard.

Figure 18.1 The About Tablet screen.

Cleaning the Screen

The Nexus' glass touchscreen has a special coating that does its best to repel fingerprints, but eventually it will accumulate oils, glazed sugar, sunscreen, or whatever else you have on your hands. To clean the screen, wipe it gently with a soft, lint-free cloth—the same kind that you use to clean eyeglasses or camera lenses.

To clean the rest of the Nexus, unplug it from any docks or USB cables and then turn it off. (Press and hold the Power/Lock button for a moment and then tap Power Off.) You can use a cloth that's dampened lightly with water, but never use window cleaners, household cleaners, anything from a spray can, alcohol- or ammonia-based cleansers, solvents, or abrasives. Don't get any moisture in the Nexus's openings.

Restarting Your Nexus

The Nexus does a good job of fixing its own problems, but it can accumulate software baggage with time and use. **Restarting** your Nexus (powering it off and then back on again) can quickly solve many common problems, including unexpected app failure, short battery life, odd hardware behavior, slow app or Android response, and sync issues. A restart does all the following:

- Safely quits all active applications, and processes and closes all open files, preserving your data
- Frees CPU and memory (RAM) resources
- Powers off all hardware components

Figure 18.2 The Power/Lock button on the Nexus 9 (left) and Nexus 7 (right).

To restart your Nexus:

1. Press and hold the Power/Lock button (Figure 18.2) for a moment until a window opens.
2. Tap Power Off.
3. After your Nexus shuts down, press the Power/Lock button again to power on your Nexus.

Managing Apps and Services

The Apps screen lets you manage individual apps and services, and change the way your tablet uses memory. To open the Apps screen, tap Settings > Apps. At the top of the Apps screen are three tabs, each showing a list of apps and services. Tap a tab name or swipe left or right to switch tabs:

- **Downloaded**. Lists apps that you've downloaded from Google Play or elsewhere.

- **Running**. Lists all apps, processes, and services that are now running or that have cached (temporarily stored) processes, along with how much RAM (memory) they're using (Figure 18.3). The graph at the top of the Running tab shows the total RAM in use and the amount free. To switch lists, tap Show Cached Processes or Show Running Services in the top-right corner of the screen.

- **All**. Lists all apps that came with Android and all apps that you downloaded from Google Play or elsewhere (Figure 18.4).

Tip: To sort the lists in the Downloaded or All tab, tap ⋮ > Sort By Name or Sort By Size.

Figure 18.3 The Apps Running screen.

Figure 18.4 The Apps All screen.

188   Google Nexus 7 & 9

Figure 18.5 The App Info screen.

To view details about an app or other item listed in any tab, tap its name. The App Info screen opens (Figure 18.5). To open App Info quickly, on the Home screen, tap ⊕ and then drag an app icon to App Info at the top of the screen. (The words *App Info* appear when you drag.)

The available information and controls vary by item but commonly include the following:

- **Force stop**. Stops a misbehaving app, service, or process. If your Nexus stops working correctly after a stop, restart your Nexus.

- **Uninstall**. Deletes the app and all its data and settings. You can't uninstall Android's built-in system apps.

- **Uninstall updates**. Uninstalls all updates to the app, rolling it back to its original version.

- **Disable**. Prevents the app from running but doesn't uninstall it. This option is available for some apps and services that can't be uninstalled.

- **Show notifications**. Toggles notifications for the app or service.

- **Clear data**. Deletes an app's settings and other data without removing the app itself.

- **Clear cache**. Clears any noncrucial data that the app is storing temporarily in memory.

- **Launch by default**. Lets you change your mind if you've configured an app to launch certain file types by default. You can clear that setting here.

- **Permissions**. Lists the kinds of information about your tablet and the data to which the app has access.

Resetting App Preferences

After you set options for a large number of apps on your Nexus, it can hard to determine which apps are changing which functions on your tablet. By resetting all app preferences, you can troubleshoot from scratch. To reset app preferences to their original settings (without losing your app data or files), tap Settings > Apps > ⁝ > Reset App Preferences. A small warning window opens, listing which preferences will be reset. Tap Reset Apps.

Monitoring Internal Storage and RAM

Apps use two types of memory: **internal storage** and **RAM**. Each app, whether it's running or not, uses internal storage for itself and its files, settings, and other data. When it's running, each app also uses RAM (random access memory) for temporary storage and fast access to some data.

You typically don't need to worry about managing memory yourself. The Nexus's internal storage—where the system files, apps, and most data for those apps are stored—is protected for your privacy. You can't see this part when you connect your Nexus to a computer via a USB cable. The other portion—where music, media, downloaded files, and the like are stored—is visible.

Android also manages how apps use RAM. It usually caches things you've used recently, to enable quick access if you need them again, but it erases the cache if it needs the RAM for new operations. If an app freezes or otherwise jumps the rails, you can monitor its RAM usage and stop it by using the Apps and App Info screens in Settings.

You affect the way that apps use internal storage when you install, use, or delete apps; download, create, or delete files; copy files to or from a computer; and so on. To see how internal storage is being used, tap Settings > Storage (Figure 18.6).

Figure 18.6 The Storage screen.

Tip: To manage files directly on your Nexus, download a file-manager app (such as ES File Explorer or File Manager Explorer) from the Google Play store.

Optimizing Data Usage

To monitor the amount of data uploaded or downloaded by your Nexus during a given period, tap Settings > Data Usage (Figure 18.7). Near the top of the screen is the **data usage cycle**, a date range for which the graph displays data usage. To choose a different cycle, tap the dates.

The list below the graph breaks down data usage by apps and services. Tap an item in the list for more details (Figure 18.8). Some apps transfer data in the background when you're not actually using them. Some apps also let you restrict data usage from the app's own settings, which you can access by tapping App Settings (if available). To restrict background downloads, tap ⋮ > Network Restrictions.

Tip: You can reduce data usage by syncing your apps manually and only when you need the data, rather than relying on autosync. To toggle autosync, see "Configuring Sync Options" on page 76.

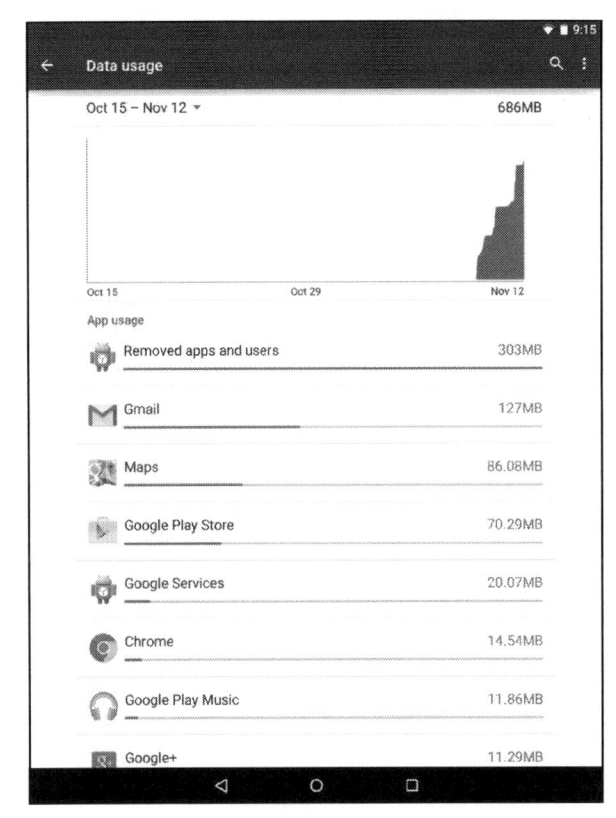

Figure 18.7 The Data Usage screen.

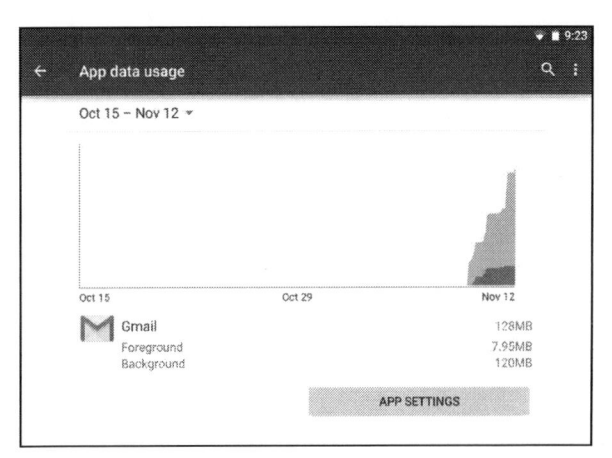

Figure 18.8 The App Data Usage screen.

Resetting Your Nexus to Factory Settings

The nuclear option for troubleshooting is resetting your Nexus to factory condition. A factory reset erases all your personal data and settings from your Nexus, including your Google Account; other accounts; system and app settings; network settings; downloaded apps; and your media, documents, and other files. Tap Settings > Backup & Reset > Factory Data Reset > Reset Tablet. After resetting your Nexus, you must go through the setup process again (see "Setting Up Your Nexus" on page 16).

Tip: You should factory-reset your Nexus before you sell it or give it away, so that the new owner can't access your stuff.

> **Setting Developer Options**
>
> To view or change advanced Android options, tap Settings > Developer Options. Many of these settings are designed for professional developers, so be careful. If Developer Options isn't visible, tap Settings > About Tablet and then tap Build Number repeatedly to enable Developer Options.

Index

A

accounts. *See also* Google Accounts
  adding 74
  editing 75
  removing 75
  syncing 76
airplane mode 72
alarms 98, 152
albums, photo 182
All Apps screen 29
ambient light sensor 33
Android. *See also* Nexus
  about 8
  changing font size 8
  data usage 191
  developer options 192
  factory data reset 78, 192
  Google Play Edition devices 8
  internal storage and RAM 190
  managing apps and services 188
  pure Android 8
  restarting 187
  settings 22
  shorthand instructions 9
  system information, getting 9, 186
  updating 10
  versions 10
Android Beam 71
Android Device Manager 46
appointments. *See* Calendar app
apps
  about 27
  All Apps screen 29
  backing up and restoring data 78
  clearing data 189
  default 115, 189
  digital certificates 48
  disabling 189
  finding 158
  folders 30
  Home screen
    adding to 29
    rearranging on 28
    removing from 29
  installed 188
  installing 159
  managing 188
  notifications 189
  permissions 159, 189
  resetting preferences 189
  returning for refund 159
  screen pinning 44
  sharing 159
  stopping 189
  switching 28
  uninstalling 160
  updating 160
  verifying 48
  voice actions 98
attachments, email 128

B

Back button 14
backing up data 78
battery. *See* power
Battery Saver 40
bezel 13
Bluetooth connections 68
Bluetooth printer 60
bookmarking webpages 112
brightness, screen
  adjusting 33
  ambient light sensor 33
browser. *See* Chrome web browser
buttons. *See* navigation buttons

C

Calendar app
  about 144
  accounts 145
  events
    adding 146
    deleting 146
    editing 146
    searching for 147
  invitations 147
  settings 148
  sync options 145
  using 144
  viewing calendars 145
  voice actions 98
Camera app 183. *See also* photos
capacitive screen 13
cellular (LTE/HSPA+) networks 66
checklists. *See* Keep
Chromecast 23, 41
Chrome web browser
  address bar 106
  bookmarking webpages 112
  cookies 116
  downloading files 114
  file-type associations 115
  navigating webpages 108
  omnibox 106
  opening 104
  private (incognito) browsing 111
  searching the web 106
  settings 116
  signing in and out 105
  sync options 105

tabs 110
typing tips 106
URLs 107
using 104
voice actions 98
Clock app
  alarms 152
  settings 153
  stopwatch 153
  timer 153
  using 152
  voice actions 98
  world clocks 152
Contacts app
  about 136
  contacts
    deleting 142
    editing 142
    exporting 140
    favorite 138
    filtering 138
    importing 140
    joining 143
    multiply sourced 142
    separating 143
    sharing 141
    viewing 138
  read-only accounts 142
  using 137
  vCard (.vcf) format 140, 141
conversations, Gmail 122
cookies in Chrome 116

D

data usage 191
date and time 32
  viewing in Clock 152
default apps 115, 189
developer options 192
dictating text 59
digital certificates 48
display. *See* screen
double-tap gesture 13
downloading files 114, 184
Downloads app 114
drag gesture 13

E

earphones 37
email. *See* Gmail app
email accounts, adding 74
Email app. *See* Gmail app
encrypting a Nexus 48
events. *See* Calendar app
external display 41

F

factory data reset 78, 192
Favorites tray 27
file-type associations 115, 189
flick gesture 13
folders 30
font size, changing 8

G

gestures, multitouch 13
gesture typing 52
Gmail app
  about 122
  adding contacts 139
  attachments 128
  bulk operations 128
  conversations 122
  inbox 123
    categories 125
    priority 125
  labels 122
  messages
    archiving 126
    deleting 126
    forwarding 130
    muting 126
    reading 126
    replying to 130
    sending 130
    writing 130
  non-Gmail accounts 122
  settings
    account-specific 133
    general 132
  voice actions 98
Google+ 16, 98, 101, 134
Google Accounts. *See also* accounts
  adding and removing 74
  backing up 78
  changing home and work locations 91
  erasing 78
  importing and exporting contacts 140
  Nexus setup 17
  privacy settings 100
  restoring 78
  syncing 76
Google Cloud Print 60
Google Earth 179
Google Maps. *See* Maps app
Google Now
  changing home and work locations 91
  controlling location privacy 89
  customizing 91
  displaying and managing cards 90
  opening 88
  setting reminders in 92
  settings 100
  turning on and off 88
  using 88
Google Play Edition devices 8
Google Play Store. *See* Play Store
Google Search
  changing home and work locations 91
  hotword detection 95
  sample search queries 96
  settings 100
  using 94
  voice actions 98
Google Settings app 24
Google Wallet 17, 157
guest users 19

H

Hangouts app 134
Home button 15
Home screen
  about 26
  apps and widgets
    adding 29
    rearranging 28
    removing 29
  folders 30
  showing 28
  switching 28
  wallpaper 34
hotword detection 95
HSPA+ networks 66

I

IMAP and POP3 email 122
input devices 53
international keyboards 56
IP address 65

K

Keep
  about 149
  audio notes 150
  creating and managing notes 149
  setting reminders in 151
  using 149
keyboards. *See also* text
  dictating text 59
  gesture typing 52
  hiding 50
  international 56
  physical 53
  switching 51

text, selecting and editing 58
typing on 50
typing options 54

L

labels, Gmail 122
landscape view 35
locating a missing Nexus 46
Location services 180
Lock screen
  about 44
  notifications 85
  Smart Lock 45
login screens 65
long press gesture 13
LTE networks 66

M

MAC address 62
Mac, USB connection to 81
Maps app
  about 165
  changing home and work locations 167
  Compass mode 171
  directions 178
  distance units 167
  finding locations 170
  Google Earth, opening 179
  internet connection required 167
  location details 169
  Location services 180
  maps
    moving 168
    rotating 168
    tilting 168
    zooming 168
  navigating 179
  offline maps 177
  search history 175
  searching for locations 174
  signing in and out 167
  status bar icon 167
  Street View 172
  traffic view 176
  using 166
  views 176
  voice actions 98
messaging 134
micro-USB cable 2
Miracast 41
mirroring, screen 41
mobile hotspots 62
mouse, using 14
multitouch gestures 13

N

navigation buttons
  about 14
  Back 14
  Home 15
  Overview 15
  revealing when invisible 31
networks. *See also* wireless connections
  airplane mode 72
  cellular (LTE/HSPA+) 66
  virtual private networks (VPNs) 67
  wi-fi 62
Nexus. *See also* Android
  Bluetooth devices, connecting 68
  cleaning the screen 186
  data usage 191
  developer options 192
  earphones, using with 37
  encrypting 48
  factory data reset 78, 192
  Google Account 17
  hardware 2
  Home screen 26
  input devices 53
  internal storage 190
  locating missing 46
  locking screen 44
  mouse, using with 14
  multitouch gestures 13
  navigation buttons 14
  owner (user) 18
  physical keyboard, using with 53
  powering on and off 11
  Power/Lock button 11, 45
  printing 60
  RAM 190
  restarting 187
  restricted profiles 21
  selling 17
  settings 22
  setting up 16
  sleep, activating 11, 44
  speakers, using with 37
  specifications 2
  system information, getting 9, 186
  updating Android 10
  users 18
  volume buttons 36
  waking 12
NFC (near field communication) 71
notes. *See* Keep
notifications. *See also* status bar
  apps 189
  Lock screen 85
  managing 85
  muting 85
  viewing 84

O

omnibox, locating in Chrome 106
onscreen keyboards. *See* keyboards
orientation, changing screen 35
Overview button 15
owner (user) 18, 45

P

People app. *See* Contacts app
photos
  albums 182
  Bluetooth transfers 184
  built-in camera 183
  copied from computer 184
  displaying in Photos app 182
  downloading 184
  editing tools 184
  getting onto Nexus 182
  image formats 181
  managing 184
  screenshots 184
  sync options 182
Photos app 181. *See also* photos
physical keyboard 53
pinch gesture 13
Play Books 163
Play Games 159
Play Movies & TV 162
Play Music 98, 161
Play Newsstand 164
Play Store
  about 155
  apps 158
  books 163
  games 158
  magazines 164
  movies 162
  music 161
  news 164
  payment methods 157
  refunds 159
  TV shows 162
  using 156
POP3 and IMAP email 122
portrait view 35
power
  Battery Saver 40
  charging the battery 38
  conserving 40
  powering on and off 11
  Qi wireless charging 38

Power/Lock button 11, 45
printing 60
proxy server connections 64

Q
Qi wireless charging 38
Quick Settings 23

R
reminders
   setting in Google Now 92
   setting in Keep 151
   setting with voice actions 98
resetting app preferences 189
restarting Nexus 187
restricted profiles 21
rotate gesture 13

S
screen
   bezel 13
   brightness 33
   capacitive 13
   cleaning 186
   external display 41
   full-screen mode 31
   landscape view 35
   locking 44
   mirroring 41
   pinning apps 44
   portrait view 35
   rotating 35
screen pinning 44
screenshots 184
search. *See* Google Search
Settings app 22
settings, viewing and changing 22
setup, Nexus
   changing settings after 17
   first-time 16
shorthand instructions 9
SIM card 66
sleep, activating 11, 44
slide gesture 13
Smart Lock 45
SMS/MMS messaging 134
sounds
   muting notifications 85
   screen lock 45
   touch sounds 13
   volume, adjusting 36
speakers 37
spelling, checking 55
status bar 31

stopwatch. *See* Clock app
Street View 172
swipe gesture 13
switching keyboards 51
syncing account data 76
system information, getting 9, 186

T
tap gesture 13
Tap & Go 17
tethering 62
text. *See also* keyboards
   dictating 59
   emoticons 51
   gesture typing 52
   positioning insertion point 58
   selecting and editing 58
   spell-checking 55
   typing 50
   typing options 54
text messaging 134
text size, changing 8
time and date
   setting 32
   viewing in Clock 152
timer 98, 153
touch and hold gesture 13
touchscreen. *See* screen
typing. *See* keyboards

U
updating
   Android 10
   apps 160
URLs 107
USB charging unit 2
USB connection
   to Mac 81
   to Windows PC 80
users
   about 18
   adding 19
   deleting 20
   guest users 19
   Lock screen info 20
   modifying 20
   owner 18, 45
   restricted profiles 21
   switching 20

V
vCard (.vcf) format 140, 141
verifying apps 48
vibration 13, 54

video chat 134
videos
   playing on Play Movies & TV 162
   playing on YouTube 119
virtual private networks (VPNs) 67
voice actions 98
volume, adjusting 36

W
waking Nexus 12
wallpaper, changing 34
web browser. *See* Chrome web browser
widgets
   about 27
   adding 29
   rearranging 28
   removing 29
   resizing 28
Wi-Fi Direct (ad-hoc) connections 65
wi-fi networks
   about 62
   airplane mode 72
   closed 62, 64
   connecting to 63
   forgetting 63
   IP address 65
   login screens 65
   MAC address 62
   mobile hotspots 62
   printing via 60
   proxy server connections 64
   settings 64
   signal strength 62
   tethering 62
   turning connections on or off 63
   Wi-Fi Direct (ad-hoc) connections 65
   Wi-Fi Protected Setup 63
Wi-Fi Protected Setup 63
Windows PC, USB connection to 80
wireless connections. *See also* networks
   airplane mode 72
   Android Beam 71
   Bluetooth 68
   NFC (near field communication) 71
world clocks. *See* Clock app

Y
YouTube app
   channels 119
   finding videos 119
   playing videos 119
   using 118

Made in the USA
San Bernardino, CA
09 August 2015